Vierke's Aquarium Book

...the way the Germans do it

Vierke's Aquarium Book

...the way the Germans do it

by Jorg Vierke
Translated by Annemarie Lambrich
Edited by Dr. Herbert R. Axelrod

Front endpapers: A Southeast Asian aquarium stocked with tiger barbs, harlequin rasboras, danios, loaches, and other characteristic tropical Asian fishes. Photo by B. Kahl.

Back endpapers: A heavily planted South American aquarium with angelfish and rosy tetras. Photo by B. Kahl.

Title page: The elegant Congo tetra is excellent in large schools in a heavily planted aquarium. Photo by B. Kahl.

CONTENTS

INTRODUCTION

Few people can resist the fascination of a beautifully equipped aquarium. However, many renounce the acquisition of an underwater world in a glass, believing themselves incapable of maintaining an aquarium. Isn't this hobby very expensive in terms of money and, even more so, time? Others, on the other hand, have put their aquarium back into the basement from boredom or disappointment after a short time. They had been promised a "perfect aquarium," a number of gadgets were going to assist them — yet it did not turn out according to their wishes.

Aquarium keeping is a very individual hobby. If you like plastic plants you can use plastic plants. If you want to mix Asian gouramis with Mexican swordtails, then you can feel free to mix them. At least this is the way American hobbyists think of their hobby. German hobbyists are much more formal in their arrangements and tend to deplore artificial anythings.

I can promise that the maintenance of an aquarium does not require any water, chemical, or biological studies and that it can be done with much less work and expense than is commonly supposed. Nevertheless, a certain basic knowledge of the necessities of life of the pets and of the problems that *may* possibly be encountered is, of course, required. With this book I would like to pass on my experiences based on long-time aquarium practice — experiences that will enable the layman to begin with this wonderful hobby and to become familiar with it.

In addition, I would also like to give some tips and suggestions to experienced hobbyists that will help them to enjoy their fishes even more and will encourage them to try more exotic fishes, or to make an attempt at breeding fishes.

J. Vierke

BASICS OF AQUARIUM CARE

This book deals only with the freshwater aquarium. Although sea fishes are often much more colorful, they are suited only within limits for the amateur aquarium: for one, most species grow quite big and require, therefore, larger aquaria; in addition, their requirements regarding the composition and quality of water and food are considerably greater and much more difficult to meet than those of freshwater fishes.

The dream of a beautifully planted underwater coral reef will also be difficult to fulfill, because, with very few exceptions, we cannot keep plants in a marine aquarium. Even the experienced hobbyist will only rarely turn to the marine tank since this area will regularly deprive him, with only a very few exceptions, of the most thrilling experience of success: breeding.

In some books the beginner is advised to use cold-water fishes for his start with aquarium keeping. Be cautioned about this! Cold-water fishes are more difficult to keep, in the long run, than tropical, warm-water fishes. Beyond a doubt, a stickleback aquarium is very beautiful for a few weeks in the spring; it is possible to enjoy these lively fish for many hours and to study their most interesting reproductive behavior. In the long run, however, native fishes are difficult to keep in the home. They require the temperatures of their waters in the wild; they are only rarely comfortable with room temperatures. Although this is true in many instances of tropical, warm-water

fishes, it is still a lot easier to heat an aquarium than to cool it! Indeed, it was the tropical freshwater fishes that caused the rise and blossoming of the hobby. They are the really decorative fishes.

For a tropical freshwater aquarium, fewer technical accessories are needed than commonly supposed. Thus, we can do in most cases without aeration, for instance. It is necessary only in a few cases, usually is only a more or less attractive luxury, and in some causes is even harmful. The most important accessories are the heater that maintains the water temperature at a predetermined level and the aquarium light, without which the plants cannot survive. In addition, at the beginning we need only a cover, an aquarium thermometer, and — when everything is installed — of course, plants and fishes. Not too many fishes, please, even though the temptation is powerful! If we can resist the temptation to stuff the aquarium full of fishes, we can even do quite well without a filter, but if you can afford a pump and filter, by all means get them.

Part of the care for an aquarium involves regular feeding and an occasional partial change of the water during which at the same time the debris is siphoned off the bottom and the front pane is cleaned. From time to time, plants should be thinned. Detailed instructions for these maintenance jobs are given later on. Do not think that a smaller aquarium is easier and quicker to take care of than a larger one. On the contrary, the smaller the tank the faster the water quality may deteriorate. For this reason the beginner is advised not to economize in the size of his first aquarium! One should not have one's first experiences with an aquarium of less than 10 gallons (38 L)!

Aquarists versed in biology sometimes have the idea that things should even be more simple than described above. They think of the often used and abused term "balanced aquarium." Indeed, the animals and plants are part of a mutually complementary ecological system. In addition to light, the plants also require for their growth animal excretions such as droppings and carbon dioxide and in turn they furnish the fishes with oxygen and food. Consequently, shouldn't it be possible to leave a sensibly equipped aquarium completely alone? **No!** In nature, the circumstances are completely different from those in the limited situation of an aquarium. In nature, in an enormous mass of water there are comparatively few plants and even fewer fishes. Those places in open waters where there are large schools of fishes must be averaged with the many areas where fishes are few or absent. We neither can nor want to imitate these ratios in the aquarium.

Our aquarium is more than a section of a tropical stream in the virgin forest. A better comparison is a greenhouse or a garden; an aquarium requires constant corrections on our part.

But don't worry; our care measures need not degenerate into work. On the contrary, most aquarists need to hold back so that they won't offer too much of a good thing in their zeal.

AQUARIUM TECHNIQUES

The Aquarium

In the pet trade, different types of aquariums are offered, from the simple all-glass aquarium to the perfect aquarium furniture with all the accessories built in. The choice is determined mostly by the tastes and the wallet of the purchaser.

Basically, all-glass aquariums are more frequently in use than plastic ones. Not every plastic material remains crystal-clear and transparent for years. In addition, the danger of scratching the panes during cleaning is usually greater in plastic aquariums than in glass aquariums. On the other hand, the aquariums manufactured from plastic or plexiglass have the advantage of a markedly lower weight. Further-

This is how an all-glass tank is put together. For purposes of clarity the thickness of the glass is exaggerated. We also need a glass bottom and clamps to hold the sides in position.

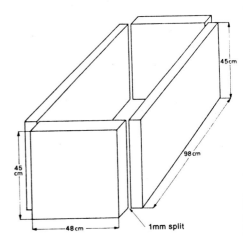

45cm

98 cm

45 cm

48 cm

1mm split

Height of Aquarium (cm)	Length of Aquarium (cm)								
	50	60	70	80	90	100	120	150	200
30	6	6	6	6	6	8	8	10	10
40	6	6	6	8	8	8	10	10	12
50	6	8	8	8	10	10	10	12	15
60	8	8	10	10	10	10	12	12	15
70	8	10	10	10	12	12	15	15	18

Determination of glass thickness needed for various lengths (top line) and heights (left column) of all-glass aquarium. All measurements are metric, the glass thickness given in millimeters. For a tank 100 cm long by 50 cm high, you would need glass 10 mm thick.

more, plexiglass aquariums can be made to order in any desired shape, such as round, triangular, or arched, with curved or straight panes, with a built-in filter, and with many other possibilities. Beware of the illusion, however, that plastic is cheap. Plastic tanks are usually more costly than glass aquariums!

Formerly, glass aquariums were offered predominantly with stainless steel frames. Nowadays, they have been replaced almost completely by the cheaper all-glass tanks, glued together with silicone rubber and often furnished with edge moldings for decoration. Well-glued tanks last for years without problems. However, as a precaution, newly purchased aquariums should be filled with water before decorating them. Nothing is more aggravating than to find that a newly-bought aquarium, decorated with love, is not water-tight!

Even with a minimal amount of skill, an all-glass aquarium can be made at home without problem. Usually the glazier will cut the panes to order in the desired sizes. However, find out first what the cut panes will cost, add the price of the silicone rubber, and determine whether the expense is really worthwhile! It rarely is!

There are many methods for gluing together an aquarium. In the following, a method is described that can easily be used even without the assistance of another person. As an example, we use an aquarium with the outside dimensions 100 × 50 × 45 cm and a pane thickness of 1 cm. For the front and rear walls we require panes with the dimensions of 98 × 45 cm each. The two side panes are 48 × 45 cm each. The bottom pane is to be glued between the four vertical panes. Since we want to subtract 3 mm on each side for the glue bead, we arrive at the measurements of 97.4 × 47.4 cm for the bottom pane. For stabilization we need two glass strips that we will fasten in the ends as crosswise braces. They can be used at the same time as supports for the cover. The glass strips must be 47.4 cm in length and can be between 3 and 6 cm in width.

The glass panes need not be ground at the edges. It is sufficient to smooth the sharp edges at the ends with sandpaper. (Take care to account for the necessary thickness of the glass panes! Using the accompanying table, the correct thickness can easily be determined.) As glue, use a one-component transparent silicone rubber. Silicone rubber is available from your local pet-shop.

Before gluing, we have to clean the panes in the area of the places to be glued with a rag soaked in acetone. (Acetone is available in some drug-stores.) The least little fingerprint may keep the grout from sticking (grease spots!), and the aquarium will later leak. After a thorough cleaning, we fasten the four vertical panes with masking tape. The tape is fastened on the inside, so that the outside corner can be completely filled with rubber later on. During fastening, take care that the panes do not touch directly in the corners — a gap of easily 1 mm should remain. This is easiest to do by inserting wooden matches at the top and bottom when taping two adjacent panes together. Don't forget to remove the matches before gluing.

We now set the bottom pane on a piece of paper and carefully set our unstable taped glass construction onto it in such a manner that a gap of 3 to 4 mm remains on all sides.

To avoid smeared glue edges, the edges beyond the groove to be grouted should be covered with masking tape before grouting! The application of the glue itself should be done fluidly. Immediately afterward, the mass must be smoothed with a putty knife or a finger and should be pushed in a little. In order to keep the silicone rubber from sticking to the putty knife or finger, the "tool" must be continually dampened during smoothing using warm water to which a squirt of detergent has been added. Our work must be completed in a few minutes; the silicone rubber hardens rapidly.

Do not add water right away. Wait for at least a week before doing a water test. Possible leaky places must then be carefully marked. For waterproofing them, the aquarium must be completely emptied and the places in question must be well dried, cleaned with acetone, and then glued again. Large tanks may also be given a bead of silicone glue on the inside.

In the same manner, older frame aquariums may also be waterproofed. Puttied frame aquariums easily become leaky if they stand empty for some time. Before re-use, they need not be reputtied, but the interior edges may be cleaned carefully with acetone and grouted with silicone rubber. The tank is then ready again to be used for many years!

The Position of the Aquarium

Today nobody would put his aquarium in front of a window any more — with the light shining through, plants and fish are not very attractive. To the contrary, we prefer a relatively dark place, and the tank will be displayed all the better! Artificial aquarium illumination makes us independent of natural light and even allows us to regulate the light in such a manner that an infestation with algae can be largely avoided.

When looking for a suitable stand, let us not forget that an aquarium has considerable weight. A tank with di-

$$\text{Volume (in liters)} = \frac{\text{Length x Width x Height (in cm)}}{1000}$$

mensions of $100 \times 40 \times 50$ cm has a volume of 200 liters (50 gallons). A liter of water weighs 1 kg. For the aquarium of 100 cm length used as an example, we may assume an overall weight of about 220 kg (484 pounds), since added to the weight of the water is the weight of the tank, the sand, and the decoration materials. Together with the stand or shelf on which it will stand, this could amount to more than 250 kg. A tank that is twice as long, however, does not weigh twice, but about four times as much — an aquarium measuring $200 \times 60 \times 70$ cm contains 840 liters! Together with the weight of the tank, the decorative material, and the stand, the total weight could be more than a ton. In many apartments, however, the admissible load on the ceiling is only 150 kg/m^2. Of course, the strength of the ceiling along the wall is considerably greater than in the middle of the room. Before setting up a large aquarium, these things must be carefully considered.

As support, a stable table or a commercial aquarium stand is recommended. In old houses, you should check with a level to see whether the floor is really level.

The aquarium is not placed directly on the wood or the stand; we first put down a soft, spongy pad of felt or styrofoam. For small or medium-sized aquariums, solid foam blocks are extremely well suited as supports. They are light, offer an unbroken surface, and are easy to camouflage. The support should be selected in such a manner that the aquarium can be comfortably observed from a sitting position. When you are sitting down it should be at eye level. Occasionally it is forgotten in the planning stage that the aquarium needs to be easily accessible from above, since otherwise, the work of caring for the aquarium becomes a despised torture. This mistake becomes evident, at the latest, during the decoration of the aquarium, but by that time it may already be too late to move it without a major effort.

Light in the Aquarium

In twilight it might still be possible to observe the fish, more or less, but no plants would grow. Remember: with the help of chlorophyll, the plants fabricate from carbon dioxide and water the energy-rich substances that serve as building and energy materials. This process (photosynthesis) can only take place in the light because it is the light that furnishes the energy. An aquarium light is necessary, therefore, unless we decide to do without plants or use daylight. The latter is very disadvantageous, since in the summer we usually get too much light, while in winter the brief light periods are insufficient to adequately maintain the tropical plants.

For our purpose, there are three basic types of illumination: incandescent light bulbs, fluorescent lamps, and mercury vapor lamps.

The incandescent bulbs that once were used almost exclusively are still used occasionally. They serve in very small aquariums and are occasionally used in larger aquariums as spotlights to illuminate certain group plantings.

In most aquariums, fluorescent lamps are in use. With the same consumption of current, fluorescent lamps are about four times as bright as traditional light bulbs. The lamps are available in different colors, not all of which are suitable for aquarium use. Basically, fluorescents give off only a part of the spectrum of daylight. Daylight, which is white to our eyes, is a mixture of the spectral colors violet, indigo, blue, green, yellow, orange, and red. The plants require especially the blue-violet and red components of the spectrum for their growth (blue-violet mainly for cell division, red for the growth of the individual cells). Nurseries successfully use lamps that radiate these color components, and these lamps are often used by aquarists. Beginners are especially fascinated by the violet twilight that these lamps radiate, strongly emphasizing the red and blue coloration of the fishes. Unfortunately, the algae also grow especially well under these lights — so the initial enthusiasm of many aquarists for this type of lamp has become somewhat subdued! Both pleasant to the eye and advantageous for the plant growth are warm-toned lamps (light color 30 or 32); the light is somewhat yellow and quite similar to that of an ordinary light bulb.

Today mercury vapor lamps and mercury high-pressure vapor lamps are used in increasing numbers. They are not housed in light hoods or strips lying directly on the aquarium like fluorescent tubes, but usually hang free

Plants need a lot of light, and not just any type of light. Fluorescent tubes especially balanced to meet the needs of plants are available in your pet shop. Photo courtesy Dr. D. Terver, Nancy Aquarium, France.

above the aquarium. Their use is a matter of taste. They are more expensive than tubes but more economical in the long run, since the output of the lamps barely falls off even after prolonged use.

Two decisive questions still need to be answered: how long should we illuminate, and how strong should the light be? The duration of the illumination should not be less than 12 hours a day. A shorter period of illumination cannot be made up by higher light intensity! Since in our latitudes the winter days are considerably shorter than 12 hours, we cannot keep tropical plants in daylight exclusively in the winter. There are no objections to a longer period of illumination. On the other hand, we should not extend the "aquarium day" to more than 16 hours; more does not agree with either the fishes or the plants. If you use a timer, it is best to set it for an illumination period of 13 hours per day.

In relation to optimal plant growth, most aquariums get too little light. There are pronounced bright-light plants, such as the *Alternanthera, Cabomba,* and *Rotala,* as well as plants that can easily be kept in dim light, such as some *Cryptocoryne, Vallisneria,* and Java fern. A rule of thumb may be helpful here: for each liter of aquarium water, 0.5 watt of light is needed. A 120-liter tank thus needs at least 60 watts of illumination.

When calculating the minimum wattage, we should not be too stingy. An excess of light intensity is not harmful! In addition, the actual amount of light is often not completely used. Just consider that a dirty cover glass can filter out up to 20% of the amount of light! During the purchase of a lamp, we should pay attention to

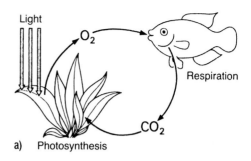

a) Photosynthesis

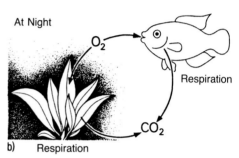

b) Respiration

Aquarium photosynthesis (a) and night respiration (b). In photosynthesis light striking the leaves of the plants produces oxygen used by the fish, which in turn produce carbon dioxide used by the plant. At night both the fish and the plants compete for the oxygen, with both producing carbon dioxide as a waste product.

whether the lamp hood or the lamps themselves are furnished with a reflector; if not, more than half the light is lost. This situation is often easily remedied by covering the upper part of the hood with aluminum foil.

The average aquarist changes his fluorescent tubes only when they begin to flicker. After replacing them with new tubes, he notices that the aquarium has become considerably brighter. As a matter of fact, fluorescent tubes lose about 50% of their light intensity after about 5000 hours use. With a daily illumination of 14 hours, this amounts to about a year. After one year, at most, all tubes should be replaced!

15

Heating

The temperatures in an aquarium with tropical decorative fishes and plants lie — depending on the requirements of the fishes — between 22 and 30°C (generally, median values of 24 to 26°C — 75-79°F — are used). Since these temperatures are higher than normal room temperatures, the aquariums must be heated. Only the fortunate aquarists who can afford a special fish room in which they have set up several aquariums may heat the aquariums by means of a suitably elevated room temperature. In addition to the high temperature, because of the aquariums this fish room also has a commensurately elevated air humidity — the room can also be used as a plant nursery. However, the room can only be used within limits for other purposes.

The majority of aquarists will not have a special room at their disposal for their hobby, and they will have to see to it that the temperature of the aquarium water is always somewhat higher than the room temperature.

Submergible (wand) heaters are the simplest and cheapest heaters for the aquarium. They consist of a heater spiral and a thermostat enclosed in a water-tight glass tube filled with sand. This type of heater can be placed in the aquarium in any position, the most advantageous being a horizontal position directly above the sand. The heater is fastened to the side panes by means of rubber suction cups. In this horizontal position the heat is distributed most evenly, allowing the warmer water to rise in a broad front. Since these heaters are not exactly ornamental in the aquarium, they may be camouflaged by a suitably large rock or root. Be careful not to put the rock or root directly on or against the heater.

Under no circumstances must the heater be buried in the substrate because it cannot give off heat rapidly enough and there is danger that the glass tube of the heater will burst or that the heating coils will melt. The same will also happen if the heater is allowed to operate out of water. For this reason we should develop the habit of always pulling the plug on the heater before changing the water.

The required heat output is essentially dependent on the amount of the water to be warmed and on how much higher the water temperature is to be than the room temperature. In the table you will find information about how many watts of heat output are needed for a given aquarium, positioned out of drafts and well-covered.

It is usually not immediately noticeable if a heater becomes leaky. The fish act normally, since they are not in direct contact with the ground. A person who touches the metal parts of the aquarium or reaches directly into the water is in danger, however, unless the heater and regulator are grounded! Unfortunately, this is usually not the case. It is urgently recommended that the aquarist use only equipment with a safety ground (they are recognizable by the three-pronged plug).

In addition to submergible heaters, heating cables are also available. They are more expensive but have the advantage of being able to be installed almost invisibly in the substrate. Thus, they do not have to be hidden laboriously behind decorative pieces and warm not only the water but at the same time the substrate. This is very advantageous for plant growth, since our aquarium plants, as a rule, do not like to have "cold feet." The slight current through the substrate that is caused by the heat-

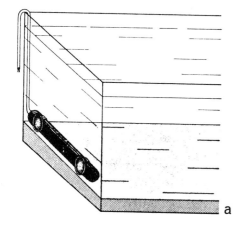

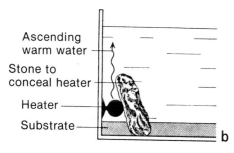

Ascending warm water —

Stone to conceal heater —

Heater —

Substrate —

a

b

Aquarium heaters with separate thermostats are usually submersible and may be mounted inside the tank just above the bottom (a). They are readily hidden from sight by rocks or other decorations (b). The thermostat probe should be mounted in another corner away from the heater to assure even heating.

ing cable also encourages the plants to thrive.

Another heating possibility is the use of heating mats. These heating mats consist of plastic foil into which a heating element has been placed in a watertight manner. The mats are put between the styrofoam or felt pad and the bottom pane of the aquarium; *i.e.* the aquarium is placed directly on the heating mat, with the styrofoam or felt insulation toward the support. With framed aquariums, care must be taken to equalize the air space caused by the thickness of the frame with an additional layer of felt or foam, since the heating mat must lie snugly against the bottom pane of the aquarium to guarantee a reliable radiation of heat. These heating mats are available in all customary aquarium sizes; they are relatively expensive, however.

Unfortunately, there are many recent reports about the heating mats causing the bottom panes of the aquariums to burst. Apparently the heat output (watt per cm^2) of many of these bottom heaters is too high. The use of heating mats is also problematic in those cases where we want to put larger rocks directly on the bottom pane. Here we always have to expect the possibility that the pane will become hotter in those places where the rocks are, thus coming under stress and breaking. For these reasons, I personally prefer the cheaper submersible heaters.

On the other hand, heating mats have evident advantages. First is electrical safety, since no part of the heater any longer has to be placed in the water. In addition to complete invisibility, the beneficial influence of this type of floor heating on the plants also must be noted. Better even than with a heating cable, with the use of heating mats the substrate is evenly flooded by the rising warm water and inflowing somewhat cooler water. This steady circulation constantly carries new nutrients and oxygen to the plant roots.

The trade offers numerous other heating possibilities for aquariums. For instance, there are modern power filters that also contain a heater and thermostat. There are exterior heaters that can be installed behind the outflow of the filter pump of different manufacturers. In these cases the filtered water

Size of tank in liters	Number of degrees the aquarium temperature will be raised above room temperature									
	1°	2°	3°	4°	5°	6°	7°	8°	10°	12°C
10	1	3	4	5	7	8	10	11	14	17
20	2	4	6	9	11	13	15	17	22	26
40	3	7	10	14	17	20	24	28	35	42
60	4	9	13	18	22	27	31	35	45	54
80	5	11	16	22	27	33	38	43	54	65
100	6	13	19	25	31	38	44	50	63	76
120	7	14	21	28	36	43	50	57	70	85
150	8	15	25	33	41	50	57	66	83	98
200	10	20	30	40	50	60	70	80	100	120
250	12	23	35	46	58	70	80	93	115	140
400	16	32	48	63	80	95	110	130	160	190
600	20	40	62	83	104	124	145	166	200	250
800	25	50	76	100	126	151	176	200	250	300
1000	30	60	88	117	146	175	205	235	290	350

Determining the required wattage of a heater according to tank volume (right column) and number of degrees Centigrade by which you wish to exceed the average room temperature. For example, assume a tank holding 200 liters in a room with an average temperature of 20 °C. If you wish to hold the water temperature at 25 °C, then you would need a 50-Watt heater.

is sent through a heating container before flowing — warmed — back into the aquarium. However, we should not make-do with a heater alone: a thermostat frees us from having to supervise the heater all the time.

Thermostats are regulators that maintain the desired water temperature automatically by switching the heater on or off according to need. Thermostats are available either separately from the heater or as an integral part of the heater. The advantage of a separate regulator lies mainly in the fact that these thermostats can be used to regulate the heaters in several aquariums at once. In this manner, several aquariums of different sizes can be maintained, if the heating efficiency is calculated according to the table.

There are other reasons for a separate heater and thermostat. In one-piece thermostatically controlled heaters, the regulator is usually heated directly by the heating element positioned directly below, causing it to switch on and off frequently. The wear can be considerable, shortening the life expectancy of the thermostat accordingly. With separate appliances, if one becomes defective only that one needs to be replaced. Should we purchase a larger aquarium, for instance, we will only have to buy a suitably stronger heater; we can continue to use the quite expensive thermostat. Alas, one piece heater-thermostat combinations out-sell all other heaters combined!

To leave enough latitude for regulation, the wattage output of a heater

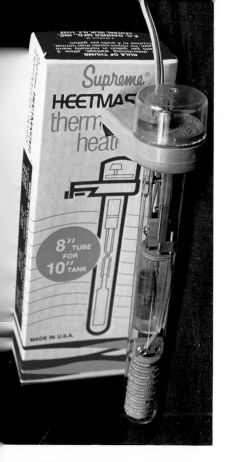

While Europeans tend to use submersible heaters with separate thermostats, Americans prefer an all-in-one heater that is attached at the top rim of the tank (left and below left). These heaters contain their own thermostat and are easily regulated with a simple knob, making them very convenient and almost foolproof to use. They also tend to be cheaper than submersible heaters. Recently several temperature alarms have become available (below right). These provide a signal when the aquarium water becomes either hotter or colder than preset temperatures.

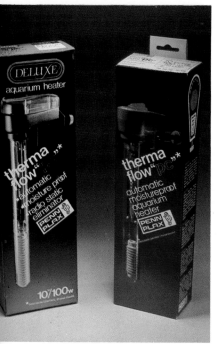

should be calculated according to the table by the following rule:

The wattage of the heater should be such that we could attain maximally 5C more with it than we actually want. For example, if we want to maintain a water temperature of 25°C, we should get a heater that will warm the aquarium to 30°C at an average room temperature of 22°C. In this manner we can be sure that even should the thermostat be defective, our fishes will not be cooked. (Most fishes and plants can stand 30-32°C for a short time.) This rule should be followed whether we want to use the regulator to maintain one or several aquariums.

There are two types of thermostats available in the stores: bimetallic thermostats and electronic temperature regulators. Bimetallic regulators are much cheaper but unfortunately also much less reliable. The desired temperature can be set with an adjustable screw. This screw should be as water-tight as possible, but it should be easy to use, and these two requirements are not always easy to bring together in one gadget. It is best always to fasten even so-called "water-tight thermostats" in such a manner that the adjustable screw sticks out of the water!

Much more recommended, safer to use, and much more attractive because they are less noticeable are the electronic regulators — however, they cost about three times as much as a good bimetallic regulator. In the long run, this expense is certainly worthwhile, because the life expectancy of an electronic thermostat also is much greater! The appliance itself remains outside the aquarium, and only a thin cable with a temperature sensor is put into the water. This cable can, of course, be placed in a spot where it will not disturb the viewer and which, in addition, is as far as possible from the heater. Outside sensors are also available that are fastened to the outside of the aquarium glass but they measure the room temperature more than the water temperature.

The switching accuracy of the elec-

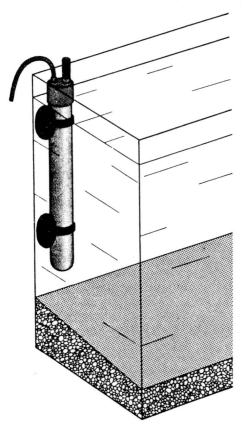

Heaters with self-contained thermostats are mounted vertically, usually in a back corner. The setting dial or screw must remain above the level of the water for safety of operation, even if the unit is sealed.

tronic regulators lies around 0.1 to 0.3°C, but these values should not impress us too much! Slight temperature variations are absolutely advantageous for our fishes because in the wild there also are slight differences in the day and night temperatures of the water. Of course, these variations can be quite different. In flat, standing, sunny puddles, the day- night difference is naturally considerably greater than in a shaded river in the virgin forest.

To check the water temperature we need an aquarium thermometer. Most stores offer both the inexpensive liquid thermometers, which can be bought either as floating or stick thermometers, and heat-sensitive resin thermometers that attach to the outside glass.

Floating thermometers have the negative habit of always floating into corners in which they cannot be read. A suction cup prevents this and will fix the thermometer in a handy place. For this, it is best to select a readily visible spot on the side glass in which the thermometer is least in the way. Stick thermometers are stuck into the substrate and can be displaced only by strongly burrowing fishes. These thermometers will register the temperature right at the substrate.

Aeration

A beginner considers an aerator (air pump) an important, even essential, accessory. This opinion was shared for a long time by the "old hands" at aquarium keeping. This is no surprise, because when the fishes stand gasping and obviously breathless under the water surface, only a few minutes of strong aeration will help them. But what does aeration really do?

The gases dissolved in the water (here only the biologically important gases, oxygen and carbon dioxide, are of interest) are normally in a state of equilibrium with the air gases: at 20°C, a liter of water contains 8.5 mg oxygen and 0.48 mg carbon dioxide. This state cannot be changed even by the strongest aeration! The living things in our aquarium, however, cause variations in the proportions of the gases to each other. In the light, the plants use carbon dioxide and give off oxygen (photosynthesis). The animals, on the other hand, follow the reverse process: when breathing, they use oxygen and excrete carbon dioxide. This process (use of oxygen, giving off carbon dioxide) also takes place in plants in the dark: at night the plants are no longer manufacturers of oxygen, but are instead oxygen-users, thus in competition with the fishes! This is the reason why, particularly in beautifully and richly planted aquariums, the fishes may have considerable trouble breathing at night. Actually, this is rarely due to a lack of oxygen, but rather to an excess of carbon dioxide that is manufactured at night not only by the fishes, but also by the plants. The absorption of oxygen can only happen with simultaneous giving off of carbon dioxide, but this is possible only when the carbon dioxide content of the water is not too high. To be specific, this means that the exchange of gases can only take place if a certain concentration gradient is present. In this case, only the expulsion of carbon dioxide can make possible a sufficient absorption of oxygen — the aerator has to be switched on to remove the carbon dioxide.

The problems described appear only in aquariums that are very well planted and at the same time overstocked with fishes or in hopelessly crammed tanks. If, in addition, doses of carbon dioxide are added at night by means of diffusors to help the plants grow, losses of fishes may occur.

In a well-planted aquarium, we can do without aeration at least during the day, since it forces out the carbon dioxide that is so important for photosynthesis and thus also limits the production of oxygen. Carbon dioxide fertilization in a well planted tank would make much more sense during the day.

The circumstances are different in more or less under-planted aquariums or in markedly overstocked tanks. Here the exchange of gases between water and air must be mechanically accelerated, and this can be done by means of an aerator. The movement of the water caused by the aerator bubbles that rise from the nozzle favor an optimal composition of the gases dissolved in the water. However, if we use a filter that in its turn sees to an adequate turnover of the water, the aerator is superfluous here also!

For ordinary use, a filter will be preferable to an aerator in most instances. With its use it is not necessary to return the water to the aquarium in a manner that causes air bubbles to appear. The exchange of oxygen or carbon dioxide takes place mostly on the surface of the water. This is another reason why a turnover of the water is so important! It keeps the water from sitting in dead corners and lower layers for any amount of time.

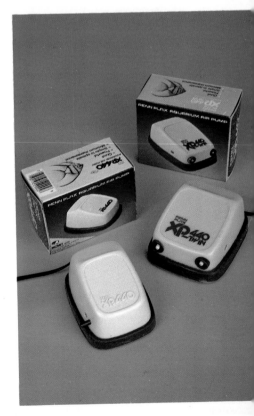

Air pumps come in a multitude of sizes and designs. Small vibrator or diaphragm pumps are satisfactory for most aquaria and are generally cheaper to purchase and repair than are piston pumps and air compressors. As shown here, vibrator pumps are available with one or more air outlets and in a variety of case styles.

Above: A small motor-driven filter unit with a filter box that hangs outside the aquarium. *Below:* Small and very large vibrator pumps to fit any common aquarium demands.

Below: A variety of gang valves are necessary to accurately direct and control the flow of air from the pump to various other pieces of air-operated equipment and the airstone.

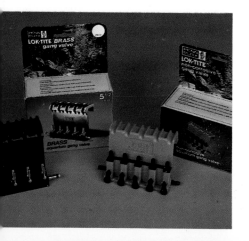

On this occasion, let me point out another positive effect of water turnover: it prevents the formation of warm zones. In completely quiescent waters, the surface is often several degrees warmer than the bottom. This temperature difference is advantageous for neither fishes nor plants.

All this shows that people who have a filter can well do without an aerator. I myself use my aerator only when preparing my fishes for breeding, when raising young, and for the operation of my brine shrimp hatchery. An air pump is also required for the operation of an ozonizer.

The most important part of aerating equipment is the electrically operated air pump. It is connected by means of an air hose to an airstone. The airstones are made of fused sand, glass, plastic, or wood. Wooden air releasers produce particularly fine air bubbles. By means of plastic tubing, which should be furnished with air valves, several aquariums can be served by one pump, especially if it is powerful.

Diaphragm air pumps operate on the oscillating membrane principle — the membrane of the pump chamber is moved back and forth in front of a magnetic coil. Pumps of this type of construction are quite tough but sometimes also quite noisy. Even the sound of a pump described as "amazingly quiet" can be quite disturbing in the long run. If we house the pump in an insulated box that we then set inside a closed cabinet (holes for the air hoses are, of course, necessary!), the noise can be considerably abated. Occasionally it is even recommended to install the pump in an adjacent room. This is sometimes necessary for a different reason — if someone is smoking in the aquarium room, the tars and nicotine would constantly be pumped into the water via the air pump. Many fishes react sensitively to this type of pollution.

When positioning the pump, we should bear in mind that it should be placed higher than the water level. Otherwise, in case of a malfunction or if the hose should become detached from the pump, the flow of aquarium water in the pressureless hose might be reversed and the aquarium emptied on the siphon principle. If the pump has to be placed lower, we should install an antireverse flow safety valve in the air hose.

Oscillation dampers (mufflers) are available commercially that are also installed in line with the air hose. Oscillation dampers serve to reduce the oscillations of the air and thus a part of the operating noises of the aerator and pump.

For larger aquarium set-ups, special high-output diaphragm compressors as well as large piston pumps are available.

Filters

"Aquarium filters merely make sewage-infiltrated water appear crystal-clear!" This is usually asserted by malicious tongues, and even if I cannot subscribe to this statement, I must admit that it contains a grain of truth. It is true that a mechanical filter cannot remove all dissolved noxious substances from the water! What use, then, is a filter, and what can it do?

Filters easily remove small particles (tiny pieces of debris) from the water, which, however, are not harmful to the fishes under ordinary circumstances but which hinder plant growth since they more or less filter out the light. In addition, the filter causes a favorable exchange of gases by water movement

and helps at the same time to prevent undesirable warmth layers. Under certain circumstances, filters perform more than just a mechanical cleaning.

Filter fibers serve merely to filter out detritus and other particles. Thus, they are only able to clean mechanically and are sometimes put in front of other filter media to prevent their premature soiling.

Filter charcoal may be able to filter larger organic molecules, dyes, and aromatic matters, as well as medication from the water. Unfortunately, the quality of filter charcoal is not uniformly the same everywhere, and this can lead occasionally to dangerous changes in pH values and to chemical changes of the water. In any case, filter charcoal is exhausted after at most 24 hours of use and should then be exchanged for other filter material.

Filter peat gives off humic acids and tannins that lower the pH of the water and give the fishes an environment that is similar to their natural habitats. The characteristic yellow coloring caused by the acids of the peat is described by many aquarists as "typical virgin forest water," and rightfully so; however, it reduces slightly the effectiveness of our lighting system.

Peat is exhausted after a few days and should not remain in the filter for more than a week. Be careful with peat sold for gardening purposes! This is often mixed with fertilizer additives and is, therefore, not at all suitable for the aquarium.

Filter materials such as coarse gravel, basalt splinters, lavalit, and ceramic tubes serve as biological filters. First, they serve for mechanical cleaning. In the interstices, water whirls and quiescent zones are formed in which the dirt particles are deposited. In a

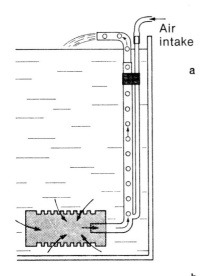

Air intake

a

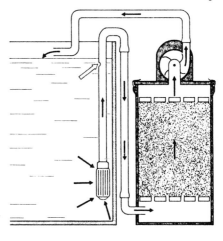

b

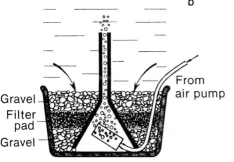

Gravel
Filter
pad
Gravel

From
air pump

Types of filters. a) A simple sponge filter using a foam core and running off the air pump. b) Box filters are quite efficient in a small tank and can even be made at home. c) Diagram of a basic outside power filter. The water returns to the tank in a healthy current just above the surface of the water. Take note of the hole in the suction tube about 5 cm below the water level (open arrow).

few weeks these materials become covered with a bed of bacteria. This bed of bacteria and other micro-organisms performs an important function, because it decomposes all deposited organic substances. It lives off the protein remnants, the organic refuse of the aquarium. This is described as biomineralization. The end products of this process are oxygen, water, nitrates, sulfates, and phosphates, materials that are absorbed again by the plants as nutrients. The biological filter thus is, so to speak, the missing link that is needed for the maintenance of the biological equilibrium.

However, certain things must be taken into consideration: the ratio of plants to fishes and bacteria is never balanced in an aquarium environment. Even very efficient biological filters cannot prevent the need for an occasional partial change of water. Another factor is also extremely important: the bacterial bed requires oxygen. This normally reaches the bacteria, which are growing firmly attached in the substrate, via the water streaming into the filter. As soon as the filter is turned off for several hours, the bacteria suffocate and die. A biological filter should never be turned off more than one or at most two hours!

In newly-equipped aquariums, we must be economical in the stocking of fishes and also with feeding, because especially in the beginning the bacteria are numerically too few and are unable to completely convert the organic wastes. The nitrification bacteria, which convert the highly toxic nitrites manufactured during the conversion of the nitrogen- containing organic substances into non- toxic nitrates, are obtained by inoculating the filter or the aquarium bottom with a handful of the corresponding substrate from a well-established aquarium. If this is not possible, irrigate some garden soil in a pot, let everything stand for a few minutes, and then pour the water, which is clear or only slightly murky above the soil, into our aquarium. It often takes several weeks before an optimally composed bacterial bed becomes established. This usually happens all by itself.

Even with a biological filter, the filter mass has to be cleaned occasionally. During cleaning only the debris is rinsed off with cool or luke-warm water. Overly intensive cleaning or boiling would destroy the valuable bacteria. To be on the safe side, we should always leave a handful of the substrate uncleaned in the filter so that the bacterial cultures can regenerate themselves relatively quickly. Considering the wide range of commercially available types of filters, it is impossible to look at all types individually. Here I would like to explain only some well-proven standard types. I will also forego an explanation of the method that uses the entire substrate of the aquarium as a filter mass. This may be considered outdated, since the soil pores become clogged.

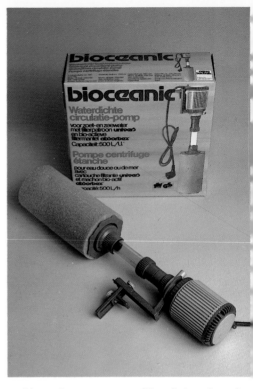

Above: A power sponge filter. *Below:* One of the more complicated power filter systems now available.

Above: An improved design of sponge filter with greatly increased surface area.

Below: Filter cartridge designed to hold activated carbon.

Basically, we distinguish between inside and outside filters. Inside filters are put *into* the aquarium. Their main advantage is that there can be no mishaps with leaky hose couplings. Disadvantages are the limited size and the need for hiding the filter somewhere because they are all not exactly ornamental. Because of their limited dimensions, inside filters are not suited as biological filters, either.

An effective inside filter can easily be constructed at home from a flowerpot or a plastic cup, a funnel, and a matching plastic pipe. The accompanying illustration shows such a filter operated by means of an air pump. As filler, coarse gravel is most indicated, perhaps with a layer of filter "floss" in the middle zone.

Outside filters can be of any size. If in doubt, select the one with the greatest capacity! This is more important than the water turnover capacity of the pump, because what good is it if the pump forces the entire water contents of the aquarium through the filter hourly, but the water is only partially cleaned?

Depending on the construction, filters can be operated either with an air pump or with a circulating pump.

Let us consider the first case: inside filters work especially well with an air pump. With the use of air valves and air lines, several small aquariums can be filtered with one air pump. The air bubbles flowing into the water pipe riser cause the water to lift and bring it above the water level. The water that rushes to fill its place streams through a filter cartridge and is well-cleansed mechanically by its passage through the fine membrane pores. The dirty cartridge should be cleaned weekly.

I would like to advise against the use of inside filters run by circulating pumps. I also do not recommend the small outside filters operated by means of an air pump that are hooked to the rear and side walls of the aquarium like a backpack. If a really effective outside filter is needed for a larger aquarium, a circulating pump should be selected. It is almost noiseless, virtually maintenance-free (the mechanism, not the filter itself!), and enormously effective. Here, too, there are two basic, different methods of circulating pump construction available: closed and open filters.

Stores offer mostly closed circulating filters. They have the undisputed advantage that they can be operated in any position and at a greater distance from the aquarium. They are linked with the aquarium by two hoses, the intake and the outflow hose. These filters can easily be housed under the aquarium in a cabinet or behind a cover. Two disadvantages of closed filters are the sometimes quite complicated process necessary to change the filtering material and the fact that occasionally the hose connections become leaky. Be careful about this, because the aquarium might be completely emptied. However, a trick can prevent the worst: into the water intake pipe that hangs in the aquarium, drill a small hole about 3 mm in diameter about 5 cm below the water surface. The water cannot flow out below this point. If the water level sinks to the level of this hole, the pump can then only suck in air. Of course, this is fatal for the circulating pump (which is cooled by the water), but on the other hand, once the entire aquarium has run empty, the moment will also come when only air is sucked in!

Fortunately, such mishaps do not often occur. Closed outside filters are easy to use as biological filters, but again, they should have as large a filter chamber as possible filled with gravel or other solid filter material and must absolutely never be turned off for more than a few hours!

The ideal filter for me is an open outside filter of as large a size as possible, driven by a not-too-strong circulating pump. An experienced handyman can build the filter with a plastic tank with glued-in walls and pipe conduits that match a purchased circulating pump (but it is usually cheaper to buy this type of filter rather than build one). The filter itself consists of two chambers. The aquarium water is sucked by an intake pipe into the first chamber, which may also contain a heater. From here the water flows into the actual filter chamber, which is best filled with sand and covered on top with a layer of foam to catch the worst dirt. This foam layer can easily be removed. It should be washed every week, during which the filter may remain in operation. Through an intake pipe extending deeply into the gravel, the filtered water is moved back into the aquarium by a circulating pump. In an emergency, the method described initially for inside filters run by means of an air pump would be sufficient for pumping. However, this will not obtain a sufficient mixing of the waters in the aquarium.

The advantage of this open type of filter over the closed ones lies particularly in the possibility of making it larger. It is also easier to clean, especially if the filter mass is set into a filter basket that simply has to be lifted out for cleaning. In addition, all connections to the aquarium can be made leakproof via solid plastic tubing. Of course, this system also has a disadvantage: it is not always easy to position the filter in such a manner that it does not obtrude. After all, it is not exactly a room ornament, and it must be positioned in such a manner that the water level of the filter is the same as that in the aquarium.

Automatic Lamps

Automatic lamps are practical gadgets. With a timer, the aquarium lamp is switched on and off at predetermined times. The steady rhythm of illumination caused by this is better for the plants than the irregular switching on and off that cannot be avoided with manual operation. Appliance stores offer timers that can be connected to different aquariums. Automatic lamps are absolutely essential for people who have to leave their aquariums alone for two to three weeks during vacations. Steady light or steady darkness would be equally harmful for the fish, but even more for the plants.

Automatic Feeders

Automatic feeders for dry food and food tablets are available in pet stores. Most of these appliances also can switch on the lamps at the same time. Someone who goes away for several weeks on vacation may want to care for his fishes in this manner. For weekends, however, the automatic feeder should not be used. One or two fasting days per week are veritable "cure days" for all adult fishes that we should grant them. Healthy fishes can even survive two or three weeks without any problems in a well-established aquarium. Daily feeding should never be left to an automatic feeder. We need these

minutes in front of the aquarium to make sure that all the fishes are healthy and eating well!

Appliances for the Enrichment of the Water

In addition to the usual filters, pet shops also offer many other appliances for the enrichment and fertilization of the water. Many of them, however, are unnecessary for the average aquarium keeper and are not always without pitfalls in their use. Specialists also consider these articles nonessentials. Nevertheless, these sometimes not exactly inexpensive appliances are briefly listed here with their advantages and disadvantages and, where applicable, alternatives.

Ozone

Let us begin with the **ozone treatment** of the aquarium water. Ozone reliably kills bacteria and speeds the breakdown of nitrates. For this reason it can be a valuable aid for fish breeders. On the other hand, the pH value can be lowered to such an extent when ozone is used in soft water that the fishes are threatened. Ozone can also be dangerous to humans. As soon as its typical smell is noticed outside the aquarium, the equipment must be checked.

An ozonizer consists of a high tension transformer and discharge chamber through which air is conducted. Through an electrical discharge, atmospheric oxygen (O_2) is partially changed into ozone (O_3). Usually an ozonizer is simply inserted between the air pump and the air outlet. However, the air pump and the air hoses have to be "ozone proof," since ozone damages PVC and rubber.

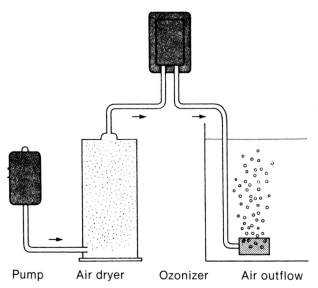

Pump   Air dryer   Ozonizer   Air outflow

Schematic of the connection of an ozonizer to an aquarium. Since ozonizers work best with drier air, this diagram shows an air dryer placed between the pump and the ozonizer. The silica gel used in most air dryers can be heated in an oven for reuse.

The output of an ozonizer depends largely on the humidity of the air: the drier the air, the more effective the work of this appliance. For this reason, it is sensible to purchase an air dryer, which is installed between the pump and the ozonizer. It is a pipe filled with silica gel equipped with a color indicator. When the coloration changes, the silica gel is saturated and has to be regenerated by drying. It can be dried in an oven at temperatures of 140 to 160 C.

Ultraviolet

Similar to ozone appliances are the effects of UV radiators or sterilizers. The radiation from special low-pressure discharge mercury lamps reliably kills bacteria and other germs that are in the water. The firmly established bottom bacteria, which are important for biological filtering are not reached by the UV rays, since the radiation in the water is effective only in the immediate surroundings of the lamp. The water must be made to flow directly by the lamp, using either an air-operated water pump or in conjunction with a filter. It is best to put the appliance between the filter outflow and the aquarium, since this will overcome the possibility of germs wrapped in dirt particles going past the UV barrier.

UV appliances have the unpleasant characteristic of reducing nitrates to toxic nitrites, thus reversing an important part of the biological reduction processes. This danger exists most of all in newly established aquariums. If some time after the initial use of the UV radiator the fishes become restless or, even worse, shoot reeling through the tank, they are probably suffering from nitrite poisoning. The fishes must be put immediately into non-toxic, aged aquarium water!

Top: A pump (power head) that can be attached to an undergravel filter to increase the rate of filtration. *Center:* Power filter assemblies that combine mechanical and biological filtration. *Bottom:* A basic undergravel filter with attached activated carbon cartridges.

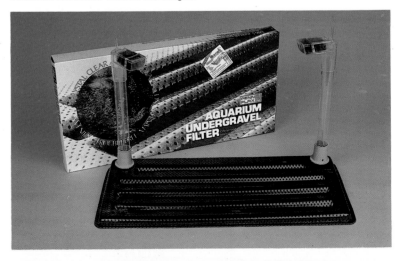

Carbon Dioxide

The growth of aquarium plants is dependent on carbon dioxide. Carbon dioxide is dissolved in the water in the form of carbonation. In the case of an undersupply of carbon dioxide, plant growth will stagnate. There are various possible ways to fertilize with carbon dioxide in the aquarium.

The simplest method, that of pouring carbonated water into the aquarium, is expensive and not recommended because of the concomitant salinization of the water. Most carbonated waters contain salt, either added for flavor or present naturally in the water itself.

There are several appliances commercially available for carbon dioxide fertilization, but I will not recommend the small diffusors. They require constant attention. The pH value especially must be constantly monitored (it should not drop below 6)! Several types of fully automated carbonation fertilization equipment have appeared on the market that are equipped with an electronic pH meter. As soon as the pH value drops below a previously set limit, the carbon dioxide supply is stopped by means of a magnetic valve.

In connection with the use of carbon dioxide, the following points must be made. Basically, carbon dioxide is beneficial only for plant growth; its use in a tank containing only fishes is senseless. Just as wrong is the operation of a carbon dioxide fertilizer and an aerator at the same time. The aerator immediately removes the carbon dioxide from the water!

Excessive carbon dioxide fertilization can lead to breathing difficulties in the fishes, especially at night and in the morning. With air breathers such as the labyrinth fishes, added caution is indicated. Since carbon dioxide weighs 1.53 times as much as air, it can collect in a layer directly above the water surface, thus poisoning the air breathers!

To take an unmistakable stand: good plant growth can absolutely be obtained *without* carbon dioxide fertilization. I consider carbon dioxide fertilization primarily a fad. However, perfectionists can obtain a certain effect with a not inconsiderable investment of money and time.

Water Softeners

For the greater part, tropical decorative fishes come from extremely mineral-poor waters — soft waters. The water flowing from our taps, however, is always harder, often even considerably harder. Many aquarium fishes can be easily kept in hard water and some even breed there. However, if you want to keep or even breed problem fishes, you need soft water; *i.e.,* you must reduce the hardness of the tap water.

The purchase of demineralized or distilled water becomes expensive and is only an emergency measure for short-term problems. Demineralized or distilled water must never be used unmixed, or our fishes will die! It is best to harden the distilled water somewhat with our tap water to the desired value. Many aquarists collect rain or snow water. This is quite adequate in many instances, but in industrial regions this water can sometimes be dangerous because of atmospheric pollution! Think of *acid rain!*

Suitable for a technical softening of the water are, above all, the ion exchangers. The anion exchangers exchange only anions such as chloride ($Cl-$), sulfate (SO_4-), and nitrate

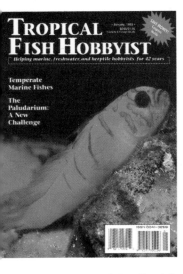

(NO$_3$−) for hydroxyl (OH−) ions; kation exchangers exchange cations such as sodium (Na+), potassium (K+), calcium (Ca++), and others for hydrogen (H+) ions. When the exchange resins are exhausted, they must be regenerated. Most areas have water softener companies. Check your telephone directory.

For more demanding aquarists, there are cartridge gadgets that operate on the mixing-bed principle. They can be attached directly to the freshwater tap. They can also be equipped with a meter measuring electrical conductivity, which will indicate the degree of hardness of the produced water right away. It goes without saying that these appliances are not exactly inexpensive. However, they are very well suited for breeders and aquarium shops.

Other Useful Accessories

In conclusion of the technical part, here is a listing of simple, usually inexpensive small accessories that simplify the maintenance of the aquarium. As an example, the purchase of a window cleaner is essential unless we want to use the razor blade in our bare hands. Also recommended is the purchase of an algae magnet. This consists of a pair of magnets, of which the one in the aquarium can be controlled by the one on the outside of the pane of the aquarium, allowing the removal of loosely clinging algae from inside the tank. However, in the long run even here an adhesive film will develop that can only be removed with the blade cleaner. Owners of plastic aquariums should do without algae magnets, since the danger of scratching the plastic is too great.

Furthermore, we need nets, since it will occasionally be necessary to get a fish out of the aquarium. Nets with a small mesh are not as suitable as nets with a larger mesh. To catch a fish, it is best to use two nets by trying to steer the fish with a moving net into a stationary one.

For the removal of debris, so-called bottom cleaners are available that can be hooked up to an air pump with an air hose and used like a vacuum cleaner. Actually, these appliances are superfluous, because it is quite sufficient if we remove the debris with a hose during the regular partial change of the water. This leads us to some further, important accessories. For the partial water change, we need a hose and, of course, one or two pails. The hose should be transparent, at least 2 m long, and should have a diameter of about 1 cm. There are automatic water changers on the market in America. Dr. Axelrod says they work very well, but I have no experience with them.

Automatic water changers are marvelous for providing a continuous exchange of new water for old. Some experts swear that they make spawning and raising of many formerly difficult fishes simple.

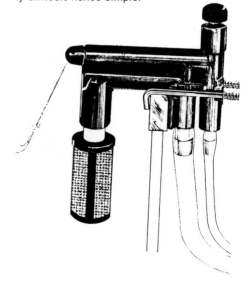

THE AQUARIUM WATER

The environment of our fishes and plants is water. Every aquarist knows that all waters are not equal. If algae are taking over or if the fishes won't breed, he looks for the reason first in poor water quality. Of course, other factors may be responsible for failures, but the composition of the water is indeed often of decisive significance in our hobby. Unfortunately, this recognition leads many aquarists to occupy themselves more with the chemistry of the water than with their actual hobby. Successful aquarists normally try to get by with as little chemistry as possible. For beginners especially, water chemistry is unnecessary ballast!

However, if someone wants to keep or possibly breed especially sensitive fish, he will need to familiarize himself with *some* basic facts of water chemistry, as follows.

Electrical Conductivity

There is no such thing as completely chemically pure water. Water always contains small amounts of dissolved gases, salts, minerals, and acids. The amount of substances dissolved in the water determines the electrical conductivity: a nearly chemically pure water is the distilled and demineralized water that can be purchased or manufactured with softening filters. This water has a conductivity of almost zero microSiemens (uS); *i.e.*, it barely conducts electricity. However, it cannot be used unmixed, since animals and plants would die after a short time in this water.

Most of our aquarium animals and plants come from tropical regions in which the water is markedly low in minerals. For this reason, some of these species are adaptable only within narrow limits in other water values; for

Kits containing all the equipment you need to start your aquarium hobby are available at most pet shops — sometimes at a savings from purchasing the items individually.

their proper care, but especially for breeding, they require suitable water. Our tap water is usually little suited for these species. Measurement of its conductivity would usually result in values between 150 and 800 microSiemens. By mixing with distilled or demineralized water, however, we are able to lower these values. Even in extreme cases, we need and should not go lower than 50 microSiemens (although fishes of the virgin forests sometimes occur in water even much poorer in minerals).

To a certain degree, the level of conductivity also depends on the water temperature. MicroSiemens indications normally are given for water temperatures of 20°C. Otherwise, the measurement temperature in °C is added to the indication.

"Problem fishes," such as these cardinal tetras, are difficult to breed or in some cases even keep because of their strict water condition requirements. Many problem fishes come from very soft, acid water with few dissolved minerals. Photo by H.J. Richter.

Water Temperature (in °C)	Correction Factor
16	1,10
18	1,05
20	1,00
22	0,96
24	0,92
26	0,84
28	0,79
30	0,75

Dependence of electrical conductivity on temperature. The conductivity is usually converted to 20°C; this table gives the necessary correction factors.

Conductivity meters are expensive appliances and are a poor investment for the care of a living-room aquarium. However, someone who wishes to breed problem fishes more frequently will soon be unable to do without his electrical conductivity meter.

Hardness of the Water

While the measurement of conductivity includes all substances dissolved in the water, the measurement of the water hardness only includes the amount of the calcium and magnesium salts, the so- called hardness formers. A comparatively strongly conducting water because of a high tannin content may have a low degree of hardness. However, hard water *always* has a high conductivity value.

The hardness of the water is made up of different components. Carbonate hardness indicates the total amount of all calcium and magnesium carbonates, including hydrogen carbonate. This hardness is easy to get rid of by prolonged boiling, since calcium and magnesium carbonates are precipitated as a sediment. For this reason, we speak of them causing *temporary hardness.*

The usually greater part of hardness-forming calcium and magnesium ions, however, are not bound to carbonates but to other anions. The most frequent such anions are sulfates and, in smaller amounts, also chlorides, nitrates, phosphates, and others. Since the water hardness caused by these salts cannot be eliminated by boiling, they are called *permanent hardness.*

The total of the calcium and magnesium salts dissolved in water is referred to as overall hardness. Its definition is that 1 degree German hardness (DH) equals a content of 10 mg calcium oxide (lime) in 1 liter of water.

Purely mathematically, the sum of carbonate hardness and non-carbonate hardness must be the same as the overall hardness. Because of technical problems with fine measurements, this may not always be so in practice, since the reagents for the determination of carbonate hardness indicate merely the amount of carbonates, no matter to which cations they may be bound. In the majority of cases they are really the hardness formers calcium and magnesium, but if there is much sodium carbonate in the water — as is the case in some East African lakes — it can happen that a much higher value is measured for carbonate hardness than for over-all hardness. The measuring reagents for the overall hardness indicate exactly the amount of hardness formers.

To classify the degrees of hardness, the following values are customary:

very soft water	0 - 4° DH
soft water	5 - 8 DH
medium hard water	9 - 12° DH
fairly hard water	13 - 18° DH
hard water	19 - 30° DH
very hard water	above 30° DH

Most tropical fishes prefer relatively soft water. (Generally, some African cichlids and some livebearers can be mentioned as exceptions.) The aquarist should know the degree of hardness of his tap water — a call to the water company might help. Values up to 12° DH are best suited for average aquarium purposes. Even with a hardness up to 20° DH, most fishes can be kept without problems. For the breeding of many fishes, however, it is necessary to soften the water by mixing it with demineralized water. The degrees of hardness can be determined without much trouble by means of chemical reagents (several kits are available in the stores). For measuring, we add to a small water sample drop after drop of the reagent until a color change indicates that the measuring is completed. The number of drops required for this corresponds to the hardness of the water. Each kit contains complete instructions.

The Acidity of the Water

As is commonly known, chemists call water H_2O. This means that water consists of molecules composed of hydrogen (H) and oxygen (O). All non-distilled water is dissociated to a minimal degree; *i.e.*, some water molecules (H_2O) have become decomposed into positively charged $H+$ ions and negatively charged $OH-$ ions. The product of these two kinds of ions remains constant.

In neutral water, $H+$ ions and $OH-$ ions are available in exactly equal amounts. One liter of neutral water contains one-tenth of a millionth gram of hydrogen ions, expressed more clearly as 10^{-7} g. To simplify this representation even further, merely the negative logarithm is used, and we say that the water has a pH (percent hydrogen ion) value of 7.

If the water contains ten times the amount of $H+$ ions, the corresponding concentration of $OH-$ has to be lower, since the total of the two kinds of ions remains constant. In this instance, we have a millionth g $H+$ ions in one liter water, or 10^{-6} g $=$ pH 6. A predominance of $H+$ ions, such as in this case, causes the water to react acidly; a predominance of $OH-$ ions makes it react alkalinely.

Our calculation shows that the dropping of the pH value by one degree of acidity makes the water ten times as

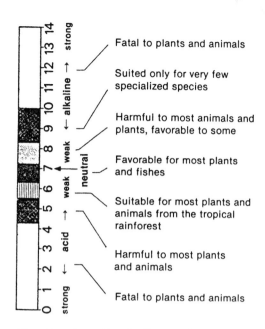

The pH scale and its significance for plants and animals.

acid. It is important to know that water with a pH value of 7 is neutral; that values below pH 7 are increasingly acid; and that values above pH 7 are increasingly alkaline.

Most tropical fishes find pH values between 6 and 7 in their home waters. Our tap water, on the other hand, is most frequently neutral to alkaline, but it is certainly possible to make the water somewhat acid to meet the requirements of the fishes. For this, filtering through peat or the slow, gradual addition of commercial humus preparations is particularly suitable. In general, however, the fish adapt quite well to our water conditions. On the other hand, since they often react sensitively to rapid changes of the pH value, we should warn against rash manipulation. Just remember that water with a pH value of 6.6 is twice as acid as that with a value of 6.7!

37

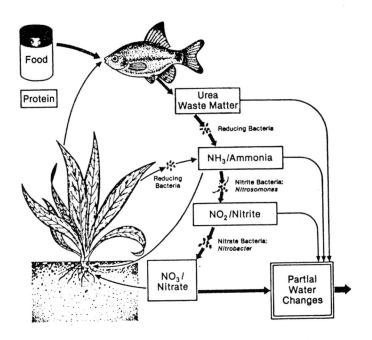

The nitrogen cycle in the aquarium. Through constant additions of protein in the form of fish foods, the nitrogen content of the aquarium rises steadily. Bacteria change the ammonia and nitrates to less harmful nitrates, which are partially absorbed by the plants. The rest must be removed by regular partial water changes.

An increase of acidity can be achieved with diluted phosphoric acid. However, this must be done with considerable care and, above all, outside the aquarium! If phosphoric acid is poured directly into the aquarium — unfortunately, this happens quite frequently — it will almost always cause damage.

In the normal aquarium, values between pH 6.5 and 7.2 are desirable, and there should be no experimentation beyond these values. For measuring the pH value, electrical equipment and standard chemical tests are available. For aquarium purposes, the chemical methods are usually sufficiently exact.

The Nitrogen Cycle

Decades ago, aquarists guarded their "old water" like a treasure. They believed that it was especially good for their fishes. It is a fact that old, established aquariums function much better than newly equipped ones because of their content of nitrogen-reducing bacteria — at least for a while. The higher plants are growing, and with this competition the algae don't have a chance and the fishes do well. But without a regular partial renewal of the water, the nitrogen- reducing substances increase to an extent dangerous to the fishes. How does this happen?

The element nitrogen (N) is an important component of protein and thus of all living substances. In every aquarium, organisms die and decompose after a short time. These are not necessarily dead fishes that have been overlooked — it is also true of plants and uneaten fish food. Protein reduction products are also given off regularly as part of the excretions of the fish (droppings, urine). In an old, established aquarium, an army of millions of bacteria is busily reducing these protein substances through different intermediate steps. The final step is nitrates, which in normal concentrations are completely non-toxic and are absorbed by the water plants as an important nutrient. This cycle, which in an undisturbed natural environment can be used as an excellent example of ecological equilibrium, can never be duplicated perfectly in the aquarium. Even in the best-equipped plant tank with a minimal number of fishes, the density of fishes is so great that the plants cannot use the nitrate completely. Even if the fish can stand nitrate in a relatively high concentration, the danger point will be reached sometime. Only a change of water can help here! Even the best filters cannot remove nitrates, which, by the way, do not indicate their presence by murkiness of the water or a certain coloration of the water. In order to avoid nitrate problems it is better to do frequent partial water changes rather than complete water changes at long intervals.

In addition to a change of the water, there is only one other sensible method for removing nitrates from the aquarium. As previously stated, nitrates are valuable plant nutrients. Some room plants, such as philodendrons, form long, strong air roots. If there is a possibility of placing these plants in the immediate vicinity of the aquarium, as many air roots as possible should be guided directly into the aquarium. There they will branch out very attrac-

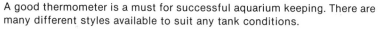

A good thermometer is a must for successful aquarium keeping. There are many different styles available to suit any tank conditions.

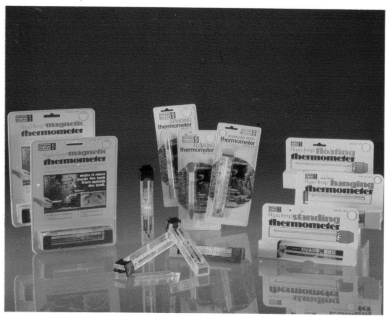

tively and remove a considerable portion of the nitrate from the water. However, since these plants, like all house plants, need light for their leaves in order to thrive, this possibility cannot be realized in many instances. Even if the use of these special "bio-filters" can extend the intervals between partial water changes, we will not be able to do without them entirely!

The reduction of proteins to nitrates occurs through different intermediate steps that are achieved by the work of different kinds of bacteria. Unfortunately, some of these intermediate products are highly toxic for the fishes, such as ammonia and nitrites. Dangerous concentrations of these substances occur only through uninformed meddling with the water. For this reason I always caution against excessive experimentation with the aquarium water!

Proteins usually are reduced via amino acids to ammonium salts and then further to nitrites and finally nitrates. Ammonium ions (NH_4+) are non-toxic. Under certain circumstances, however, they combine with the hydroxyl ion $(OH-)$ to form the highly toxic ammonia $(NH_3 \cdot H_2O)$. Logically, this happens especially when there are large amounts of free hydroxyl ions in the water; in other words, in alkaline water. To put it differently: as soon as the water reaches higher pH values, dangerous ammonia may be formed. The danger is especially great if, during the change of water, we add to very acid water the usually alkaline tap water.

If, after a partial water change, the sensitive fishes act in a troubled manner, breathing quickly at the surface as if they were suffering from a pronounced lack of oxygen, only a total change of water can help. Luckily, such instances occur only if the fishes are kept in a very acid environment but the water flowing from the tap is very alkaline.

Nitrite has a toxic effect on the fishes even in small amounts. With a too highly elevated nitrate content, the customary reduction processes in the aquarium may occur partially in reverse order. In that case the harmless nitrate turns, by reduction, to nitrite again! Here again a regular change of water will help. As a precautionary measure, we should feed only sparingly so that no remnants of food are left over that will decay.

Nitrite and nitrate content of the water can be determined easily by test kits. With some experience, however, a partial change of the water is barely more trouble than the determination of the water values. Since lower nitrogen contents are most reliably achieved by regular water renewals, such measurements may be unnecessary for most aquarists.

THE EQUIPMENT OF AN AQUARIUM

Basic Guidelines for the Aquarium Equipment

In the design of his underwater garden, the aquarist may use all his imagination. Here, I will answer only some basic questions.

Before thinking about the design of the aquarium, we first must determine what kinds of fishes we want to keep. It depends on their needs whether we will require many hiding places, whether a plant jungle can be planted, and many other things.

A fish breeder must equip his aquarium in a completely different manner from someone who will do behavior research, the latter differently again from a fish photographer or someone who wishes to set up a display aquarium as decoration in a room.

Here we will talk about the equipment of a simple home display aquarium, no doubt the most popular type. Such a display tank is certainly the most sumptuous as far as its furnishings are concerned. In many countries it is a "must" to decorate such an aquarium with plastic divers, underwater castles, and dragons. Of course, this is purely a matter of taste, since the fishes don't care one way or the other. I am glad that such aberrations are taboo among real aquarists in central Europe. The introduction of large scallop shells or corals into a freshwater aquarium also is not exactly the mark of an experienced aquarist, not to mention the fact that this will harden the water.

Let us be clear about the fact that the fishes could not care less about the decoration, whether in good taste or not. Of course, the interior decoration helps considerably to determine the structure of the living space. It is most important for many fishes to find hiding places in caves or to find shelter from view from above under roots or large-leaved plants. For other fishes, it is important to have sufficient open swimming space; others again require a plant jungle, and many need the opportunity of not being in constant visual contact with their cohabitants. This shows that the fishes are not totally indifferent to the equipment in their aquarium. Further hints are given in the descriptions of the genera and species.

Again and again, aquarists believe that the aquarium is a mirror image of nature in miniature. If you ever have the opportunity of seeing the plants and fishes in their natural habitat, you will quickly see your error: the water is by no means always crystal-clear, and most fish habitats are completely free of plants. Where plants are found, they form uniform, large clumps. Many streams are overgrown only with *Cryptocoryne* or *Vallisneria* covering the surface. In addition, many of our "water plants" in the wild grow mostly in swampy ground but exposed to the air (emersed). An aquarium established strictly following the dictates of nature is not decorative, quite in contrast, by

the way, to the natural marine aquarium. For this reason it is totally senseless to take into account geographical considerations when selecting the water plants. For the functioning of the biological processes it does not matter at all whether there are plants of one region only or whether African, Asian, and American plants are associated with each other. The main consideration is that their environmental requirements harmonize with each other.

A strict geographical orientation in the selection of the fishes is just as senseless. It must be clear to everyone that it is easier to combine small South American tetras with small Indian zebras than the zebras with the fish-eating snakeheads from the same range. This need not always be quite as evident as here, where a ravenous fish is paired with its prey.

Decorations

The most important and at the same time decorative materials in an aquarium are live plants. For many aquarists they are even more important than the fishes. For this reason, a separate chapter is devoted to the plants, their placement, care, and aquarium suitability; let me just point out here that they are much more than decorating materials.

Not every aquarium can be planted to the desired extent with plants. Some larger fishes dig so violently in the substrate that no plants will thrive; other fishes even are plant-eaters. Aquariums with these fishes can usually be equipped attractively only with decorative stones and roots. However, some plants may be placed even in these aquariums. For this I recommend above all ferns, since most fishes will eat them only reluctantly. Suitable ferns are the various horticultural forms of water sprite, *Ceratopteris thalicroides*, which form floating leaves that will also extend into the air space and whose long, densely branched roots extend deep into the water; *Bolbitis heudelotii;* and the Java fern, *Microsorium pteropus*. The last two ferns are tied in bundles with rubberbands or nylon thread to pieces of wood, bark, or rocks and will anchor themselves to their substrate after a while.

Whether we have a planted tank or not, our aquarium will need a substrate, a decorative rear wall, and rocks for decoration.

Substrate

The selection of the correct substrate is a source of many arguments. Much is a matter of faith: many things that have been tested and approved will fail with extensive use or with different water conditions. One thing is certain, however: the formerly defended opinion that the substrate should be fertilized with humus or peat like a garden is absolutely wrong! This leads to rotting spots in the substrate that cause the plant roots to die.

Safe and inexpensive manufactured duplicates of natural decorative items such as old logs and rock caves are now readily available in any pet shop. They require no soaking or special treatment to make them suitable for the aquarium and last virtually forever. The components of rock caves often firmly attach to each other, making accidental collapse impossible. Nature can definitely be improved upon.

Fine gravel (with a grain of between 1 and 5 mm) has proven itself most suitable for good plant growth. The individual grains should be rather larger in size than too small. Grains that are too fine will render a water current through the substrate impossible in the long run because the fine pores between the grains are quickly clogged up with debris. As a result the plant roots no longer get any oxygen and the plants sicken and finally die.

It is often considered advantageous to cover the substrate with a layer of somewhat coarser gravel. Just like other types of substrate layers, this layer is unstable in the long run. With the planting of new plants, the gravel-shifting activities of snails, and especially because of fishes that dig, the layering will soon be mixed up.

For many fishes, gravel with a diameter of more than 1 mm is unsuitable. Many catfishes and dwarf cichlids need fine sand for digging and grubbing. We may allow these small fishes to dig since they cannot cause much damage to the planting. For many fishes that care for their broods, a gravel bottom could destroy the entire brood, since the eggs or the helpless fry might fall between the pebbles and no longer be reachable by the parents. In these cases, finer sand is indicated. If some Malayan snails are put into the aquarium, we do not have to be afraid of a lack of oxygen in the substrate. The snails live in the substrate and are constantly busy plowing and loosening it without damaging the roots of the plants. In the aquarium the Malayan snail fulfills the role that earthworms play in the garden. The Malayan snail propagates well (sometimes too well) without our help and in addition are no disturbance at all while living on the bottom. They are ideal helpers that also remove debris and small overlooked dead animals.

When selecting the substrate, we should try to obtain shades as dark as possible. The danger of an overgrowth of algae on a dark background is smaller and the fishes are usually considerably more effective over a dark bottom, since they then are usually more brightly colored.

Fertilizer

Should we add fertilizer to the substrate or not? This is disputable. We should remember, however, that artificial fertilizer furnishes an excess of mineral salts, which are required only in minute amounts. It is a fact that we regularly have an unnecessary, even harmful, excess of these nutrient salts, which forces us to remove these substances by a change of water. On the other hand, with the addition of fresh water, trace elements are constantly added to the aquarium and can be absorbed by the plants. In many cases a frequent change of water is completely sufficient to supply the mineral needs of the aquarium. I should not forget to mention that the tap water is also more or less enriched with trace elements, depending on its origin. Nitrogen sufficient for most purposes in the aquarium comes from the plant and animal wastes.

Many plants absorb the mineral salts in dissolved form from the water with their leaves. Others — usually not genuine water plants but rather swamp plants that are kept under water, such as *Cryptocoryne* — depend mainly on their roots for the absorption of nutrient salts. These plants often react quite favorably to additions of fertilizer. If they are to grow optimally and we want to do without fertilization, for the time being we should not be too thorough when washing the substrate. Muddiness that appears when washing the fresh sand or gravel bottom normally consists of clay. It is thus sufficient to wash out only the coarsest muddy substances from these sands. We should then cover the substrate with a finger-thick layer of the same material, but this time extremely well washed. We may now certainly wait for a year before adding fertilizers!

Rocks

Rocks are almost essential in the decoration of an aquarium. They are used in the partitioning of the tank, for the construction of caves and hiding places, for the construction of terraces, and for shaping the substrate. Not all rocks are suitable for aquarium purposes. Many give off hardeners after prolonged soaking in water. Someone who wishes to keep hard-water fishes will not need to restrain himself in the selection of rocks — he can even use chalky rocks that often come with holes and bizarre shapes. In most cases, however, use rocks that will not harden the water, such as granite. Calcium-free slate, sandstone, and quartzite are also suitable.

Since few aquarists are also geologists, it is useful to know a method for determining whether a rock contains undesirable calcium components. This is the hydrochloric acid test. A few drops of diluted hydrochloric acid are put on the rock or gravel sample. If gas bubbles form in the acid or if it foams, the rock or substrate is unusable for our purposes!

We should refrain from looking for geological rarities among the rocks. Rocks with enclosures of unknown minerals may lead to poisoning of our fishes. Do not use any sharp-edged rocks in the aquarium.

Roots, Cork, Peat, and Reeds

Dead tree roots that have been in the water for some time are excellently suited for the aquarium, especially the roots of alders, oaks and beeches. Especially advantageous is the bizarre bog pine wood, the roots of pines that have rested in the soil of peat bogs for a long time. Before we put the roots into the aquarium, we have to boil them thoroughly. On one hand, this kills undesirable germs and small living things; on the other, it forces out enough air so that the roots lose their buoyancy in water. Dry roots will become heavy enough for use if soaked in water long enough for them to become water-logged. Always select the smaller pieces of wood — it is easy to over- estimate the capacity of the aquarium in this regard.

All roots, even some of the petrified woods that are sometimes commercially available, give off humic acids. However, this takes place only to a quite limited degree and may ultimately even be viewed as a positive addition to the aquarium water.

I would like to point out once more that it is quite useful to guide the air roots of certain houseplants into the aquarium. They branch out very attractively and remove some noxious substances (mostly nitrates) from the water.

Cork bark is also suitable for decorating. Cork is chemically neutral and does not give off any noxious substances. However, cork does not lose its buoyancy even after prolonged soak-

Dense jungles of aquatic plants are preferred by some aquarists, but probably most hobbyists would just like to have a good growth of a few species to provide an interesting background for their fishes. The fishes must have room to swim and behave normally, and few aquarium fishes are normally inhabitants of dense weedbeds. However, a growing number of aquarists are finding that keeping plants to the exclusion of tropical fishes can be very interesting, a practice already widely accepted in Europe.

Opposite: The beauty of aquarium decorations is in the eye of the beholder—if you like mermaids and treasure chests, then use them (top). German aquarists consider such things to be rather immature, however, and prefer more natural scenes such as could be obtained with carefully printed and prepared backgrounds (bottom).

ing. Therefore, we have to either glue it in place or weigh it down with rocks. Cork boards are also very well suited for the construction of terraces or of rear walls.

Peat should be put into the aquarium only in exceptional cases. In the moors of Europe and the northern U.S. one sometimes finds very decorative peat boards interwoven with wood that — set vertically against the rear wall — are very suitable for background decoration. Formerly, entire rear walls were constructed from peat boards. However, peat has the characteristic that, depending on its consistency, it will disintegrate completely after a rather brief period of time. In addition, peat gives off tannic acid that acidifies the water and colors it yellow or brownish.

To imitate a tropical rice paddy, it sometimes may appear attractive to imitate reeds standing vertically in the water. For this, thin bamboo sticks or pepper reeds are particularly well suited. In contrast to our local reed stems, these materials are fairly durable in water. They appear most natural if the stems are of varying thicknesses and are planted in irregular groups.

Shaping the Rear Wall

Most aquariums are put up with one long dimension against the wall. So that we do not end up with the wallpaper as background decoration we have to provide a suitable rear wall. We have here two basic possibilities:

We may fasten the cork wall dry, so to speak, to the outside of the aquarium or we may put it directly in the aquarium. If this should prove sensible and necessary, we may, of course, decorate the sidewalls also.

It is easiest to cover the back wall of the aquarium on the outside with paper or fabric. (Dark velvet often is most effective here.) Of course, the simplest course is to use one of the printed backgrounds available in pet shops. Not all of these rear walls are tasteful, but if our aquarium is sufficiently planted in the rear later on, even these rear walls appear quite attractive. It also is possible to buy printed plastic back walls that are strongly textured and have a three-dimensional appearance. These are quite effective because of their structure and shadow effects.

With some talent as a handyman it is possible to construct very beautiful exterior rear walls that additionally give the aquarium an added appearance of depth. For this, we build from plywood or other suitable materials a shallow box to the size of the aquarium rear wall. For a smaller aquarium, we may also cut down a sturdy cardboard box to the desired size. Depending on the size of the aquarium, the depth should be between 5 and 15 cm. Into this box we glue, according to taste and the character of our tank, sand, gravel, peat, small and larger bits of cork bark, flat roots, twigs, and reeds. The roots and some other materials should extend into the front of the box in order to obtain an appearance of depth. In any case, we should see to it that the interior decoration continues without a visual break into the rear shadow box.

It is sensible to restrain ourselves in the selection of the materials. A box covered only with cork may be very effective. Additional effects can be achieved by illuminating the rear wall with a small lamp installed for this purpose. Be careful to consider the problem of possible overheating in the box and provide the necessary air holes! Safety comes before decorativeness! Let us also not forget that it is easy to

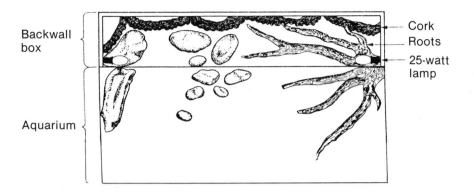

Backwall box

Aquarium

Cork
Roots
25-watt lamp

Diagrammatic view from above of a rear wall decoration box. The dry decorations in the box should continue the decor of the aquarium without a gap.

go overboard and produce a cluttered, distracting background. It often is readily apparent that the rear walls fastened behind the glass are dry, so it is sometimes helpful, especially in the shadow box just described, to cover the decorative materials with a transparent but reflective varnish.

Rear walls that are positioned directly in the aquarium are often more effective. The rear wall fastened on the inside also has the advantage that we may tie different water ferns (*Microsorium, Bolbitis*) directly to it with threads and they soon will root themselves there and make the rear wall more lively.

What materials are suited for the interior wall? Above all, they must be non- toxic, should not give off any substances into the water, and should be easily worked. When preparing the interior wall, we must take special care to prevent the fishes from being able to swim between the rear wall and the aquarium pane and getting stuck there!

Styrofoam has proven to be an easily worked and shaped material that also is completely unobjectionable biologically. This material may be purchased in hobby and building material stores in many different sizes and thicknesses. The slab may easily be a few centimeters in thickness. The thicker it is, the more three- dimensional can we make it.

First we cut the styrofoam to the exact measurements of our aquarium rear glass. Then we work over the slab with a cigarette lighter or a candle flame; with larger blocks, this job is easier and faster with a blow torch. Styrofoam does not burn, but it does melt under the flame, so we may sculpt caves and ledges according to our taste; at the same time, the flame hardens the surface of the material and the slab will no longer crumble.

Now we can paint the rear wall. Of course, we will select drab shades for this — gray, brownish, or solid black is very effective. Non-soluble paints that

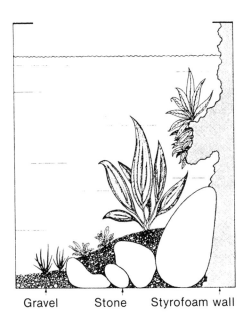

Gravel   Stone   Styrofoam wall

Cut away side view of a formed Styrofoam wall in piace in the aquarium. Styrofoam is easily shaped and provides a fine base for mosses and ferns.

generous with the substrate and it helps to in addition lean one or two rocks against the rear wall so that the wall cannot be pushed up laterally from below. It is easy to underestimate the force with which a styrofoam rear wall strives to reach the top! To get a feel for this, first test the anchoring of the styrofoam wall in a full aquarium with the substrate and rocks before adding plants and animals! If we have miscalculated, the damage thus is not as great. If you like this method of shaping but the risks of a styrofoam interior wall seem too great, you may, of course, form an outside rear wall by this method.

Artificially decorated tanks are just as attractive in the eye of many hobbyists as are natural tanks. Certainly the fishes cannot tell the difference between a plastic plant and a real plant unless they try to eat it, and rock caves have no obvious advantages over formed ceramic ones.

dry in about 24 hours or less and are harmless to animals and plants must be used of course.

Before filling the tank with water, we must firmly glue or wedge the styrofoam rear wall into place. This presents the disadvantage of this otherwise very recommendable method: styrofoam has an immense buoyancy! This is one reason for not exaggerating the thickness of the slab. Styrofoam is suited largely for those aquariums in which the rear wall can be jammed under a projecting upper frame. Larger glued glass aquariums have a center or at least side wall braces, under which we may fasten the rear wall. If the rear wall fits snugly against the bottom pane, it will not have to be additionally fastened. In any case, we have to be

SETTING UP
THE AQUARIUM

As is widely known, many paths lead to success, and many an expert may proceed individually according to a different plan from the one shown here. I intend this chapter as an assist for those who have little experience concerning the setting up of an aquarium. The following tips should help the beginning aquarist to end up with a beautiful and functional aquarium with as small an investment as possible.

In the installation of an aquarium, some basic ground rules have to be considered. Also, a certain sensible sequence should be followed when working. Beyond that, it is recommended that you follow rules of esthetics in the decoration.

If you are installing a larger aquarium for the first time, you should not forego the trouble of making a floorplan sketch of your aquarium before beginning with the work. On this sketch you will note how you plan to arrange the decorative materials. A part of this is to think about the placement of the plants. Professionals would not bypass planning the interior decoration in a sketch before beginning the work, particularly with a very large aquarium.

The choice of the proper site for our aquarium has already been discussed. Next we have to obtain a pad of styrofoam or felt that will be trimmed to the dimensions of the bottom of our tank. If we have a bottom heating mat, it will be placed on the pad. Remember, we must turn the heater on only after the aquarium has been filled with water!

Now we collect our installation and decoration materials: substrate, roots, rocks, bark, and plants. Then the great scrubbing begins, preferably under running water. First, the aquarium is cleaned as thoroughly as possible. Normally, its disinfection is not necessary. Existing algae and calcium rings possibly are best removed with a sharp razor

Cryptocoryne ciliata is one of the larger crypts and should be planted in small groups. On the rock in the background is a group of Java fern, *Microsorium pteropus*. Photo by J. Vierke.

blade; calcium rings may also be rubbed off with a rag soaked in vinegar. Roots and rocks must be thoroughly brushed under running water to be freed of dirt and algae.

Now we fit the interior rear wall. It must fit precisely, so that no fish can get between the wall and the back glass pane to get stuck there. If we prefer an exterior rear wall, it is best to fasten it on now, too.

Next, the rocks are put into the aquarium. The large rocks should be placed to the sides or rear of the aquarium. So that they cannot be undermined and caused to fall over, we set them directly on the bottom of the aquarium (being very careful when using a heating mat). If you want to construct a cave from several rocks, you may glue the rocks to each other with silicone sealant. This is very sturdy, is not visible later if we work carefully, and we can be sure that our work will remain stable. Such caves should be glued togther several days before the actual installation of the aquarium because they require time to harden in air.

Many aquarists now distribute smaller pebbles on the floor of the aquarium. They serve only indirectly as decoration by preventing the immediate leveling of the substrate by the activity of digging fishes and snails. Even if we do not wish to construct real terraces, it is more attractive if the substrate of the tank inclines toward the back. If we put in a sufficient number of stones whose height is about the thickness of the substrate, we will get mini-terraces that are barely noticeable later on but which will help to stabilize the slope of the bottom.

Now to the substrate. Many pet stores offer pre-washed natural gravel in several grain sizes and in different colorations (best is dark gravel with a grain diameter of 1-5 mm). If you would like it cheaper, you may get the gravel from the building material trade or directly from outdoors, but you must be prepared to invest much time in the washing of such gravel! The washing of the gravel may test our patience quite severely. Even pre-washed gravel must be washed again!

In summer it is best to wash the gravel directly in the yard (if you have one!), otherwise the bathtub must be pressed into service. For washing, put the gravel in small portions into a bowl or pail and spray it with a strong stream of water. As a substitute we can use an old cooking spoon or our hand for stirring up the gravel. The water above the gravel is poured off and the entire procedure is repeated until the water remains clear. The first one or two bowlfuls of gravel need not be rinsed out quite as thoroughly; it is even desirable to get some clay into the bottom — it will profit the growth of the plants! This coarsely washed layer of gravel should be covered with a layer of very well washed substrate.

We fill the bottom at the front of the aquarium to about the level of the lower frame; in frameless tanks we go to about 5 cm in height. Toward the back, the bottom may rise to about 15 cm. Usually we underestimate the quantity of gravel: for a 100-liter aquarium, we must assume 15 liters of gravel, for a 300-liter aquarium as much as 60 liters of gravel!

Now we install the technical appliances: heater (if we do not have a heating mat), regulator, filter. These appliances are not to be turned on yet!

The heater is fastened with suction cups directly above the substrate on a side or rear wall. Since a heater is not exactly a decorative element, we will try to camouflage it with a rock or root of suitable dimensions. We proceed similarly with our temperature regulator (thermostat), which we install, if possible, in the vicinity of the rear wall, in the corner farthest removed from the heater.

When placing the rocks and roots in the tank, the planned planting must be taken into consideration. For esthetic reasons, a too symmetrical arrangement is to be avoided. Large rocks or striking roots should never be placed directly in the center of the aquarium, but should be shifted toward the side or should be placed directly along the side. With stones we have to avoid an excessive collection of different kinds of rocks. Our aquarium should not turn into a geological display case! It is best to stick with one kind of rock.

With planting, we should take our time. We could begin to plant now, but we might lose the overall view very quickly. It is best to fill in a quarter to a third of the water now. We have to pour in the water very carefully so that the substrate is disturbed as little as possible. For this, we first cover the bottom with newspapers and guide the stream of water onto the paper or into a small bowl that has been placed on the paper. The filling is done by means of a pail or with a long water hose that has been connected directly to the tap. Take care that the water is slightly warm when filling. In any case, never heat up water that is too cold by adding a few liters of boiling water — there is considerable danger that the aquarium might crack!

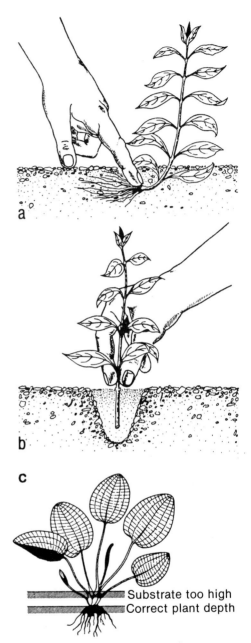

Substrate too high
Correct plant depth

Stemmed plants are not just pushed into the substrate (a). They are set into prepared planting holes and filled from the side (b). The roots and leaves should not be covered by soil. In plants that spring from a basal rosette (c), the leaf bases should not be covered by the substrate, which should just barely cover the roots.

Aquatic mosses provide much of the background for this impressive group of African tetras and other fishes in a very large tank. Notice how simple is the design of this aquarium, with just large groups of plants, driftwood as a place of attachment, a simple bottom, and plenty of swimming space for the fishes. Photo by Dr. Herbert R. Axelrod at Nancy Aquarium, France.

When we have filled in about one-third of the water, we pause and wait until the water reaches room temperature. Now we plant. With the initial planting, we cannot do too much of a good thing in regard to the amount of plants we put in. Sensibly, we will at first use mostly fast- growing, inexpensive plants. When after three to four months the aquarium has been "broken in" and we can gradually replace these plants with slower growing and more valuable plants. First we group the plants according to species. When

planting, follow the planting plan and the following guidelines. With the exception of a few especially beautiful accent plants, we should always plant our plants in groups. If necessary, the bunch plants are cut off at the bottom if they have already lost their leaves there. We need not pay any attention to roots; they will grow again in a short time. When planting the bunch plants, one mistake is often made that leads to the rotting of the lower stem parts. Never simply push the stem into the substrate with the finger! This literally crushes the soft, large-pored parts of the stem. Instead, poke a hole into the substrate with your finger, into which you stand the cutting. Then fill in the sand from the side.

Even when we place the plants in a group, we should always put only one cutting into a planting hole. The distance from one slip to the next should amount to at least twice the length of the leaf. In a too dense stand, the lower leaves get too little light and die off.

Broad-leaved plants must be treated differently. Their sometimes well-formed tap roots, as in *Cryptocoryne*, we leave untouched. They contain nutrients that help the plant to overcome the stress of transplantation. On the other hand, the smaller roots, especially in tightly rooted plants, are more harmful than useful. They die off after planting and new roots are formed. In newly planted plants, too many and too long roots may begin to rot and interfere with the formation of new roots. As a rule, therefore, cut back the roots to about one-third of their original length. Use the remaining roots to anchor the plant in the substrate. Besides, the plant can draw some nutrients from them.

Above all, we must not plant the broad-leaved plants too deeply in the substrate. The crown, the so-called heart of the plant, always must peek out above ground! For this reason, the plant should be set into the ground only to the very tops of the roots.

Once all the plants have found their place in the aquarium and the water has remained more or less clear, we again cover the water surface with two or three layers of newspaper and add water. In frame aquaria fill to the lower edge of the upper frame; in frameless

This interesting specimen of *Cryptocoryne korthausi* is not in the best of condition. Many aquarists have trouble keeping crypts and similar plants very long in the aquarium, although some hobbyists have no trouble at all with these plants. Be careful not to injure the tap root when replanting crypts. Photo by R. Zukal.

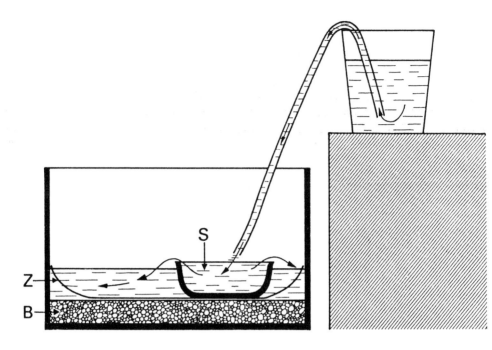

One method of filling the aquarium. A pail of water is placed above the level of the tank and water led into the aquarium by a siphon. To prevent disturbing the substrate (B), cover it with newspaper (Z). By directing the water into a bowl first (S) it will not dig a hole in the bottom.

aquaria fill to about 3-5 cm below the upper edge of the tank. An initial slight murkiness of the water disappears after a few days, and the air bubbles that form on the glass disappear even more quickly.

However, if the murkiness of the water after planting or after the last filling should be very disagreeable, change the water completely. Take a water hose — an indispensable aid when changing the water — and put one end into the aquarium water; suck on the other end until the water begins to flow, according to the siphon principle. (This principle works only if the other end of the hose is lower than the water level.) We run the water into a pail or, if the hose is long enough, directly into a drain. If we refill the aquarium with new water very carefully, following the method described initially, the water now should be clear.

After the aquarium has been filled with water, the plants usually lie haphazardly. With the hand or a wooden stick, put them back into the desired position. This is also the moment for replanting those plants that perhaps were pulled from the substrate during filling.

Now we can install the thermometer and put the lighted hood into position, and switch on the light and heater and possibly other appliances. There is only one thing we should not do now: put the fish in right away!

It is most sensible to leave the aquarium completely without fish for the first three or four days and only moderately lighted. If we put the fish in immediately, we risk the fish being damaged by gas bubble disease or suffering chlorine poisoning — sometimes they even die from these damages! In addition, adding the fish during the first few days encourages a possible infestation of blue- green algae. They also often interfere with the undisturbed rooting of the plants (this is particularly true of the algae- eaters, which are most welcome after a week to fight against blue-green algae). Their excretions and excess food may cause dirtying of the water.

It is important in the freshly installed aquarium to during the first days cut back the amount of light initially to half the normal value or even less. Be aware of the fact that the plants first have to form new roots — this phase lasts for two to ten days, depending on the kind of plant. During this period the plants live largely off their stored food — light for photosynthesis is not important now. The reaction of green and blue-green algae, which are always present in small numbers, is different: with immediate bright lighting they can leap from virtually nothing to a mass propagation. Against the competition of numerous, well-rooted higher plants, however, they have a much tougher stand. For this reason, then, our aquarium should operate for the first four days with a markedly reduced light output until the majority of the plants have rooted. An initial fertilization would be disadvantageous in any case — it would only work in favor of the algae! On the whole, it is much better to err on the side of too little when fertilizing!

When the tank gets full light after four days and the fish are added, we should follow one rule: at first, we should replant as little as possible! It is best to leave the tank alone as much as possible. Only if a slimy green or blue-green film forms on the lighter spots should it be attacked. However, though these blue-green algae can be fought mechanically only to a limited degree, once our aquarium is really broken in — this can take three months — they will disappear by themselves.

As I have described repeatedly, a "broken-in aquarium" implies a community that functions well based mainly on healthy plant growth and a well balanced bacterial flora. If you do not reach this goal, you will not enjoy your aquarium. Many an aquarist got rid of his aquarium because he was too impatient and took apart the aquarium at the first sign of blue-green algae, washing and disinfecting the bottom, not allowing any bottom bacteria to establish themselves. Others who spent a lot of money on fish saved on a sufficiently dense initial planting under the motto "the shoots will grow by themselves!" This method works occasionally, but by no means always.

To get a functioning bacterial flora as soon as possible, we should, if possible when equipping a new aquarium, add a bit of the substrate from a well-established aquarium, rinsing off only the coarsest dirt in cool or luke-warm water. The best experiences have been made with such a "bacterial breeding stock." As a substitute, small amounts of garden soil may also be used.

Regular Care

The amount of work caused by an aquarium to its owner was and is still often overestimated! Frequently aquaria fail to thrive in which too much fussing takes place. I know one aquarist who had been seduced by incessant advertisements to install a super-perfect aquarium at great financial sacrifice, with all the technical refinements: filter, carbon dioxide diffusor, special substrate. The plants were fertilized. The water chemistry was constantly being tested for all kinds of different factors and then carefully regulated. However, he was not happy with his aquarium. The plants would not grow and the fishes refused to thrive. Only when he had to leave his aquarium for a few weeks for job-connected reasons and his wife only did what was absolutely essential, when this aquarist thought that algae, diseases, and water pollution would take over completely, that was when his aquarium became balanced. The water remained clear, the plants showed healthy growth, and the fishes got good colors.

With this description I do not wish to cause the impression, however, that all work with an installed aquarium is harmful, that the technical aids and water checks are unnecessary. That would be nonsense! I only wish to warn against excessive zeal. Experience shows that the danger of an aquarist neglecting his fully equipped aquarium is less great than that of his fussing it to death.

More important for the thriving of the entire system than the work in the aquarium is primarily patient observation in front of the tank. We might as well be aware that this calls for an attitude that is in contrast to our performance-oriented society. In our society

If you have trouble keeping living plants, then artificials are better for your aquarium than the real thing — at least they won't turn brown and die.

the "doer" is in demand, not the remote, quiet observer. However, it is just this quiet contemplation that gives meaning to our aquarium hobby; it allows us to take a break from the everyday demands of our job.

Seen in this light, this part of our hobby, the daily observation of our pets is not work, even though it is part of the regular care. We should allow nothing to interfere with the 10 or 15 minutes that we spend sitting quietly in front of the aquarium. After all, this is the reason why we have it! Usually we will devote ourselves to our fishes in the evening or afternoon, when we return from work, when we feed them and observe their behavior. In this manner we will soon get to know our fishes and have the possibility of intervening in case of unusual behavior or appearance.

Daily Care and Feeding

Both daily and monthly jobs are part of the care for our aquarium. The daily care should not be considered "work" at all. It virtually takes care of itself as part of the daily observation period. Three things should be checked during the daily maintenance: the water temperature, the lighting, and the behavior and appearance of the fishes during feeding. It is obvious that you will additionally discover other things, for instance with the plants. Our activities should be consciously restrained, and we should by no means doctor the plants daily.

The check of the water temperature and the lighting is as easy as possible and practically incidental if we have a thermostat for the heater and an automatic timer for the light. In the long run, we should not do without the purchase of these two appliances. Never-theless, we should daily check the functioning of the heater — a glance at the aquarium thermometer is sufficent!

If you do not have an automatic light timer, you must turn the light on and off every day, if possible always at about the same time. The plants require light for at least 12 hours per day. However, many must not be lighted for more than 14 hours; some plants resent this.

A group of callistus tetras and swordtails during feeding. The few neons at the bottom of the crowd will obviously be able to get only the leftovers. No matter how much food you put into the aquarium, it will not help the fishes if it does not get to them — remember to take into account the feeding patterns of every species. Photo by B. Kahl.

It will be most practical to combine the daily observation of our fishes with their feeding. Abnormalities in the behavior of our fishes are most easily apparent at that time. Fishes that are not feeling well are often apathetic and refuse to eat. For this reason alone, we should not purchase an automatic feeder — besides, it is fun to watch the fish eat. I will deal later with the kinds of food available in greater detail. Let me just state here that if possible (at least on high holidays!) we should occasionally give our fishes live food.

It is easy to make mistakes in feeding. In most instances, the beginner will put much too much food in the water. This holds true particularly for dried and frozen foods. By the way, the latter should always be given completely thawed!

Let us make it a rule to never give more food than is eaten in five minutes! If we really have the feeling that our fishes are not getting enough, we can without hesitation give them some more, and perhaps after another five minutes a further small portion. In this way we will soon get a feel for the right amount of food. Under no circumstances must the left-over food be allowed to remain lying on the bottom of the aquarium for any length of time. It will rot and spoil the water in the aquarium. At first, the beginner will almost always feel sympathy for the "hungry" fish that constantly "beg" for food. He can give them several portions of food per day, as long as he sticks to the five-minute limit!

Even if our fishes always appear to be hungry, one fasting day per week is good for them. In the wild, tropical fishes do not always find their table well set. Indeed, one of the predominant reasons of premature death in aquarium fishes is fatty liver degeneration!

Changes in the appearance or the behavior of our fishes, of course, are reason for concern. Fishes that show damaged fins or injuries of the skin are certainly being bothered by fishes of the same species or other fishes. Here we first have to watch until the attacker is identified. Then we have to determine whether we want to risk waiting for the matter to get settled by itself or whether we need to separate the fishes in question.

Some of the most frequently apparent changes are small white dots on the fins and the skin of the fishes. This is a symptom of the most frequent fish disease in the aquarium, *Ichthyophthirius*, often called "ich." This disease is caused by tiny one-celled parasites and is not dangerous with immediate countermeasures. The same is true of *Oodinium*, even smaller parasites that often appear like a fine white velvet cover on the fishes' skin. At the first appearance of the symptoms, one of the commercially available medicines for ich should be used (follow instructions exactly!). The treatment takes place in the aquarium, since usually all fishes are infected, even though the symptoms cannot be seen on all of them. Someone who misses the first signs of these diseases might easily lose his entire stock of fishes!

Fishes with undefinable illnesses should be isolated in a special individual tank. Only in this manner can an excessive spreading of the disease be avoided. Dead and dying fishes must be immediately removed from the aquarium, since on one hand they give off noxious substances into the water, and on the other they may infect other fishes.

Monthly Care

In addition to the daily care, there are other caretaking jobs to be done at greater intervals. It will prove advantageous to get accustomed to a regular schedule for these jobs and checks.

I consider it sufficient to roll up my sleeves once a month and get done with a partial water change and cleaning of the aquarium. Only with very sensitive fishes do I change the water partially every two weeks. In tanks used for raising young, even one-week intervals for care are required.

Parts of the monthly care are:
Cleaning of the aquarium glass
Renewal of about ¼ to ⅓ of the aquarium water
Siphoning off of debris
Thinning of the plants
Cleaning of the filter.
At first this seems to be a long list, but some of these jobs are done quite simply. After a while you will acquire a certain routine and will need only about half an hour for a medium-sized aquarium.

It is best to begin with the partial water change. However, before we begin to do anything in the aquarium, the heater and possibly the filter and other appliances are switched off. If the setup of our aquarium allows it, we work best with the lighting turned on. However, in many cases this will not be possible without danger. Rather than expose ourselves to risks with lamps, it is better to be satisfied with less advantageous lighting when cleaning. A light falling into the aquarium could endanger our lives!

Since we are changing only a part of the water, the siphoning of the water and the refilling take place with all the fishes and plants remaining in the aquarium.

Partial water changes can be made by using a siphon even if the aquarium is swarming with fishes and densely planted. The surface debris should be siphoned off with the water.

For siphoning, one end of the hose is put into the aquarium; the other is held lower and sucked on strongly. Initially there will be some small accidents — water in the mouth, water splashed around, etc. — but we will soon become accustomed to this method. If you do not wish to suck the water up with your mouth, you may first fill the hose with water and bring it — both ends held shut — into the described position. The aquarium will now drain by itself until the higher end of the hose is lifted out of the water.

We must put the siphon hose in the water in such a manner that the suctioning action can be stopped instantly. It is sufficient to hold a thumb or index finger in front of the hose opening. In this manner we can prevent curious fishes from getting into the hose. Of course, we could do this also by putting a net or a sieve (such as are avail-

All types of little gadgets are available to help care for the aquarium. *Top left:* battery-operated tank vacuums; *top right:* automatic planting tongs; *bottom left:* lead plant anchors; *bottom right:* combination glass cleaner and planting stick.

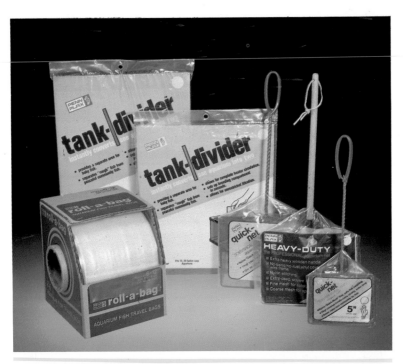

More gadgets. *Above:* various sizes of aquarium nets, tank dividers (essential for spawning many fishes), and plastic bags. *Below:* a large, fancy breeding trap often used with pregnant livebearers.

able for the intake pipes of outside filters) in front of the hose opening. But a sieve would prevent removing anything other than water. Together with the siphoning of the water, the debris that has collected on the bottom should be removed. For this we put the hose opening directly above the aquarium bottom and regulate the distance so that only debris — if possible no gravel — is siphoned off. Of course, this distance depends on the force of the current, which ultimately depends on the diameter of the hose and the level of the lower end of the hose.

This very simple method is usually sufficient to remove the accumulated debris. A "bottom vacuum cleaner" such as is available in pet stores is a mere toy, in my opinion. One might consider it an advantage that it can be used without siphoning off water at the same time, but I consider this just a disadvantage: one is constantly tempted to put off the overdue water change even longer, since the aquarium appears clean. In addition, the "bottom vacuum cleaner" is a constant temptation for many people to keep the aquarium spick and span. At the appearance of the slightest speck of debris, it is cleaned off — if possible every other day! That these constant disturbances can have negative consequences for our aquarium has already been explained in a different place.

If coarser gravel has been used for the substrate, we can construct a "suction bell." It consists of a plastic cup attached to our siphon hose. The connection from hose to cup is made of a rigid piece of plastic pipe attached with silicone sealant. With this cup we can stir up the substrate during siphoning and suck up the debris without any gravel getting into the hose. This

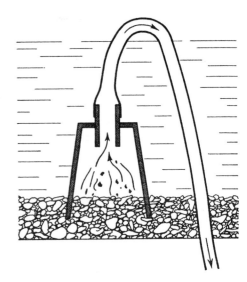

A homemade suction bell consisting of a plastic cup or small flowerpot, a short piece of plastic pipe covered with silicone rubber, and a siphon hose of the necessary diameter and length. Very useful for removing coarse debris from gravel.

method is particularly well suited for lightly planted large cichlid tanks, which often become very dirty. The best depth for the cup depends on the force of the suction and the size of the gravel grains. The optimal dimensions must be established by trial and error. Automatic water changers are fine but they do not remove debris. After siphoning off one–fourth to one-third of the water, we begin with the cleaning of the glass while it is still damp. If necessary, briefly moisten the portions that are above the water. The algae that grow on the glass above the water should be carefully scraped off in such a manner that as little as possible falls back into the aquarium. Each aquarist develops his own tricks for this; some prefer to clean the glass before siphoning off the water and to siphon off the fallen algae together with the other debris.

Now refill the tank with fresh water. For this purpose, spread a newspaper over the surface and fill the aquarium with a hose. You can connect the hose directly to the mixing tap in the bathroom. However, this method usually requires a partner who will open and close the faucet at the proper time. We could attach the hose with a U-pipe to the edge of the aquarium in such a manner that it doesn't slip, but it is better if we constantly have our hand on the outflow end of the hose to check that the water is neither too warm nor too cold. At the same time, our hand held in front of the stream helps prevent damage to the decorations in the aquarium from the force of the stream.

A thermometer is *not* required to check the temperature when refilling. The heat sensitivity of our skin is sufficient to warn us of extreme temperatures. If, as a result of our partial water change, the aquarium water is only 3° warmer or cooler than before, we need not worry. Such temperature differences are tolerated by all fishes — and even sensed as pleasurable by many. During the course of the next few hours, our thermostat will regulate the temperature to the original level.

A water change by means of pails is done in principle in the same manner, although it requires more work. It is usually not good to pour the lukewarm water directly from the pail into the aquarium, since this can cause havoc with our decoration. Here again, it is best to proceed according to the siphon principle. In this case, the filled pail with the siphon hose must be higher than the aquarium.

You may be wondering whether this might not be a good time for measuring the nitrate and pH values and running a hardness test or a CO_2 check. If the water had not been manipulated previously, such as by the addition of acid, this is not normally necessary. These checks may be quite interesting (occasionally) for the owners of community tanks — even more so for the manufacturers of the required chemicals! — but basically, they are just a game. However, I do not wish to hide the fact that many of these reagents are essential for fish breeders, for people interested particularly in ecology and water chemistry, and for the few aquarists who live in areas with very hard water. They, however, are not the *average* aquarists addressed in this chapter. Let me tell these aquarists that it is the purpose of regular water changes to maintain the water quality within the limits beneficial to the fishes. This makes a check of the water values unnecessary. The partial water changes make it possible to keep the hardness of the water low. Even more important is keeping low the nitrate and nitrite values. These and other constantly forming nitrogen combinations are harmful and must be constantly diluted by partial water changes.

Usually, the tap water can be put into the aquarium just as it comes from the tap — assuming that the temperature has been set correctly and the water is added very slowly. We may speed the process of chlorine diffusion by aerating the water with an automatic water changing device available in your pet shop. In old established aquaria, it is occasionally useful to add plant fertilizer to the water according to the instructions for use (*Cryptocoryne* reacts especially favorably to this).

It is part of the monthly care to inspect the plant growth and — if necessary — to intervene and correct the landscaping. With the fingernails or scissors, remove unsightly brown leaves. Shorten the stem of plants that have grown too tall by cutting the shoots immediately below the stipules, removing the lowest leaves, and replanting the newly formed shoot. The less attractive, rooted lower parts of the stems can be removed and thrown out unless you want to propagate these plants. In that case, leave the stem parts in the sand, and they will usually soon form side shoots. Check that the plants, carefully formed into groups, do not send runners into other groups and become intertwined. If you really like your underwater garden, you can spend a lot of time with its care. However, this also calls for the necessary sensitivity. Each growing thing transplanted to another spot needs time and strength to become rooted. Follow the principle: *"Transplant only when really necessary!"*

The purpose of thinning out is to let more light into the aquarium. Those plants and plant parts that float on the surface absorb much light, which the plants in the lower water layers then lack. As decorative and beautiful as floating plants are, we must keep their numbers low in the interest of the other plants. The often accidentally introduced little water plant known as duckweed should be fished out completely with a net! We can also cut off a part of the leaves of the *Vallisneria* drifting under the surface. However, we must be clear about the fact that every such thinning represents a loss of plant vigor, that the *Vallisneria* will now grow and propagate more slowly!

A general guideline about thinning:

Nothing is more important for the functioning of the community aquarium than healthy, rich plant growth. We should

Thinning the tops of the leaves of *Vallisneria* just below the surface of the water will prevent it from forming an unsightly jungle of twisted leaves, but it will also reduce the vigor of the plant and cause it to grow more slowly. Photo by R. Zukal.

thin only when it is really necessary to get rid of excessive plants, trying to maintain at the same time the grouping of the plants. Once the tank is well established, we can replace those plants and plant groups that appear less decorative with other more valuable and beautiful plants. However, in the first three months after a new set up, I would touch the plants as little as possible.

Now we come to the cleaning of the filter. Small inside filters often need to be cleaned more frequently than once monthly. A large bio-filter, on the other hand, can usually function for several months without any cleaning whatsoever. As a rule, we should not wait this long. Rinse the filter material carefully, without stirring it up too much, until the water runs off clear. Refrain from using too warm or even hot water in order to preserve the bac-

terial flora as much as possible. Such a gentle treatment of the filter may initially repulse a cleanliness fanatic, but it has its definite purpose.

Once the filter is reinstalled and connected, the cover glass can also be cleaned and put back. The lighting is once again turned on, and the last chore remaining is to clean the aquarium glass from the outside.

This tank of Southeast Asian fishes may have been thinned too much. Notice the scraggly appearance of many of the plants and their less than robust condition. Even the large group of attractive gouramis and barbs cannot overcome the feeling of barrenness given by this tank, a feeling that well-planted tanks just do not present. Perhaps if some of the fishes (several of them plant nippers) were removed temporarily the plants might gain a better foothold. Photo by Dr. Herbert R. Axelrod at Nancy Aquarium, France.

Reestablishing an Aquarium

Every aquarist will have the happy experience of discovering that an aquarium requires less work the longer it has been established. Indeed, an aquarium does not have to be emptied for years if we do not pass up its regular care. For this reason, a reestablishment of a tank will usually only take place in order to try new ideas, to do something different. Perhaps a catastrophe has occurred because of carelessness — a fish disease has spread into an epidemic or possibly algae have overgrown the entire tank.

In the case of disaster, especially if there has been an epidemic, we have to change the substrate and clean and disinfect the plants, the appliances, and the aquarium very thoroughly before redecorating. Disease germs are easiest killed by strong heat or chemicals.

For disinfection, wood, nets, and other sturdy items are thoroughly boiled. Water plants are treated with potassium permanganate. The shiny dark purple crystals or deep red solution is available in one form or another at pet stores. For disinfection, the plants are put for five minutes in a solution of one gram of potassium permanganate crystals in 20 liters of water and frequently moved about. The appliances and the aquarium itself are treated with a stronger permanganate solution (3 g to 1 liter of water). After this treatment, the aquarium will be covered with a dark film that can be removed easily with a squeegee — this film is not in any way harmful. Sodium bisulfate removes purple permanganate stains from fingernails, etc.

However, in most instances, disinfection of the tank is not necessary. To the contrary, we will try to leave as much as possible of the well-established micro-life, so that the newly established aquarium will function again as quickly as possible. For this reason, after the electrical appliances (heater, etc.) have been turned off, use about one-fourth to one-third of the old water again. Siphon this water from the upper half of the aquarium before having stirred up any debris by removing any plants or similar items. For safety reasons, filter this water through a fine cloth. You will be surprised to see the residue left behind.

Next take out the appliances and the plants. Sort the plants according to species in bowls or pails filled with water. Then remove the rocks, roots, and — if present — the interior rear wall. Now it is no problem to catch the fishes in the bare tank and put them into a large container (pail, tub, plastic bag). Remember: cover the container — otherwise, some of the fishes might easily jump out!

Now remove the remaining water and the substrate, which is put into containers. Obviously it is necessary to prepare a sufficient number of bowls and pails in advance. The substrate is rinsed with cool water until the rinse water runs off clear. In consideration of the bacteria, refrain from using hot water.

Now you can plan once again the decoration of the aquarium.

Weekends and Vacations

It is beneficial for our mature aquarium fishes to have one fast day per week. For this, Saturday or Sunday is fine. If we take good care of our fishes, it does not matter if we leave the aquarium completely alone for an occasional weekend. If we should ask a friendly but inexperienced neighbor to help, we will frequently find on our return from a trip that with good intentions he has done too much of a good thing: food leftovers lie rotting on the bottom, perhaps with dead fishes, and the tank is a murky, smelly broth!

Although it is easy to see that the fishes can survive a fasting weekend without any problems, it is difficult to see how they can do without our daily care even during vacation. Indeed, many an animal lover would not get an aquarium if he didn't think that the fishes required his constant presence. However, this is an error to which even some experienced aquarists still subscribe! The fishes can easily survive even three or four weeks without any care at all. However, some rules must be observed:

1. For a few weeks before beginning the vacation we should not acquire any new fishes and, if possible, should not move any into other tanks. This could lead to excessive fighting among the fishes and, above all, infectious diseases might be brought in whose eruption we would not notice in time to correct.

2. During these weeks we should not breed any young fishes, because they would not survive a long fasting period.

3. Only healthy and well-fed fishes in a well-established aquarium can be left alone in good conscience. This means that we must feed a good and varied diet — remember live food also — during the last few weeks before our vacation. It is evident that it is not recommended to leave the fishes completely alone for a month without previous long-range planning.

4. Two days before departure, monthly chores should be done. The partial water change and the cleaning of the filter are particularly important.

It is obvious that we have to make sure of the correct functioning of our equipment during this period.

5. Since fishes, as cold-blooded animals, have a much slower metabolism in lower temperatures, we should lower the water temperature by a few degrees for the period of our absence. Most fishes are not harmed by a temperature lowered by about 4°C. Thus, we set our heater dial somewhat lower and keep a close watch on our thermometer for the last two days before our vacation. It is even better, however, if we can do entirely without an aquarium heater during our absence. After all, there is always the possibility of a malfunction of the thermostat, and even if we have selected our heater so that our fish will not be cooked, the end result is always in doubt. Especially during the summer vacation, we can do without our aquarium heater. In the cold city of Husum, Germany, where I practice this procedure almost annually, I have never experienced a mishap in this regard. In winter, of course, we can also turn off the aquarium heater if we maintain the thermostat-controlled room heating at comfortable room temperature levels. The danger of overheating or overcooling is reduced, at least, even though this method of heating is a greater burden for our bank account.

6. We may, of course, use an automatic feeding device during the vacation period. I personally do not think much of this idea, since breakdowns could occur relatively easily.

7. We should not make do without an automatic light timer. This — as I have emphasized repeatedly — is also very useful for daily use. Plants as well as animals suffer almost as much from constant light as from constant dark-

ness of similar duration. Light timers are also practical, since — in contrast to the automatic feeders — one piece of equipment may be used for a number of aquaria.

8. On the day of departure, the fishes get their normal food. Beware of giving them a multiple of the customary portion out of sympathy! Check once more for the perfect functioning of the equipment that cannot be turned off. The filter connections should be tested for a tight fit of their hose connections!

Upon our return from vacation, check the fishes as soon as possible. During feeding, you will notice that the fishes will not throw themselves at the morsels of food as if they were starving. To the contrary, they are usually markedly less greedy than normally. As soon as possible, the tank should be returned to its normal temperature again and everything can proceed as usual.

It certainly is possible that we will miss one or another of the smaller fishes — the snails will have taken care of its body. But after all, the fishes also die when we check the aquarium daily. It goes without saying that we should keep a special eye on our aquarium during the first days after our return from vacation, that we should see to the good feeding of our pets, and that we do not put off for too long the monthly cleaning that is due.

Many types of automatic fish feeders are available in several price ranges, and most are quite reliable. There is always the possibility of the feeder breaking down, however, either providing no food (not a very major problem in most situations) or dumping in all the food at once (a major disaster).

AQUARIUM PLANTS

The Significance of Plants in the Aquarium

Aquaria are often represented as ecosystems. Ecosystems such as lakes, rivers, and virgin forests represent natural units on the basis of a biological balance that regulate themselves and have a certain self-sufficiency because of cyclic processes. In nature, the green plants assume a very predominant position: only they are in a position to store the sun's energy in the form of high energy substances (sugar, fats, proteins) that in turn serve as the nutritional basis for all vegetable and animal life. The process by which the plants synthesize energy-rich substances (carbohydrates) from the sun's energy and energy-poor substances (water and carbon dioxide) is called photosynthesis. As a byproduct of this process, oxygen is produced — also a basic necessity for the life of animal organisms. In ecology, plants are thus considered producers, animals consumers.

Only plants are equipped to transform simple inorganic elements into energy- containing nutrients with the help of light. However, the minerals accessible to plants would very soon be used up were their supply not constantly ensured by microscopically small organisms. These "reducers" (bacteria, fungi, etc.) break down dead organic substances into their mineral elements again to serve as building blocks for the plant for the production of photosynthesis products.

If we look at our aquarium from this point of view, we will see very quickly that it can only be a very imperfect ecosystem. In strictly scientific terminol-

Java moss is a standard spawning substrate for many types of fishes from all areas because the twisting stems and small leaves provide a good background for the eggs. Combining the South American *Paracheirodon innesi*, the neon tetra, with as Asian plant like Java moss would be regarded as in poor taste by some aquarists. Photo by J. Elias.

ogy, as an artificially established and therefore unnatural unit it could not be called an ecosystem at all. This system can only be maintained in balance by constant interference and regulation from the outside — man has to add food and perhaps fertilizer from the outside, he has to remove dead plant parts and animals, and he must take away waste products by changing the water and siphoning off the debris. Let us not deceive ourselves! Our aquarium plants do nothing decisive either as oxygen producers or as nitrogen consumers.

Oxygen constantly gets into the water in large amounts from the air through the water surface. If this were otherwise, unplanted aquaria could not exist at all without aeration. Many tanks for large cichlids prove, however, that this is absolutely possible. In these cases, however, a large filter should maintain a constant current in the water in order to transport the water to the water surface, where an effective exchange of gases can take place. The role of the plants as consumers of nitrogen is also often overestimated. Even optimally planted aquaria cannot deal with the production of nitrogen- containing protein waste products; they rely on the regular partial water change.

Therefore, as producers plants are not needed in the aquarium at all. Nothing proves better than this that our aquarium is not a real ecosystem. Nevertheless, healthy underwater vegetation assists our attempts to supply the fishes with oxygen and to keep the concentration of nitrogen from rising too rapidly.

However, plants do serve a definite purpose in the aquarium: every attentive aquarist knows that aquaria that are too sparsely planted are in constant danger of being overrun by algae. A healthy planting is the best preventive measure against unpopular algae. For this reason, we should never do without plants when establishing a new tank. However, someone who wishes to plant his tank from the start in the manner in which it should look in its final state must be prepared to spend a lot of money! More sensible is another method: the aquarium is planted initially with the least expensive plants (*Vallisneria* and bunch plants), but they should be planted in masses. Fortunately, the cheapest plants are also the best- growing. Once the aquarium is properly established, these plants often multiply in such numbers that we don't know where to put them all.

When our aquarium with "bunch plants" is really thriving after some weeks or months, we can gradually replace the plants that appear less attractive with more expensive and attractive ones.

Our plants also have the function of subdividing the free water space, thus giving the fish an opportunity to hide or to form territories. Those fish that have many possibilities of hiding tend to seek their hiding places less frequently than others. They feel more secure, and we can enjoy them more.

However, the decorative aspect is probably the deciding factor for aquarium planting. Just as we enjoy the growing and thriving of house plants, as we enjoy garden flowers and bushes, we will find joy and satisfaction in our underwater garden. A word on the subject of plastic plants: the fishes don't care whether they swim around an "easy-care" plastic *Cryptocoryne* or a real plant. In a breeding tank, plastic plants may sometimes even be sensible.

In a display aquarium, on the other hand, this is quite a different matter. "Plastic plants, yes or no?" is not a biological question, it is a question of taste.

Stemmed plants with different leaf positions: a) alternate (Hydrocotyle); b) opposite (Hygrophilia); c) whorled (Myriophyllum).

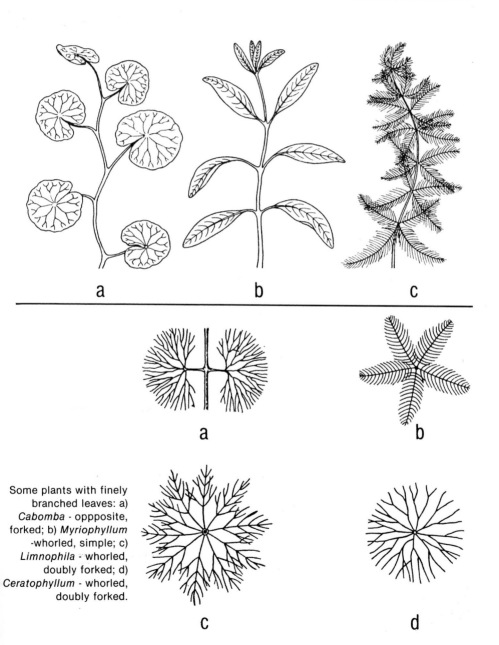

a   b   c

a   b

Some plants with finely branched leaves: a) Cabomba - oppposite, forked; b) Myriophyllum -whorled, simple; c) Limnophila - whorled, doubly forked; d) Ceratophyllum - whorled, doubly forked.

c   d

Plastic plants were once of relatively low quality and often came in bizarre colors that bore no resemblance to the originals. However, today the better plastic plants are completely life-like in both form and color (above). When carefully chosen and placed they can imitate even the most complex grouping of living plants, such as the jungle of mixed plants on the facing page...and they never die or turn brown, nor do they have to be thinned or fertilized.

The Different Types of Plants

Bascially, we differentiate between stemmed and basal rosette plants. Stemmed plants have a stem that grows more or less upward and is leafy. As exceptions, there are also stemmed plants with stems that grow along the ground. The leaves grow singly (alternate), in pairs (opposite), or several (whorled) from particular points on the stem, the nodes. The part of the stem that lies between two nodes is called an internode.

If we imagine the internodes shortened to such an extent that one node practically sits atop another, we can see how basal rosette plants developed. Their leaves and roots appear to spring from one center.

Another category of water plants is formed by floating plants that grow without connection to the ground. They, too, can be either rosettes or stemmed.

Many aquarium plants are actually not even typical water plants. They are swamp plants that customarily grow in the air and bloom there (emersed plants). Since they have adapted, however, to the floods that are frequent in the tropics, they can also be cultivated under water (submersed). These plants have the characteristic of readily growing out of the aquarium. Many can be kept under water only by constant cutting back.

The aquarist is now faced with the following questions: Does the plant require much light, or can it do with less light? What temperature requirements does it have? Does the plant remain small therefore suited for planting in the foreground, is it suitable as a solitary plant, or does it grow so quickly that it is better to put it into the background?

Popular Aquarium Plants

The number of useful aquarium plants can be placed at around 200. Of course, only a limited selection can be presented here. I have taken care to treat in greater detail those plants that are frequently kept or are popular for other reasons. Someone wishing to cultivate more exotic plants that are not listed separately here should get an aquarium plant book.

Algae

As the simplest plant inhabitants of our aquaria, almost all algae are unwanted guests that we will never ever get rid of entirely, but which can be kept in check by observing some basic rules.

In every aquarium there are few to many algae of several different kinds. When appearing in masses, algae are very unattractive and can destroy entire groups of certain plants. In order to combat the algae, it is first necessary to recognize the different forms of algae.

BLUE-GREEN ALGAE

Blue-green algae are the most frequent and most disturbing algae. The name "blue-green" algae is totally misleading because these algae frequently have an ugly greenish, brownish, or blackish coloration. Often, they actually are colored blue-green. They appear as slimy, often thick masses and prefer to grow in the brightest areas of the aquarium. They grow preferentially on the bottom, but also grow on the plants. If the water's surface is undisturbed and provided with floating plants, blue-green algae are found there, too. The algae cover plants and equipment with a moldy-smelling slimy layer within a short period of time and suffocate the entire vegetation. Fortunately, blue-green algae are relatively easy to combat.

GRAVEL ALGAE

Because of their brown color, gravel algae are often called "brown algae." They cover aquarium panes and rocks with a thin slimy film but are not a great nuisance. Their appearance indicates that the aquarium is *insufficiently lighted* and also has a too high pH-value. In stronger light gravel algae disappear on their own. In addition, loaches and sucker catfishes like to eat them.

RED ALGAE

Most red algae live in the ocean. Since the red pigments of our freshwater red algae are covered by chlorophyll, they appear blackish green to black on casual observation. The major type of red algae, black brush algae, is easily recognized. If an entire tuft of small branched, blackish threads comes from a single central point, we are dealing with black brush algae. The tufts are up to 2 cm high and may occur on dead objects or on the leaves of plants. They develop most frequently on the harder parts of dead leaves. As a rule, brush algae are rarely a nuisance and some aquarists even consider them decorative. The other common type of red algae in the aquarium is the beard algae. The blackish-green threads of the beard algae are barely branched and grow up to 10 cm in length. They appear like loosely falling beards and are difficult to remove since they are firmly attached to their support. They are not decorative but are not too harmful to the plants.

GREEN ALGAE

The green algae are the most highly developed algae, similar to those from which all higher plants evolved in the course of the Earth's history. Consequently, their requirements resemble those of our actual aquarium plants more closely than those of the other algae. For this reason, green algae cannot be removed well with chemicals since those chemicals would also damage the higher plants to some extent. It could be said that a healthy growth of green algae indicates that the water and light conditions actually must be ideal.

The growth forms of green algae can be very different. They may float in the water as microscopic spheres, they may drift loose in the water in the form of hair-like threads or filaments, or they may appear as fixed growth on plants, rocks, and other substrates.

To put it more simply: those algae that do not appear in slimy form (blue, gravel algae) or look blackish (red algae) must be numbered among the green algae, independent of their shape.

NITELLA FLEXILIS

This alga, widespread in the northern hemisphere, is hardly ever recognized as an alga by laymen. Its shape rather resembles that of a higher plant, and it is therefore the only "real" aquarium plant among the algae. In temperatures below 25°C and sufficient light intensity this plant is quite hardy.

The algal plague, especially the predominance of blue-green algae, has inspired horror in many an aquarist. There is virtually no aquarium without algae. We must realize that algae and higher plants are, in a sense, competitors for light, oxygen, and food. The more highly developed organisms, our aquarium plants, generally have the edge — if they are not damaged in any way!

Some aquarium plants. Top left: *Bacopa monnieri.* Top right: *Aponogeton madagascariensis,* the Madagascar lace plant. Photo by W. Tomey. Below: *Nymphaea lotus* var. Red Star, a water lily suitable more for ponds than aquaria. Photo by C.O. Masters.

Microsorium pteropus, the Java fern (broad-leaved plants in the background). Photo by Dr. D. Terver, Nancy Aquarium, France.

Name	Distribution	Plant Type	Light Requirements per 100 liters (in watts)	Planting Suggestions	Temperature (in °C)
Riccia fluitans	Cosmopolitan	Sch	35-70	–	10-28
Eichhornia azurea	Cosmopolitan	(ST) Sch	min. 70	–	22-28
Pistia stratiodes	Cosmopolitan	Sch	min. 70	–	22-25
Salvinia auriculata*	North, South America	Sch	50-100	–	20-25
Ceratopteris cornuta*	Cosmopolitan	Sch, G	40-100	S	20-30
–thalictroides*	Cosmopolitan	Sch, G	40-100	S	20-30
Bolbitis heudeloti	Africa	G	30-60	V	22-25
Microsorium pteropus*	Asian	G	20-70	V	20-28
Marsilea crenata	Asian, Australian	STK	min. 70	V	22-28
Cabomba caroliniana	North, South America	ST	min. 70	H	22-28
Ceratophyllum submersum*	Cosmopolitan	Sch, ST	40-70	H	18-28
Myriophyllum aquaticum	South America	ST	40-70	H	22-28
Bacopa caroliniana	North America	ST	min. 70	V,H	22-28
Limnophila aquatica*	Asian	ST	40-70	H	25-28
Utricularia vulgaris	Europe, North Africa	Sch, ST	40-70	–	18-22
Rotala macrantha	Asian	ST	min. 50	H	25-30
Ludwigia repens*	North America	ST	40-70	H	18-28
Elatine macropoda	Europe, Africa	STK	min. 70	V	22-28
Hydrocotyle vulgaris	Europe	STK	min. 70	V	18-22
–leucocephala	South America	ST	40-80	H	20-28
Alternanthera sessilis	South America	ST	min. 50	H	25-30
Lobelia cardinalis	North America	ST	min 50	H	22-26
Saururus cernuus	North America	ST	min. 70	V,H	22-28
Hygrophila polysperma*	Asian	ST	40-70	H	18-28
–difformis*	Asian	ST	20-70	H	22-28
–corymbosa*	Asian	ST	20-70	H	22-28
Nymphaea lotus	Africa, Asian	G	40-70	S	24-28
Barclaya longifolia	Asian	G	min. 60	S	23-30
Anubias congensis	Africa	G	40-70	S	25-28
–barteri	Africa	G	40-70	V	22-28

Name	Distribution	Plant Type	Light Requirements per 100 liters (in watts)	Planting Suggestions	Temperature (in °C)
Nymphoides aquatica	North America	G	50-80	S	20-28
Egeria densa*	South America	ST (Sch)	40-100	H	20-24
Crinum thaianum	Asian	G	40-70	S,H	22-28
Vallisneria gigantea	Asian	G	40-70	H	22-28
–spiralis*	Cosmopolitan	G	20-70	H	18-28
Sagittaria subulata*	North America	G	50-70	V,H	22-28
–platyphylla*	North America	G	min. 60	H	20-25
Eleocharis vivipara	North America	G	50-100	V,H	22-28
–acicularis	Cosmopolitan	G	50-100	V	18-26
Aponogeton undulatus	Asian	G	40-100	S	22-28
–crispus	Asian	G	40-70	S	22-28
–madagascariensis	Africa	G	min. 70	S	20-22
Echinodorus tenellus*	North, South America	G	50-100	V	25-28
–parviflorus*	South America	G	50-70	H,S	22-30
–amazonicus*	South America	G	40-70	S	22-28
–bleheri*	South America	G	40-70	S	22-28
–cordifolius	South America	G	50-80	S	22-28
Cryptocoryne wendtii*	Asian	G	20-70	V,H	22-28
–willisii (=nevillii)*	Asian	G	50-70	V	25-30
–affinis*	Asian	G	20-70	V,H	22-28
–ciliata	Asian	G	40-70	S,H	22-28
–usteriana	Asian	G	40-70	S,H	22-28

The species marked with an asterisk (*) are relatively trouble-free and recommended for beginners.
Explanation of abbreviations: ST = stemmed plants. STK = stemmed plants. Sch = stemmed plants with creeping runners. G = rooted plants. Sch = floating plants. V = small plants suitable for grouping in the foreground. S = plants growing best as individuals. H = tall plants suitable for planting in the middle and background.
Light requirements are minimal values; almost all plants will do better with stronger illumination.

A densely planted aquarium is still the best protection against algae! The higher plants use up the mineral salts and the carbon dioxide in the water so that nothing is left for the algae to thrive on. Only with excessive availability of fertilizer can the algae, too, develop strongly. In order to prevent excessive fertilization, the water should be changed frequently and the debris siphoned off at the same time. Neither should there be any left-over food. The greatest problem with the newly-established aquarium is that we simply cannot prevent bringing in algal spores or isolated cells. There develops a regular battle for dominance between the algae and the higher plants, which are at a disadvantage initially since they need time to become rooted. The final result is either a tank totally overrun with algae or a beautiful planted aquarium. In order to obtain the latter, we must do everything to ensure the unhindered growth of the plants. Therefore, do not disturb the plants by renewed transplanting. Keep the algae as much in check as possible (try to siphon off the blue-green algae with a hose!) in such a manner that the higher plants are disturbed as little as possible.

In order to keep the algae in check, certain fishes are recommended. A tank with swordtails, platies, and guppies will become less rapidly infested with algae since these fishes will continually clean away new algal colonies. The Chinese algae-eater, *Gyrinocheilus aymonieri*, and the flying fox, *Epalzeorhynchus kallopterus*, will help to restrain the growth of algae. The fishes just mentioned will, however, ignore filamentous algae. For their control, *Ancistrus*, *Otocinclus*, and *Hypostomus* catfishes are suitable. Snails, too, act as biological controls for algae.

The Chinese algae-eater, *Gyrinocheilus aymonieri*, is one of the most familiar of the algae-eaters. Young specimens are almost always available in pet shops, but they seldom grow up in the aquarium because they need large amounts of algae and other plant foods to grow to adult size. Like most fishes considered to be "scavengers," they must be fed and fed well to survive. Photo by J. Vierke.

Many catfishes are used as algae-eaters in the aquarium. The most popular are members of the family Loridariidae, a very large and confusing family. Photo by David Sands.

Once again, briefly, the most important points:

1. A newly-established aquarium should be planted as densely as possible and should be run under weak light for the first four or five days.

2. During the first weeks, the plants should be allowed to grow undisturbed and should not be fertilized.

3. Algae that may appear are carefully removed.

4. As a preventive measure, algae-eating fishes should be stocked four to six days after the tank becomes inhabitable.

5. Frequent partial changes of the water and less intensive feeding than normal see to it that the water is not overloaded at first, until the plants become rooted. Additionally, heavy feeding would make the algae- eaters grow lazy!

Rarely a well-planted aquarium that has been established for some time will suddenly malfunction. In such instances it is not always easy to find a cause for the problem. Brown algae are an indication of insufficient lighting. The countermeasure is to remove some of the floating plants and replace fluorescent tubes with stronger or at least newer ones. Other algae are an indication of excessive fertilization. The countermeasure for this is more frequent water changes. Other growths may be due to insufficient fertilization (countermeasure: fertilizer for water plants), a spoiled substrate, or too alkaline water. If a tank is exposed to daylight and is lighted at the same time with plant lights it also has a tendency toward algae infestation. It is helpful, especially against blue-green algae, to completely darken the tank for one or two weeks. Every pane must be covered with paper so that not even the slightest hint of daylight can penetrate. The higher plants and the fishes (no young fishes!) will survive this drastic treatment more or less undamaged and the blue-green algae normally will die. During this forced pause, the fishes must not be fed, of course. Several algicides are available in the trade, but these should only be used as a last resort. Every algae remedy will damage not only the algae but also the higher plants. Only blue-green algae can be fought somewhat sensibly with these algicides. When using algicides, the directions for use must be followed exactly and we must be prepared to accept the fact that some of our more sensitive water plants will be damaged.

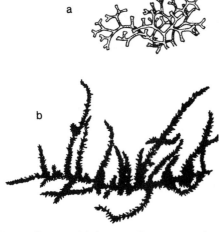

Riccia fluitans (a) is actually an aquatic liverwort, but most aquarists consider it a moss. *Vesicularia dubyana,* Java moss, is a true aquatic moss (b).

Familiar Plants
MOSSES
RICCIA FLUITANS

Riccia fluitans is a liverwort, a primitive plant distinguished by band-like, forked articulate plant bodies (thalli). *Riccia* is a very effective and easily cultivated floating plant. It is suited for temperatures between 10 and 28°C. This unassuming plant can be described as ideal inasmuch as its expansion can be kept within limits. Only the competition of other floating plants can threaten it.

*VESICULARIA DUBYANA —
JAVA MOSS*

This ornamental plant originating in Southeast Asia is among the most highly recommended of aquarium plants. It has delicate leaves of 1-2 mm in length and can form beautiful bright green underwater tufts within a quite short period of time. It is best to attach the cluster to roots and rocks or to the rear wall. These attachments are soon overgrown. For breeding aquaria, loose tufts of this moss are excellently suited as a spawning substrate.

The little plants are not very demanding either in regard to temperature or to lighting. The water quality also is not decisive for their growth. The moss is only sensitive to an excessive water current and to silt — debris is easily caught in the delicate little leaves.

FERNS

Ferns are especially well suited for aquarium planting since they are well protected against being eaten by fishes and snails because of their usually coarse leaves. In addition, some ferns are quite undemanding in regard to the amount of light required and can, therefore, grow in very shady areas.

*MICROSORIUM PTEROPUS —
JAVA FERN*

This undemanding fern with its undivided leaves is best kept attached to roots or rocks. Initially, fasten the plant to the substrate with rubberbands around its strong root stock. After a few weeks the plant will adhere by itself. This fern will also thrive on the ground, but the epiphytic growth form should be preferred for decorative reasons alone.

The fern will put forth adventitious plants from the roots and the leaves, so it can be multiplied without problems. However, only plants as large as possible should be transplanted. Strangely, this fern will grow better the more the plants are kept together.

Older leaves occasionally exhibit a tendency to have black spots; these leaves should be removed. The plant perseveres even in small amounts of light, but of course then it will grow less. It prefers temperatures between 22 and 26°C and can also be kept in harder water.

BOLBITIS HEUDELOTTI

This bizarrely feathered fern from Africa is also kept attached to roots or rocks. This fern is somewhat more demanding: it prefers a not too bright spot and moving, soft, slightly acid water. Under these conditions, the plant can grow up to 45 cm.

Aquatic ferns. a) *Ceratopteris thalictroides*, water sprite. b) *Microsorium pteropus*, Java fern. c) *Salvinia auriculata*. d) *Ceratopteris cornuta*, a floating water sprite known as horn fern.

CERATOPTERIS
THALICTROIDES —
WATER SPRITE

The water sprite and the horn fern (*C. cornuta*) are very similar in appearance and in the requirements for their care. Water sprite has more finely articulated leaves than horn fern, but the growth shape of the leaves depends very strongly on the conditions of cultivation.

Basically, both ferns are suitable as large single plants rooted in the ground as well as the more familiar floating plants. As rooted plants they need much light, however, and will soon become too large for a small tank.

If they are kept as floating plants, their requirements for light are easily met. In this form the plants appear very decorative, mainly because of their finely branched roots that hang deep into the water. Since they keep light from the plants on the bottom and multiply very quickly by means of young plants sprouting along the edges of the leaves, we occasionally have to force ourselves to thin them out thoroughly! Both *Ceratopteris* are quite large aquarium plants under all conditions of cultivation (temperatures between 20 and 30°C).

Above: *Salvinia* species. Photo by R. Zukal.
Below: *Ceratopteris thalictroides.*

SALVINIA AURICULATA

This floating fern from tropical South America is especially well suited for small and medium-sized aquaria and is distinguished by its delicate leaves. It has three-leaved whorls, of which two float on the water surface and the third grows, rootlike and finely articulated, downward. Being covered with fine little hairs, the surface of the floating leaves completely repel water.

Under favorable conditions the plant grows well and is decorative in the aquarium. Nevertheless, in consideration of the other plants, it should only cover a part of the water surface. It is sensitive to excessive currents and splashing water, requires much light, and the temperature at the surface should not exceed 25°C.

MARSILEA CRENATA —
Clover Fern

A few of these plants are sufficient to quickly grow a clover lawn for foreground planting. The plants have a creeping sprouting stem. They need lots of light and soft water.

HIGHER PLANTS
CABOMBA SPECIES

These decorative stemmed plants originate in the warmer regions of America. Their delicately shaped opposite leaves are repeatedly forked. *Cabomba caroliniana* and *Cabomba piauhyensis* have especially decorative leaves (in sufficiently strong light, the latter will even form reddish brown leaves.)

All species of *Cabomba* are demanding in every regard; they require soft (maximum 10° dGH), slightly acid, clear water and high light intensity. In addition, they like a regular change of water. They react poorly to frequent transplanting.

NYMPHAEA SPECIES —
Water Lilies

The species of water lilies available for garden ponds are, almost without exception, not suitable as aquarium plants since they become too large and in the long run cannot tolerate the temperatures of a tropical tank.

Best suited for the aquarium is *Nymphaea lotus*, which occurs in both green- leaved and red-leaved forms. As a single plant, the red form offers an

Above: *Cabomba caroliniana.* Photo by R. Zukal. Below: *Nymphaea lotus* var. Comanche. Photo by P. Stetson.

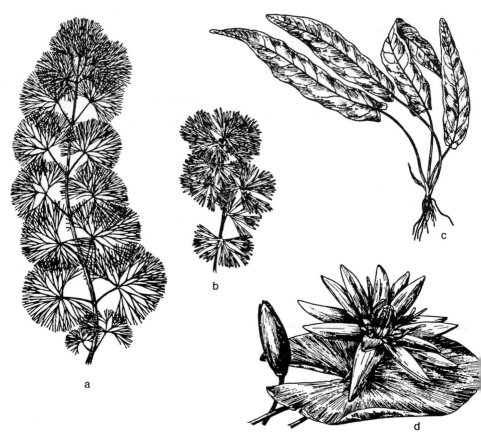

a) *Cabomba aquatica.* b) *Cabomba caroliniana.* Both these species of *Cabomba* require very strong light and clean, acid water; they seldom survive the winter. c) *Barclaya longifolia,* an Indian plant that is sometimes common in pet shop tanks. d) *Nymphaea daubenyana,* a hybrid water lily that stays small enough for use in large aquaria.

excellent center of attraction. However, like all water lilies it needs a lot of room and, above all, much light. It is best to plant them in a sand or gravel substrate that has been enriched with clay.

In the aquarium, water lilies are especially effective because of their wide underwater leaves. If the plant grows floating leaves on thin stems they should be immediately removed, since their growth takes place at the expense of the other leaves. If the plant is allowed to reach its full growth, it will soon show its majestic blossoms above water. In addition, the water lily *Nym-*

phaea colorata and the hybrid *Nymphaea daubenyana* are also suited for the aquarium.

NUPHAR — Spatterdock

The domestic yellow spatterdock (*Nuphar luteum*) is closely related to the water lily and also is suited only for large aquaria. The temperature should not exceed 24°C for any length of time. For the tropical tank, the small *Nuphar pumila* is suitable. In the requirements for their care, the *Nuphar* species resemble the water lilies.

BARCLAYA LONGIFOLIA —
Long-leaved Barclaya

This plant from the interior of India is one of the more popular aquarium plants. In contrast to the water lily and spatterdock, it does not grow any floating leaves. Its long leaves, colored reddish on the underside and wavy along the edges, make it an ideal single plant, but it will also thrive in a group. It is not rare for *Barclaya* to form blossoms in the aquarium from which fertile seeds will develop. However, its propagation is easier by means of rhizomes. The plants require high temperatures (23-30°C) and should not be transplanted too often. Occasionally, the round-leafed barclaya (*Barclaya motleyi*) is also imported.

CERATOPHYLLUM SUBMERSUM —
Hornwort

Ceratophyllum submersum is a particularly undemanding and very rapidly growing plant with fine, delicately branched leaves; it is well suited for the initial planting. This species is planted in bunches or may be allowed to drift on the surface as it does in nature. Although undemanding, it is hungry for light and should not be kept at high temperatures for any length of time.

ELATINE MACROPODA

Elatine is a ground-covering, creeping plant from the western Mediterranean region. Occasionally it is recommended for planting in the foreground, but in the long run it is not suited for higher temperatures. It requires soft water and much light.

LUDWIGIA SPECIES

The ludwigias, originating predominantly in North America, are plants that in the most favorable conditions can form dense tufts. However, in order to do so, they need a substrate rich in nutrients and sufficient light. The hybrid ludwigia (*Ludwigia repens x L. palustris*), distinguished by the red underside of the leaves, requires especially strong light. To propagate them, we simply pinch off the side shoots and put them into the ground, where they will quickly grow roots.

AMMANIA GRACILIS

This plant from tropical Africa grows long lancet-shaped red-brown leaves. It is extremely decorative in groups and is a good contrast to green neighboring plants. It likes a bright position and a regular water change.

ROTALA MACRANTHA

These plants are reminiscent of ludwigias, but the leaves are more rounded and there is no pronounced stem. In bright light the leaves turn a strong red and grow closely together. It is possible to let the shoots grow to the surface and allow them to continue growing while floating. The plant grows easily and is propagated like *Ludwigia*. It requires sufficient lighting and regular water changes.

ROTALA ROTUNDIFOLIA

This adaptable plant originates in south-east Asia. Its name (*rotundifolia* = round-leaved) is misleading; the emersed form does have round leaves, but in the aquarium it forms narrow elliptical leaves about 10-12mm in length. This delicate-leaved plant is particularly well suited for small aquariums — in large tanks it is virtually lost! *Rotala* should be planted in

Above: *Barclaya longifolia*. Below: *Rotala rotundifolia*. Photos by B. Kahl.

groups. Propagation takes place by means of shoots. After it reaches the surface, the plant may be allowed to grow floating.

MYRIOPHYLLUM AQUATICUM — Water Milfoil

This species, formerly called *Myriophyllum brasiliense*, is a very fine-leaved species and is, therefore, very sensitive to algae and debris. It thrives best in soft, slightly acid water, but it will also tolerate other water qualities as long as it gets sufficient light. Propagation takes place by means of shoots and is not difficult. There is also a red-brown species (*Myriophyllum matogrossense*), which is to be kept like its green relation. It, too, is hungry for light and loves soft water.

The species of *Myriophyllum* are distinguished from other fine-leaved plants by their whorled, simply-feathered leaves.

ALTERNANTHERA SESSILIS

This plant is notable because of the beautiful red coloration of its leaves. Under normal lighting, however, the leaves will turn green, as will those of many red-leaved aquarium plants. To preserve its beauty, the plant requires a lot of light.

This is a swamp plant that will also thrive under water. The plants are grateful for fertilization with carbon dioxide and should be kept in not too hard water.

BACOPA SPECIES

The species known as *Bacopoa caroliniana* (formerly *amplexicaulia*) and *Bacopa monnieri* are actually swamp plants. Planted in bunches, these plants are quite attractive. They make no special demands as far as the water quality is concerned, but they require a lot of light. If they are not trimmed in time, they will grow above the surface.

LIMNOPHILA INDICA

This plant, wide-spread in the tropics of the Old World, has finely divided leaves springing from the whorls. The crushed leaves are aromatic and are suspected of containing substances poisonous to fishes. These substances are released only when the plant is damaged, however when propagating by means of shoots, they should be briefly rinsed as a precautionary measure, at least for smaller aquaria. The plant needs much light!

LIMNOPHILA SESSILIFLORA

This delicate aquarium plant from southern and south-eastern Asia is with the exception of its light requirements rather undemanding. Like other stemmed plants, it is easily propagated by shoots. Its leaf whorls grow only to a diameter of about 3 cm, so it is well suited for small aquaria. This plant is effective not only alone, but also in bunches.

LIMNOPHILIA AQUATICA

This rapid growing plant with its large leaf whorls is suited only for larger aquaria. It needs a lot of light and reacts very positively to additional iron fertilization.

HYGROPHILA POLYSPERMA

Popular and proven for decades, this plant requires no special recommendation. It is easily propagated by means of shoots. By repeatedly trimming back the plant it can be stimulated to form side shoots, thus forming regular bushes. In order to obtain spectacular specimens, we should offer bright light and regular water changes.

HYGROPHILA DIFFORMIS —
Water Wisteria

This species, formerly known under

Above: *Limnophila* species, a distinctively whorled plant that may be poisonous. Photo by W. Tomey. Below: *Hygrophila difformis*, water wisteria. Photo by T.J. Horeman.

the name *Synnema triflorum,* became popular because of its large, strongly indented leaves. If it is kept in too little light the newly formed leaves develop a larger surface. It grows rapidly and is easily propagated by shoots. It is grateful for regular partial water changes. In too extreme temperature variations, disturbances in growth may appear; otherwise, it tolerates temperatures between 20 and 30 °C.

a) *Myriophyllum aquaticum,* water milfoil. b) *Limnophila indica.* c) *Bacopa monnieri.*

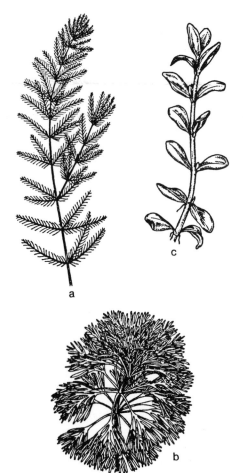

HYGROPHILA STRICTA

This species is closely related to the next but it has longer and narrower leaves that are more closely spaced. For this reason, it is as suitable as a solitary plant for planting along the edges in the background. The plant needs relatively strong light.

HYGROPHILA CORYMBOSA — Temple Plant

This large plant, long known as *Nomaphila stricta,* is among the most quick-growing of all water plants. It grows very rapidly out of the water and there sets its pale violet flowers. The pinched-off air shoots can be planted unhesitatingly directly in the water. Old plants that are trimmed too often tend to turn woody and look unattractive. They should be replaced by one of the many young shoots that are produced.

The plant is not suited to small aquaria. It is best planted in groups of several in the background of larger tanks. Since it will be satisfied with moderate amounts of light, it is also suited for taller aquaria. It may also be considered ideal as a land plant for the terrarium.

LOBELIA CARDINALIS

Lobelia is a North American swamp plant that has adapted well to the conditions of the tropical aquarium. In its appearance and care it resembles *Hygrophila corymbosa.*

UTRICULARIA SPECIES — Bladderwort

The bladderworts have very thin stems and drift on the surface. They may eventually form mats and dense tufts. The bladderwort is a carnivorous plant. The common *Utricularia vulgaris* is suitable

a) *Hygrophila difformis,* water wisteria. b) *Hygrophila polysperma.* c) *Hygrophila cor-ymbosa,* temple plant.

for cold-water aquaria, and the North American species sometimes adapt to tropical aquaria. Bladderworts might become dangerous to the fry. The small tropical species mostly catch infusoria. Bladderworts are of limited decorative value though their carnivorous habits give them curiosity value.

Swordplants and sag

At present, 47 species are counted as members of the genus *Echinodorus,* the swordplants. All are American, most coming from South America. They are mainly swamp plants. Even though only a part of them come from the Amazon region, they are all considered Amazon Swordplants. In appearance as well as in the requirements for their care, there are considerable specific differences.

Sagittaria species are grass-like underwater plants that are often confused with *Vallisneria.* Of the more than 30 species, only a few are kept in the aquarium. They differ from the *Vallisneria* species in the formation of the leaf edges and the leaf veins. The *Vallisneria* leaves are toothed in the area of the tip and their longitudinal nerves all end in the leaf tip. The longitudinal nerves of the smooth-

Many species of swordplants, *Echinodorus*, show up in pet shops, and probably all have their good points. Certainly all are popular. Shown is *Echinodorus paniculatus*, a fairly typical species. Photo by R. Zukal.

a) *Lobelia cardinalis*, a swamp plant that can sometimes be adapted to conditions in the tropical aquarium. b) *Utricularia gibba*, a bladderwort.

edged *Sagittaria* leaves end partly before the leaf tip on the leaf edge.

ECHINODORUS TENELLUS

This is a popular small plant for the foreground. In good light it will form runners and will soon produce a lawn-like growth, turning larger areas green. Usually the little plants grow no bigger then 5 cm.

Echinodorus quadricostatus (syn. *intermedius, latifolius, magdalenensis)*, which is similar in its care, grows only a little larger. Light-absorbing floating plants must be kept away from these *Echinodorus*.

ECHINODORUS PARVIFLORUS —
Blackwater Amazon Swordplant

The blackwater Amazon swordplant, originating in the high plateaus of Peru and Bolivia, has deep green darkly veined leaves. With good care, the plant will form a compact, very dense bush about 20 cm in height and is, therefore, suitable as a centerpiece for medium-sized and large aquaria. The demands of the blackwater Amazon swordplant are minimal; it needs to stand free but adapts well to lower light intensities.

ECHINODORUS AMAZONICUS —
True Amazon Swordplant

This plant, formerly also called *Echinodorus brevipedicellatus,* is one of the large species of *Echinodorus* that should only be used as free-standing single plants in medium-sized and large tanks. Their sword-shaped, downward bending, light green leaves grow to 40 cm in length and 2-3 cm in width. This robust plant readily grows runners that usually remain below the water and develop young plants. The young plants should not be

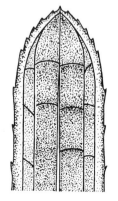
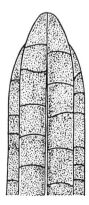

Above: The broad-leaved Amazon swordplant, *Echinodorus bleheri,* a very common species. *Below:* Comparison of the toothed leaf tip in *Vallisneria* (left) and the smooth leaf tip of *Sagittaria* (right).

separated too soon. It is best to leave the stem attached to the mother plant, bending it to the bottom and fixing it there with a rock. In sufficient light, the young plants will attach themselves well.

ECHINODORUS BLEHERI —
Broad-leaved Amazon Swordplant

This plant resembles the true Amazon sword but it is kept even more frequently and is even more robust. The leaves, gently waved along the edge, grow up to 8 cm in width.

a) *Sagittaria subulata*, the common sag or arrowleaf. b) and c) *Echinodorus amazonicus*, the Amazon swordplant most desired by hobbyists; in c) the plant is reproducing by means of a runner. d) *Echinodorus osiris*, a pseudoviviparous or livebearing species with its stem of small plants.

SAGITTARIA SUBULATA —
Common Sag

This plant, which comes mostly from the south-eastern part of North America, occurs in several forms. The *subulata* form strongly resembles *Vallisneria*. In addition to its band-like underwater leaves, it occasionally forms its arrow-like floating leaves and its small white flowers. It is completely undemanding and propagates readily by means of runners. The form *pusilla* is similar to *Echinodorus tenellus* and is suitable as a small lawn-forming plant for the foreground, but it is much more moderate in its light requirements.

SAGITTARIA PLATYPHYLLA

This robust swamp plant will grow to almost 50 cm and does extremely well in the aquarium. Its band-shaped leaves will grow to more than 2 cm in width. The plant multiplies readily by means of shoots and is undemanding in every aspect. However, the temperature should remain below 25 °C.

BLYXA

These very demanding species are decorative plants for the foreground and center. They require a lot of light and soft water.

ELODEA CANADENSIS —
Common Elodea, Anacharis

This North American water plant has been spread over much of the temperate world. It is one of the most suitable plants for the cool-water tank. It grows very quickly and is a good oxygen donor, but it needs much light. This evergreen plant is best planted in dense bunches in the background.

EGERIA DENSA —
Argentine Anacharis

This species has considerably larger leaves than *Elodea canadensis*. It, too, is very rewarding, though in the long run it will only tolerate medium temperatures.

It is best planted in larger stands in the background. However, it is also suitable as a plant floating at the surface, particularly for fish tanks in which ground plants cannot be kept (as with large cichlids). In that case, there is also no problem with the light, because, with all its robustness, *Egeria densa* is hungry for light. Its propagation by means of shoots is simple.

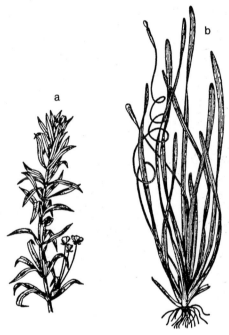

a) *Egeria densa,* a common elodea plant. b) *Vallisneria spiralis,* the very fast-growing aquarium plant that can soon overpower a tank.

VALLISNERIA SPIRALIS —
Corkscrew Val

Only a few other aquarium plants are as ready to multiply as this one. This is the ideal species for initial plantings. However, too soft water is not good for it. After a short period of adaptation it forms ground runners that will soon

Crinum thaianum is one of the few aquatic plants propagated successfully from bulbs. This water narcissus, as it is sometimes called, has leaves that grow to up to two meters in length if left untrimmed, a size that allows it to easily over-shade all but the largest tanks. Like Vallisneria, it must be kept carefully trimmed in home aquaria. Photo by T. J. Horeman.

cover the entire tank if they are not repeatedly trimmed. *Vallisneria* is best planted in groups along the sides or in the background. The leaves floating on the surface absorb much light but may be trimmed. The temperature may range between 15 and 30°C.

VALLISNERIA GIGANTEA

The giant vallisneria originates in New Guinea and the Philippines and develops leaves up to 2 m in length and 3 cm in width. For this reason it is only suited for really large tanks and should, if it is expected to live up to its name, be planted in soil containing clay. Its other requirements are minimal. It tolerates temperatures between 22-28°C.

CRINUM NATANS

This bulb plant originates in West Africa. Because of its strong leaves, which in the wild grow up to 1.5 m in length, the plant is suited only for large aquariums. It needs a rich substrate and a lot of light, but is otherwise hardy and will make do even with hard and alkaline water.

CRINUM THAIANUM

This water narcissus, which is suitable for the background and the sides of larger aquariums, is long-lived and very robust. Its leaves, 2 cm in width, grow up to 2 m in length. In the aquarium as in the wild, the leaves cover the surface and absorb a lot of light. An occasional trimming does no harm. Propagation takes place by means of tubers.

APONOGETON

The species of *Aponogeton* are among the most popular water plants. Some are truly magnificent plants. However, the purchaser should take appropriate care of them, since their numbers in the wild have already been strongly decimated through ruthless collecting of the tubers.

These plants have tuberous root-stocks. In the aquarium, a magnificent, undemanding plant will grow within a short time from such a tuber, which, however, will slow its growth after a few months and will finally stop growing altogether. The plant should then be transferred into cooler water of about 15°C and the water level should be lowered to cover the tuber by only a few centimeters. Now even the last leaves are shed. After two to four months of rest, the tuber can be returned to the aquarium, where it immediately will grow beautiful leaves again. In order to keep from having to transplant the tuber all the time, we can plant it in a flowerpot that is placed in the substrate of the aquarium. (Clay should be added to the substrate.)

Almost all *Aponogeton* species will grow readily. Most blossoms are self-fertile, their own pollen able to lead to the formation of fruits and seeds. It is best to assist in the fertilization by carefully dusting the rather spiny-looking inflorescence with a small paint brush or cotton swab in a downward motion. If the buds begin to swell after a few days, fertilization was successful. The fruit continue to mature under water. After about two months, the seeds detach themselves, float on the water for several days, and then sink to the bottom. Here they continue to grow. However, there is seldom enough room for the small plants in the average aquarium, so it is best to plant the young shoots in a flowerpot that we can place in an aquarium in such a manner that the water level above the plants is only a few centimeters. If we use a plastic container for culturing and fasten it to the top edge of the aquarium with suitably bent wire holders, we have created a simple but effective

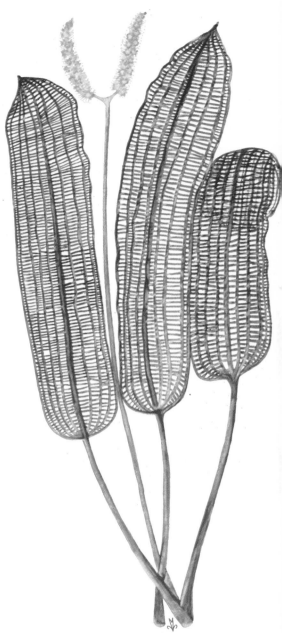

Leaves and inflorescence of the Madagascar lace plant, *Aponogeton madagascariensis*. In this spectacular species, formerly known as *A. fenestralis*, the tissue between the veins of the leave disintegrates as the leaf matures, leaving just the lace-like tracery of the leaf skeleton. A rare and treasured centerpiece.

Although most *Aponogeton* are grown from seed, in *A. undulatus* there is a more bizarre method of reproduction. In this species young plants (leaves and roots) grow from small bulblets that develop on the flower stalk.

growth bed for *Aponogeton*. If our fish exhibit too much interest in the sensitive little plants, we have to cover the bed with a translucent net.

APONOGETON UNDULATUS

This is a problem-free, beautiful plant with narrow, wavy leaves. The inflorescences usually form not blossoms but young plants complete with tubers and roots. Thus, their propagation is very simple.

APONOGETON CRISPUS

This species is frequently kept and is easy to care for. However, very hard water does not agree with it. It is frequently hybridized with other species, so several forms that resemble *Aponogeton undulatus* are available in the trade.

APONOGETON ULVACEUS

This plant, originating in Madagascar, has broad light-green leaves that, like lettuce leaves, are thin and wavy.

The plant is adaptable and will grow to a respectable size even in medium-hard water. It is suitable as a beautiful showpiece for large aquariums. Since it is rarely self-fertile, its blossom must be cross-fertilized with those of another specimen in order to be able to form seeds.

APONOGETON BOIVINIATUS

Also originating in Madagascar, this plant grows up to 50 cm in height and has very knobby leaves. As a magnificent solitary plant in large aquaria it is quite undemanding, but it does not like very hard water.

APONOGETON MADAGASCARIENSIS — **Madagascar Lace Plant**

There are two kinds of lace plants available, broad-leaved and narrow-leaved forms, both distinguished by the fact that the leaf surface between the mesh-like leaf veins is absent, leaving a fenestrate or mesh-like leaf.

Lace plants need very soft water at 20-22°C as well as a crystal-clear algae-free environment and frequent water changes. In the wild the numbers of this plant have been reduced to such an extent that its continued existence is in question.

EICHHORNIA SPECIES — **Water Hyacinths**

The water Hyacinths, with their beautiful pale blue blossoms, are not very suitable for being kept in aquaria. *Eichhornia crassipes*, originally at home in tropical America, has spread throughout all tropical and subtropical zones as a floating water weed. In the aquarium the plant does not last, since its light requirements cannot be met. *Eichhornia azurea* can also be kept underwater. It is decorative but needs much light in order to thrive.

CRYPTOCORYNES

Many popular and extremely suitable aquarium plants belong to the genus *Cryptocoryne*. They originate in southern and southeastern Asia. Since they occur there frequently in shaded forest rivers, they are satisfied in the aquarium with small amounts of light. Although mostly plants for acid, soft water, they often adapt to other water conditions when cultivated.

If cryptocorynes are to be grown successfully, they must be left undisturbed, above all else. Nothing is more harmful for them than repeated transplanting. With undisturbed growth they will form runners that in time will grow into entire forests. They grow slowly, however.

The determination of the species of cryptocorynes is not always easy. The surest method of determination uses details of color and structure of the tube-like flower, the spathe. However, since these usually do not form during the type of submerged cultivation customary in the aquarium, cryptocoryne are only rarely seen in bloom. Originally swamp plants, crypts react favorably to aquarium clay and carbon dioxide fertiization.

A sudden change in the water and the light conditions can lead to a rapid collapse of the crypt population. The leaves will rot, slowly at first then progressively more quickly. This *Cryptocoryne* rot appears mainly after a radical thinning of the cover of floating plants, a change in the type of fluorescent

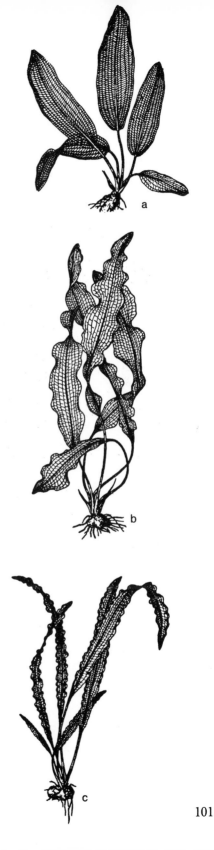

Some leaf types in *Aponogeton*. a) *Aponogeton madagascariensis;* b) *Aponogeton ulvaceus;* c) *Aponogeton crispus.*

101

Cryptocoryne lingua

Crypts, *Cryptocoryne* species, are considered by many aquarists to be the most desirable of the aquatic plants although they are often hard to cultivate. There are many species of many sizes and leaf types. Shown on the facing page is *Cryptocoryne beckettii;* two other *Cryptocoryne* species are shown above and below on this page.

Cryptocoryne wendtii

lamp or a delayed change of the fluorescent tube, or after the addition of too much plant fertilizer or algicides. However, if the cryptocoryne are spared such shocks, if they are treated patiently and virtually with velvet gloves, they can give much enjoyment. Some species that are especially easy to care for in the beginning are *C. affinis, C. petchii, C. usteriana, C. willisii, C. walkeri,* and *C. wendtii.*

CRYPTOCORYNE WILLISII

This low-growing plant was known for years under the name *Cryptocoryne nevillii*. It is ideal for turning the foreground of the aquarium green. However, many years may pass before a few plants will form a lawn! It is satisfied with less light and lower temperatures than some other species, but good light and temperatures between 25-30°C encourage growth.

CRYPTOCORYNE AFFINIS

A very frequently kept and especially undemanding plant that will grow well under almost all conditions, its leaves are sometimes slightly knobby and their undersides are frequently reddish. It will readily form shoots. It is extremely well suited for groups in the center and along the sides of the aquarium.

CRYPTOCORYNE CILIATA

This plant, which will grow up to 50 cm high, requires sufficient light for healthy growth. It is well suited for group plantings in the background. The best temperatures lie between 22-28°C, and the chemistry of the water is not that important. It will even thrive in brackish water.

CRYPTOCORYNE PETCHII

This plant, originating in Sri Lanka, has brownish, slightly wavy leaves of about 10 cm length. It is certainly dec-

a) *Eichhornia crassipes*, a water hyacinth. b) *Cryptocoryne affinis*. c) *Cryptocoryne balan-sae*. d) *Cryptocoryne wendtii*. e) *Cryptocoryne ciliata*. f) *Cryptocoryne willisii*.

orative and will readily grow shoots even in medium-hard water.

CRYPTOCORYNE USTERIANA

This species grows strongly buckled green leaves of up to 80 cm in length. The plant originates in the Philippines and is quite adaptable but, of course, is suitable only for larger aquaria. The somewhat smaller *Cryptocoryne balansae* looks similar and is also easy to care for.

CRYPTOCORYNE WENDTII

Several varieties of this species are known. The tops of the leaves are olive- green and often covered with lead-gray spots. This species is undemanding in regard to water quality, amount of light, and substrate. It is propagated by means of runners and is well suited for group plantings in the center.

LAGENANDRA SPECIES

These are swamp plants from Asia that are closely related to *Cryptocoryne* but are not nearly as well adapted to the submersed way of life. For this reason, *Lagenandra* species grow slowly in the aquarium. However, for cultivation as semiemersed plants, they are ideal.

ANUBIAS SPECIES

The *Anubias* species come from Africa and resemble in appearance and care *Cryptocoryne*, to which they are related. They are, however, less well adapted to submersed conditions. Because of their slow rate of growth, they are suited for aquarists who wish to avoid work connected with the weeding and propagating of plants. They are only suited for well established tanks! The most recommended species is *Anubias barteri* var. *nana*, originating in West Africa.

PISTIA STRATIOTES — **Water Lettuce**

Pistia is a decorative floating plant, that is less effective visually from the

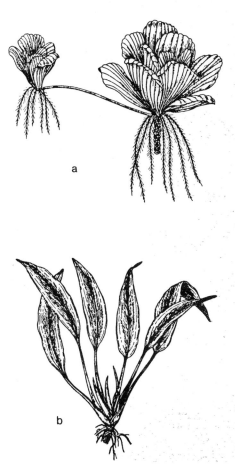

a) *Pistia stratiotes,* the water lettuce, is a popular floating plant that is best suited for ponds rather than aquaria. Although it provides very attractive greenery in the aquarium, its high light requirements mean that it often dies or gradually disintegrates in the tank. Also, the high humidity of the air above its leaves in a covered aquarium leads to brown spots on the leaves. b) *Lagenandra thwaitesii.*

usual aquarium perspective (the side) than from above. Its great light requirements may cause problems in the aquarium. On the other hand, it can be cultivated effortlessly in garden pools in the open during summer.

LEMNA MINOR — Duck Weed

Duck weed is a small floating plant that can cover ponds and aquaria in dense layers. They are frequently brought into the aquarium with live food or plants and multiply so quickly that they become a pest. They have to be skimmed off repeatedly, then after a few months they disappear by themselves. It is better to use more easily controlled plants such as *Riccia*, *Ceratopteris*, or *Salvinia* for shading the substrate.

Duck weeds are small but very rapidly growing plants that if left unchecked will soon cover the surface of any aquarium into which they are (usually accidentally) introduced. Believe it or not, duck weeds are flowering plants and actually have minute flowers and seed pods. In this picture the large plants are *Spirodela polyrhiza*, the more abundant small plants are *Lemna minor*. Photo by J. Vierke.

The larger duck weed *Spirodela polyrhiza* is less of a plague, but it also cannot be recommended as an aquarium plant. It differs from *Lemna* mainly by the reddish coloration of its underside.

SNAILS IN
THE AQUARIUM

Whether he wants to or not, every aquarist will in time make the acquaintance of water snails. They are first brought in, unwittingly, with the purchase of water plants or with live food.

Among the snails there are some that are quite welcome in the aquarium and others that should be banned as far as possible. If the snails take the upper hand, we can collect them individually or sentence them to death by snail-eating fish. Puffers, for instance, are dedi-cated snail-lovers; unfortunately, these fish may make life more difficult for other fishes, too, by nibbling on their fins.

Usually it is sufficient to collect the excessive snails. With the bait method, this is not difficult. If a large piece of a potato or a carrot is put into the water, we will find many snails there after a few hours and they can be easily collected.

An apple snail, *Ampullaria australis.* Photo by J. Vierke.

LYMNAEA STAGNALIS

This is the only common snail that will destroy our water plants. It is also at home in our outdoor ponds. It is easily recognized by its single-colored, large (6 cm) pointed shell. This species might possibly be confused with the livebearing *Viviparus viviparus*, which, however, has a brown-banded shell and an operculum that can close the opening of the shell. Both species of snails are interesting objects for pond aquaria but really are not suited for the aquarium!

MELANOIDES TUBERCULATA —
Malayan Snail

This snail has a pointed, tapered shell that is much more slender than that of the *Lymnaea*. Also, the Malayan snail grows barely longer than 1 cm. During the day they live in the substrate of the aquarium and are useful as scavengers and ground aerators at the same time. They keep the ground loose without damaging the plants. These viviparous animals sometimes multiply excessively but will not be harmful even then. If they leave the substrate during the hours the tank is lighted, this is an indication that the substrate is very dirty and requires renovation.

PLANORBIS CORNEUS —
Ramshorn

This reddish or blackish flattened, circular snail is among the most common snails in the aquarium. However, its role as an algae-eater is usually overestimated. On the other hand, it is not a danger to the aquarium plants — it can only become dangerous when present in massive infestations. Also popular are the larger red ramshorn snails, *Helisoma*, from tropical South America.

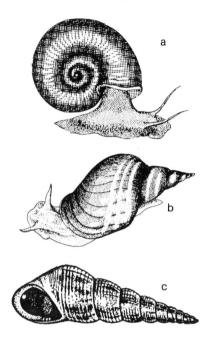

Three common small aquarium snails. a) The ramshorn, *Planorbis corneus;* b) *Lymnaea stagnalis;* c) the Malayan snail, *Melanoides tuberculata.*

AMPULLARIA AUSTRALIS —
Apple Snail

The tropical apple Snails, which grow up to 10 cm in diameter, are interesting inhabitants of the aquarium. They are capable of utilizing atmospheric air by means of a snorkel-like extrusion from the body. An apple snail deposits its eggs outside the water in groups, often on the sides or cover of the aquarium. Apple Snails also eat algae, but they need fish food, too, in order to grow well and multiply. Adult animals like to eat lettuce and will occasionally eat tender water plants. These snails are also called infusoria snails as their droppings were once used to brew infusoria cultures.

WHAT DO WE FEED OUR FISHES?

It is often believed that the quality or suitability of a fish food is indicated by the feeding behavior of the fish. Don't believe those advertisements that argue on the theme: "The fish will devour our food eagerly — therefore, it is good!" Fish quickly get used to certain kinds of food (regardless of whether or not it ultimately is good for them), and it may take some time to accustom them to a different kind, should this be necessary or convenient.

Dry Food

Probably the majority of aquarists feed dry food. This method is convenient, and the fishes indicate that the food tastes good. Dry food is available in different forms: as flakes, as pellets, and freeze-dried.

Flakes are the all-round food, and most aquarium fishes may be fed with this food alone. Flake foods are manufactured from different animal and vegetable substances, trace elements, and vitamins. A good flake food should not turn the water murky and should not fall apart into tiny bits too rapidly. Most commercially available kinds of flakes completely fill the requirements for the daily care of the fishes.

Pellets are especially suitable for larger fishes that cannot be satisfied with the usual flakes and will be able to devour the pellets with one gulp. Smaller fish also like to nibble smaller pieces off a pellet.

Freeze-dried food consists of animals such as tubifex, mosquito larvae, or brine shrimp whose water content has been removed by the process of freeze-drying. Their nutrients and taste remain fully preserved. Stored in a dry place, freeze- dried food may be kept for an almost unlimited period of time. However, this type of food is not exactly inexpensive because of the quite involved method of manufacture.

Meat

Large fishes sometimes like to have fresh meat as food. Lean meat may be given to large fishes within limits and not too frequently. Particularly well suited are beef heart cut into strips and lean boiled ham. Of course, fish meat is ideal since it is especially digestible. Fish roe is liked by smaller fishes, too. However, if the fishes are fed only with meat without also being offered live foods or other kinds of food, the appearance of certain deficiencies in the fish must be expected.

Frozen Food

Many fishes will not accept dry food but will eat only live food. However, in most instances, live food is not available all year and we will have to prepare a stock of frozen live food. The food animals are frozen alive, with as little water as possible. The more rapid the freezing (the lower the temperature of the freezer) the higher the quality of the frozen food.

Several kinds of frozen foods are available at your pet shop. They can be stored for months in the freezer.

When feeding frozen food, care must

The variety of fish food available in your pet shop is absolutely astounding. There are the usual flakes and pellets, but also an abundance of freeze-dried foods almost as good as live foods.

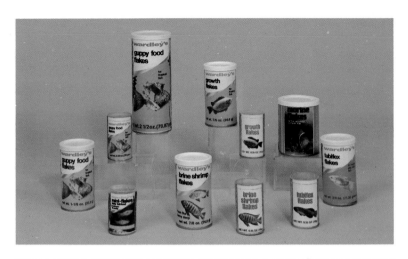

Specialty foods abound. There are special foods for cichlids and livebearers, color-enhancing foods for bettas and guppies, even mini-flakes for small livebearers and other small fishes.

be taken to have the food completely thawed — carelessness may lead to intestinal inflammation and to other illnesses in the fishes!

Live Food

Some fishes that are especially well suited for being kept in aquaria may be fed for their entire lives with dry food only: they may even be bred on a dry food diet. The majority of our fishes, however, will thrive better if they are at least occasionally offered live food or at least frozen live food. Some species of fishes even depend completely on live food, since only the movement of their prey triggers the impulse to snatch the food. In some pet shops live food is sold almost all year. It consists most often of tubifex worms or bloodworms and sometimes also brine shrimp and daphnia. For larger fishes one may get mealworms, crickets, and sometimes other insect larvae. In bait stores we can sometimes get earthworms and waxmoth larvae.

The same rules apply for feeding with live food as for dry food: we should put only as much food into the aquarium as can be eaten within a short time. It probably goes without saying that we must turn off the filter, especially when feeding daphnia.

If we have the opportunity to do so, it is best to collect our own live food.

Water fleas (daphnia) can occasionally be skimmed from the surface of lakes and ponds in large numbers. These animals feed on tiny floating particles (detritus and microorganisms) that they filter from the water by means of a sophisticated filtering system. For this reason, water fleas may very well be kept as a living filter in the aquarium. A group of water fleas can clear an aquarium muddied by floating algae within a few hours.

The nutritional value of daphnia is often underestimated. In addition to animal proteins, freshly caught water fleas also contain vegetable particles in their digestive system that are of great importance to many fishes. In addition, their chitinous carapace is also valuable as bulk.

Water fleas need quite a bit of oxygen. If too many animals are put into the aquarium at once, many will soon die. Put in a cool place, the water fleas can be kept for several days, especially with additional aeration, but the nutritional value of these animals can no longer be compared with that of freshly caught daphnia.

Copepods (cyclops) can be caught with a net during all seasons in ponds and lakes (even in winter, they are sometimes found under the ice of lakes). The small cyclops larvae (nauplii) are of great importance in the raising of young fish. However, if more of them are put into the aquarium than are eaten right away, they will grow more quickly than the fish fry and may start attacking the fry.

Brine Shrimp (Artemia) are among the most important of all live foods for the aquarist. This is especially true for fish breeding, since the commercially available brine shrimp eggs can be hatched without difficulties, offering an excellent food for the raising of the tiniest fish larvae. The hatched nauplii can be raised in salt water (15-20 g iodine-free table salt per liter of water) with commercially available special food. The hatched nauplii are best transferred into a small plastic basin or a larger bowl. The water should not be aerated; the temperature may range between 18-28°C. Special lighting is not necessary. However, the animals must be fed regularly. For this, put one

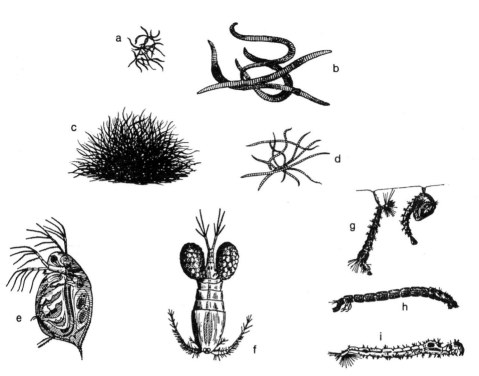

Live foods. a) Grindal worms, dwarf white-worms. b) Earthworms, readily taken by many fishes when chopped up. c) A clump of tubifex or tubificid worms. d) White-worms or enchytraeids, an underutilized food in the U.S. e) A water flea or daphnia. f) A copepod. g) Mosquito larvae (called black mosquito larvae by the Germans). h) A bloodworm or Chironomid midge larva (called red mosquito larva in Germany). i) A glassworm or phantom midge larva (called white mosquito larva in German literature).

pinch of the dust-like *Artemia* food into the water and stir. The now murky water is filtered by the shrimp in order to absorb the food. We may feed again only after the water has turned clear again. The sediment must be removed regularly.

The breeding of *Artemia* is simple once we have raised the first young animals. If the opportunity exists, we should get a breeding group of old and half-grown animals. Otherwise, the starting difficulties can be bridged with a special first food for *Artemia* nauplii. Fully grown brine shrimp become at least 1 cm in length and provide constant offspring.

Bloodworms, the larvae of chironomid midges, live in the substrate of lakes and ponds. The collection of these animals is not for the average aquarist since special tools and sieves are needed. Bloodworms are frequently offered in the trade, but they sometimes come from very polluted waters. For this reason a certain amount of caution is indicated when feeding these basically very nutritious animals. The larvae should be put in water for one or two days before feeding, at least if the fish are sensitive.

Mosquito larvae and pupae are an excellent live fish food. From spring to fall mosquito larvae are often found very plentifully in small ponds or in water-filled containers. The animals hang from the water surface with their breathing tubes up, but swim downward at the slightest disturbance. They are easily caught with an ordinary water flea net.

When feeding them, care must be taken inasmuch as the larvae develop quite rapidly in the warm water; if we feed too many (especially pupae), we could produce a plague of mosquitos in the house!

Glassworms, the larvae of the midge *Corethra,* also are an ideal fish food. The virtually transparent insect larvae are reminiscent of ¾ inch glass rods floating horizontally in the water of lakes and ponds. They sometimes appear in large numbers and are often most common during the cooler (not necessarily cold) part of the year.

Glassworms are very nutritious, increase the spawning readiness of the fish, and are very willingly eaten. They can be kept for a long period of time without aeration in a refrigerator.

Facing page: Many aquarists have come to believe (probably incorrectly) that tubifex worms carry all sorts of diseases. The ready availability of freeze-dried tubifex worms should alleviate their worries, however, as freeze-drying destroys any microorganisms likely to cause diseases. Freeze-dried foods are also easy to feed and are taken readily by a great many species. Photo by Dr. Herbert R. Axelrod.

Below: A *Corydoras adolfoi* prepares to feast on an abundance of living tubifex. Photo by Dr. Herbert R. Axelrod.

Whiteworms (enchytraeids) are white bristleworms 20-30 mm in length that are very suitable as a fat- and protein-containing growth food for rapidly growing fishes. But remember: "Avoid one- sided feeding, since the fish could easily become too fat!"

If you have enough room in your basement, you might try your hand at breeding whiteworms. For this we need a wood or styrofoam box measuring about 20 x 20 cm and about 10 cm high. Put a pane of glass directly on the bottom and then fill the box with unfertilized potting soil. The soil must always be kept moist (not wet!). On the soil put the food for the whiteworms: cooked oatmeal, bread, grated apples, grated carrots, and similar items. Then cover the box with a pane of glass. Food remnants that are not eaten must be removed in order to keep the soil from turning sour. In a healthy culture, the worms rapidly collect around the food. Since the cultures are always infested by parasites, they must be renewed regularly. It is best to keep several culture boxes going at the same time. Breeding stock is obtainable in the pet shop or by mail. In *Tropical Fish Hobbyist* magazine there are almost always such offers.

Grindal worms are dwarf whiteworms that grow to only 10 mm in length and are thus especially suitable for young fishes. They are bred at room temperatures (they also do well at slightly warmer temperatures) and need only small breeding boxes (about 10 x 10 x 5 cm). As a culture substrate, use unfertilized garden soil or peat. The care and feeding are the same as with large whiteworms.

Tubifex worms (sewer worms) are the aquarium fish live food most frequently offered in the trade. The brown to reddish worms can easily be kept for several days in cooler water if the old water with wastes is decanted every day and fresh water added. However, they keep longest and best if they are put into cosntantly and gently flowing cold tapwater. Most fishes like to eat tubifex and will tolerate this food even though it sometimes comes from very polluted waters. If the fishes are extremely sensitive, the tubifex should be cleaned in running water for two days before feeding them. Tubifex can also be chopped into small pieces with a razor blade and serve thus as growth food for young fishes.

Earthworms are a popular and valuable food for larger fishes. However, worms from manure piles should not be fed in large amounts.

115

THE COMMUNITY AQUARIUM

The community aquarium is a beautifully planted aquarium arranged decoratively with roots and rocks and stocked with many different kinds of peaceful and plant-friendly fishes. This is the type of aquarium most frequently found. For this reason, my present guidelines for the equipping and care of an aquarium are intended primarily for the community aquarium. However, let me emphasize once more: a community aquarium should not contain less than 70 liters of water, and should contain more if possible. *The bigger the tank, the easier it is to care for.*

In the combination of the plants and fishes, we should be guided by one rule of thumb: the requirements of the plants and fishes must be in agreement with the possibilities we can offer them! This is not too difficult with plants. With advance planning we can see to it that especially demanding kinds will get enough room and light and that we put together plants that can be kept in the same temperatures and water qualities.

In the combination of the fishes, much more sensitivity is needed. Some fishes that exhibit the same demands as to water quality, temperature, and planting simply cannot be kept together. While we cannot have enough plants right from the beginning, moderation is the trademark of a master aquarist when it comes to stocking with fishes.

Unfortunately, there are no rules of thumb for a correct combination of fish species, so for this reason it is difficult to state general rules. One basic relationship, however, must be clarified: we distinguish between schooling fishes and fishes that as a rule do not form schools as adults. Of course, there are also borderline types! Typical schooling fishes will get along with each other and must never be kept singly or in only small groups.

However, there are also fishes that fight bitterly with others of the same species. This is true especially for males when they are ready to spawn! Such fishes must be kept singly or in pairs. Since they usually behave themselves quite mannerly toward fishes of other species, they often can readily be kept in company with others.

There are often big discussions as to whether fishes and plants should be combined according to geographical specifications. I can certainly sympathize when someone wants to be led by geographical considerations in the choice of his fishes and plants and occasionally I do this myself, but I am not "orthodox" in this regard. Whatever might be your position regarding the geographically "correct" combination of fishes, one thing must be made clear: choice according to continents or even habitats does not even remotely lead to a harmonic, peaceful stocking. The contrary often is the case. One example may illustrate this.

In a pond in southwestern Thailand, I caught two fighting fish (*Betta splendens*), one small climbing perch (*An-*

116

abas), a blue gourami (*Trichogaster trichopterus*), and some croaking gouramis (*Trichopsis vittatus*). They were put into a (too small) aquarium in which after a few days the *Trichogaster* turned into a tyrant and became extremely annoying with its constant chasing. Once I had removed it, the male fighting fish took its place. I removed this fish, too, from the tank. Now the climbing perch began to bother the *Trichopsis!* Obviously, a common origin does not guarantee peaceful coexistence in the aquarium.

Suggestions for the Arrangement and Stocking

For the beginner, it often is not easy to arrange an aquarium well and stock it correctly without detailed help. The reader may consider the following suggestions as guidelines that make possible a favorable beginning to our hobby. Of course, there are no limits to the imagination when arranging a community aquarium, and the advanced aquarist will follow his own ideas.

As an example for the arrangement, an idea for a tank of 80-120 liters is given here. Tanks of this size are about 80-100 cm long.

Lighting: Two or three 20-watt fluorescent tubes.

Other technical equipment: One heater (40-60 watts), one thermometer, and, if possible, a filter.

Decoration: One picturesque piece of driftwood or root and three about hand- sized flat rocks. The root goes into the left side of the aquarium, where it serves as a hiding place for the equipment. Two of the rocks are used to build a small terrace in the right rear corner.

Planting: We need an *Echinodorus bleheri* (or *E. parviflorus* or *E. amazoni-*cus) and two or three stalks of *Hygrophila corymbosa* (or *H. difformis* or *H. stricta*). Of any other plants used, we should take at least five each — better more than less. There is barely a maximum limit. I have selected relatively inexpensive plants that multiply quickly and are fairly easy to get. Only the foreground plant (*Cryptocoryne willisii*) is somewhat more demanding. However, it can be replaced by *Echinodorus tenellus*.

If you can get other plants, you have the option, of course, to plant them in addition or as substitutes, taking into consideration their requirements.

When, after a few weeks, the aquarium is well established and the plants are growing, some of the less valuable species may gradually be replaced by more beautiful kinds. In many instances, we will purposely select plants which do not grow in the water, or only grow slowly, such as *Anubias* and *Lagenandra*. In this manner, we simplify the care.

In the planting, we have not followed any geographical guidelines. We have chosen undemanding and attractive plants and have combined them for their esthetic values.

Stocking with fish: For acceptable fishes I would like to give five alternative suggestions.

1. Completely unproblematic fishes from around the world:
Guppies (*Poecilia reticulata*) ...3 males, 2 females
Platies (*Xiphophorus maculatus*) .2 pairs
Zebra danios (*Brachydanio rerio*).........
10 specimens
Kribensis dwarf cichlids (*Pelvicachromis pulcher*)......................1 pair

Corydoras catfishes (*Corydoras* species)
.... 6 specimens
These are so-called "beginner fishes" whose care, however, is interesting and pleasurable. Most of these fishes are constantly on the move and attractive. Perhaps we may sometimes be able to save young guppies and platies in this aquarium, keeping them from being

Below: A diagram of a suggested planting layout and how it would look from in front of the aquarium. *Facing page:* Another diagram of a planting layout, this one with more demanding plants that in part replace and complement the planting on the other page.

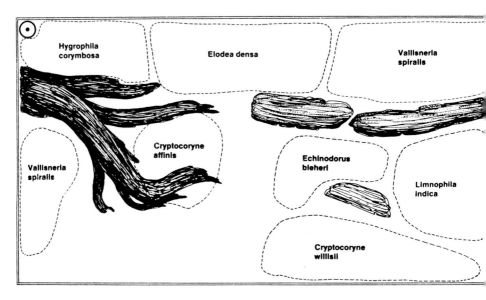

eaten by the other inhabitants. For the kribensis cichlid pair we should put a cave into the tank. For this, we may use half a coconut shell put on a slant into the substrate with its opening at the bottom so that only a small entrance remains open. Instead of the *Pelvicachromis*, we may select a pair of *Hemichromis thomasi* — these fish do not need a cave. The water temperature should be 24°C.

2. Decorative fishes from Asia and South America:

Angelfish (*Pterophyllum scalare*) ....
.... 4 specimens
Pearl gouramis (*Trichogaster leerii*). . .
.... 4 specimens
Bleeding heart tetras (*Hyphessobrycon erythrostigma*) .... 7 specimens
Fighting fish (*Betta splendens*).... 1 pair
Plecostomus catfish (*Hypostomus* species) .... 2 specimens

One name is misleading: even with a fighting fish, we have here a combination of especially quiet and peaceful fishes that are magnificent in coloration and shape. In addition to the recommended planting, we can anchor water sprite (*Ceratopteris*) in the left third of the aquarium. The water temperature should be 28°C.

3. Soft water tank for South American fishes:

Angelfish (*Pterophyllum scalare*).....
.... 4 specimens
Rams (*Microgeophagus ramirezi*)..........
.... 2 pairs
Red phantom tetras (*Megalamphodus sweglesi*) .... 8 specimens
Hockey sticks or penguins (*Thayeria* species) .... 8 specimens
Bristle-nosed catfish (*Ancistrus* species) 3 specimens

Here I have selected fishes that are not among the extreme soft-water fish. They may certainly be kept in 14°DH, although softer water would, of course, be more advantageous. The tetras may be replaced by other species. However, the fish should not be too small, since the adult angels like to eat small tetras. For this reason I have not recommended neons! (In addition, they would require lower temperatures than

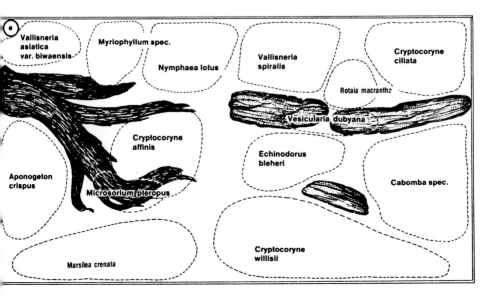

the species listed here.) The water temperature should be 27°C.

4. Fishes for hard water:

Rainbowfishes (*Melanotaenia* species)... 10 specimens

Green Swordtails (*Xiphophorus helleri*) .... 1 male, 2 females

Julidochromis ornatus 4 specimens

Archerfish (*Toxotes chatareus*) .... 1 specimen

South African mouthbrooder (*Pseudocrenilabrus philander*).............. 1 male, 2 females

Where the water flows from the tap with more than 20°DH, one will wisely decide against soft-water fish, since the necessary water preparation for larger tanks would be quite expensive and complicated. The fish listed above, on the other hand, need relatively hard water in order to be comfortable. Instead of the *P. philander,* we may also choose the *P. multicolor.* For the *Julidochromis* we should construct rock caves at the left next to the root and at right in front of the terrace. The water temperature should be about 23°C.

5. Fishes from tropical Asia:

Rasboras (*Rasbora* Species)........... 10 specimens

Coolie loaches (*Acanthophthalmus* species) .... 4 specimens

Cherry barbs (*Puntius titteya*) .... 8 specimens

Dwarf gouramis (*Colisa lalia*).... 1 pair

Red-tailed black shark (*Labeo bicolor*) . 1 specimen

Croaking gouramis (*Trichopsis vittatus*). 4 specimens

Siamese flying foxes (*Epalzeorhynchus siamensis*)...................... 3 specimens

This tank combines decorative fishes with some of the most interesting fishes. In the left third of the aquarium we should anchor a species of *Ceratopteris.* The water temperature should be between 26 and 29°C.

All these suggestions have one thing in common: with very few exceptions, these are fishes that are popular for good reasons and therefore are easy to obtain. They put comparatively modest demands on their caretaker and leave the plants alone.

I assume that with a little imagination, it will not be difficult to transfer this planning to a proportionately larger tank.

A well-planned community tank is a lovely sight to behold.

THE MINIATURE AQUARIUM

An aquarium that contains only about 15-40 liters of water is a miniature aquarium or mini-tank. However, this is by no means a tank for beginners or children! As I have expressed repeatedly, it is very much simpler to successfully maintain a larger aquarium than a smaller one. Therefore, a mini-tank is something for people who have already gained some experience with other aquaria.

A particular advantage of the mini-tank is the small amount of water. This is of importance in those cases when we need water of a special quality for our fishes, especially water that has to be obtained with a lot of trouble and, usually, expense, such as *very* soft water. Someone who would like to keep fishes that depend entirely on live food might also put them into a mini-tank. Live food is not available the year-around in larger amounts, and neither is it cheap. In a miniature aquarium stocked with only one or two species, we can feed more purposefully.

Of course, the regular partial water change also becomes a more minor chore in the mini-tank, though it must even be made at shorter intervals than usual unless we prefer to check the water quality regularly for hardness and nitrite content. Small amounts of water are less stable than large ones!

Suggestions for stocking the mini-tank

There are very small fishes that would virtually disappear in a large community tank but which we would like to keep because of their beauty or their interesting behavior. I don't mean to say that these species would be chased or even eaten in the community tank, but they remain hidden between the plants, are not flashy, are timid, and in most instances their demise would not even be noticed. Such fishes are best kept in a small dedicated aquarium in which only members of the same species are kept.

As an example, let us consider the least killifish, *Heterandria formosa*, from southeastern North America. These little fish, which grow at most to 3 cm (as a rule, the males remain even 1 cm shorter), feel happiest alone in the dedicated aquarium. We plant the mini-tank with delicately branched fine-leaved plants such as *Myriophyllum* or *Cabomba*. In addition, the tiny fish like roots overgrown with Java moss, some *Riccia*, and/or other floating plants on the water surface. The fish are given crumbled dry food, and between feedings we should always offer them some baby brine shrimp. We need not worry too much about water hardness or temperature. These livebearers need no additional heating. Even without our help their young will grow up again and again.

Everglades pygmy sunfish, *Elassoma evergladei*, which also come from southeastern North America, are also best housed in a mini-tank. They have the same minimal demands as *Heterandria* but eat only live food. Here, too, the young will usually grow up without our assistance. The black males with their

Above: Elassoma evergladei is an attractive and undemanding little fish that is readily kept and even bred in a mini-tank. Photo by B. Kahl.

Below: General layout of a scree or rocky aquarium suitable for many small fishes.

bright blue spots have a most enchanting effect during their courtship dances.

Another dwarf group that is excellently suited for the mini-tank is the dwarf cichlids. We can arrange the tank as described above but in addition put in two rock caves. Here we may observe the courtship, pairing, and caring for the brood by these beautiful little fishes. Since as a rule the young are not eaten by their parents, here, too, young fish may grow up almost without care.

Of course, the mini-tank need not be identical with the small dedicated tank. It is not only possible, but it is sometimes even recommended to combine two or three species even in a mini-tank. Discuss this problem with your aquarium store manager. He should be able to help you select from the thousands of different combinations. The presence of fishes that always swim in the open water encourages the nervous catfishes to come out of their hiding places.

As an example for such a dwarf cichlid aquarium, I would like to describe here a "scree" or rocky aquarium. The "scree" aquarium consists of about 25% rocks. The fist-sized round rocks are piled in the aquarium in such a manner that they almost reach the surface of the water in the two rear corners, while in the front corners they should reach to about half that level. In the foreground there remains a free spot in the center that is planted with delicate plants. The rocks must be wedged tightly so that our construction will not collapse, and they should be put directly onto the floor of the aquarium. Only then is the sand added. Some aquarists even glue them together with silicone sealant.

Julidochromis ornatus is right at home in a rock-strewn aquarium. Photo by J. Vierke.

In a 30-liter aquarium thus equipped, there is room for an *Apistogramma* male and two females as well as for a small school of about six small tetras such as *Paracheirodon*. The water must be soft and slightly acid, the temperature ranging between 24 and 28°C.

We may decorate a tank similarly for the small species of *Julidochromis*, dwarf cichlids from Lake Tanganyika. The water in this tank must be hard, and we can do without companion fish. Here it would look good if we used obliquely placed slabs of slate with a corresponding system of cracks. As inhabitants for such a mini-tank a single pair of *J. transcriptus, J. ornatus, J. dickfeldi*, or a similar species is sufficient. In the course of several months the offspring will take care of the extra space. Unfortunately, *Julidochromis* sexes are difficult to distinguish. I can only advise you to try to exchange uncompatible partners. First, however, the method of a separating partition should be tried, because initially some *Julidochromis* pairs don't get along. The fish are separated by a pane of glass that is put across the aquarium. When the pane is removed again after several days, the fish often have become accustomed to each other and no longer fight.

There are myriad charming combinations for a small aquarium using delicate plants, a small tree root, and some rocks as decoration. Here are some other suggestions.

A small troop of armored catfishes are easily companioned with some pencilfishes (*Nannostomus* species). These fishes need soft, slightly acid water.

Excellent and colorful combinations from Asia are honey gouramis (*Colisa chuna*) — one male and one or two females — and Day's Paradise fish, *Pseudosphromenus dayi*, or coolie loaches, *Acanthophthalmus*, and harlequin rasboras, *Rasbora heteromorpha* or *R. hengeli*.

Let us not forget the killifishes, which are suited expressly for the mini-aquarium! A small tank equipped with fine- leaved plants and Java moss and stocked with several lyretails, *Aphyosemion australe*, or other species of *Aphyosemion* is a delight for the eye. The water should be soft and slightly acid, the temperature 24°C.

Particularly rare fish also will preferably be kept in a dedicated tank since their often difficult demands can thus more easily be met. If someone is fortunate enough to find some of the rare dwarf gouramis such as *Malpulutta* or *Parosphromenus* or find a shipment of wild bettas or other rarities, he can devote special attention to them in a mini-tank.

THE SCHOOL AQUARIUM

Aquaristics and school — this is a wide- ranging field. A large, beautifully equipped community tank positioned in the main hall or the biology classroom is not only an especially attractive focal point, but it may inspire the students to observation and thus bring them closer to nature.

Since such a school aquarium must always be presentable, it must be easy to care for. For instance, the faucets (if possible, also for warm water) and drains should be nearby to facilitate water changes and enough electrical outlets for the equipment (lighting, heating, filter) must be available. Soon a sufficient number of trustworthy students will be found to take care of a part of the maintenance while under suitable supervision. They must be able to get to the aquarium without impediment, but unauthorized persons should be kept away. Nothing further need be said here about the equipping of the aquarium — the biology teacher will certainly find many options for incorporating the aquarium and its inhabitants into the courses and will stock them accordingly.

Occasionally, many different pond animals get into the hands of the biology teacher: tadpoles, newts, insect larvae, and many others. For these animals small to medium-sized plastic aquaria are very suitable. These tanks must be protected from direct sunlight and positioned in such a manner that the temperature does not exceed 20°C for any length of time. A separate lighting system is usually superfluous.

For observations over a period of several weeks in an aquarium in the spring, newts (courtship, pairing, laying of eggs) and sticklebacks (courtship, laying of eggs, caring for the brood) as well as frogs (development of the tadpoles) are especially well suited. It probably goes without saying that after the period of observation all the animals must be released in the place where they were caught.

During the other seasons, the mouthbrooding cichlid *Haplochromis burtoni* and the dwarf gourami *Colisa lalia* are excellently suited for behavior studies. These fishes have the advantage of being willing to spawn all year. In the following paragraphs, I will describe briefly some easily executed behavioral experiments. They are intended not only as guidelines for the biology teacher but also for those aquarists who are interested in behavioral observation. The ideas to be considered here concern schooling behavior, fighting behavior, and learning behavior. They also have the advantage, in contrast to experiments concerning behavior regarding the care for the brood, that they can be done without lengthy, time-consuming preparations.

Schooling behavior in fishes

A fish school is distinguished by the following relationships: the members of a school do not know each other individually, their number is without upper limit, and they seek each other's company (social attraction). The school is not tied to a special place. For testing schooling behavior, the smaller species of tetras and barbs are especially suitable.

For our tests we need about ten fish each of two species. It is evident that we should use inexpensive, hardy fishes. For our experiment, an 80 cm long tank entirely without decoration is sufficient.

Test 1. We divide the fish, separated by species, into two cylindrical glass containers of about 1-2 liters capacity, one species per cylinder. The cylinders are separated from each other in the aquarium, and the aquarium is divided into two halves by a line made with a marking pen on the front pane (careful with plastic aquaria). We now put a test fish into the middle for 15 minutes and observe how often it traverses the borders of the observation spaces and how long it stays in the different areas (as a percentage of the total observed time). We then repeat the observation with a test fish of the other species.

The presence of one or several small, simple aquaria in the classroom can be very useful in instructing children about the aquatic world and the importance of lesser forms of life. Even a young child can rapidly learn the basics of aquarium care and will surprisingly quickly pick up quite a bit on why fishes do what they do. Photo by J. Vierke.

Test 2. The execution of the test is the same as above, except that we now use only the ten fish of one species. Of these, seven are put into one glass cylinder, two into the other, and the remaining fish becomes the test fish. The same test is also performed with the other species.

Test 3. For the qualitative observation of schooling behavior, both species of fish are put loose into the tank. Do the schools mix, do they have preferred areas, are there leaders, are there fights? How do the fishes react to disturbances and to the addition of a large goldfish?

Fighting Behavior of *Betta splendens*

Animal behavior is determined by internal and external stimuli. Frequently, the internal stimuli are hormones or rhythmically self-activating centers in the central nervous system. Also of significance is the period of time in which the behavior has *not*

Many observations on the behavior of fishes can be conducted readily in a school aquarium. The gouramis, such as the spawning pair of *Colisa lalia* shown here, and other anabantoids are especially interesting in their behavior, as are the cichlids. Photo by J. Vierke.

taken place. In the fighting behavior of *Betta splendens*, the significance of external stimuli is to be determined. External stimuli that trigger an instinctive behavior are called "key stimuli."

The fighting behavior of the fighting fish males increases from approach, through spreading of the gill covers during frontal intimidation, sideways intimidation and beating of the fins and ramming. Thus, these are not mainly fights to do damage, but highly ritualized confrontations that in nature hardly ever lead to death. If one of the fighting fish has to rise to the surface in order to change the air in its labyrinth cavities, it is not attacked. The opponent usually takes advantage of this opportunity to also rise and get fresh air.

127

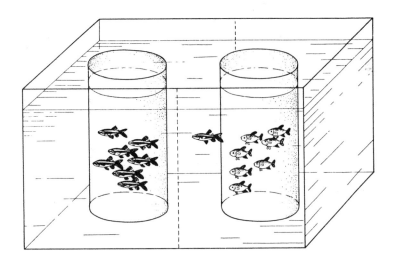

To demonstrate this behavior, two male fighting fish can be put together for short periods of time, but they must be separated again before their fins are torn! This is where cruelty to animals begins. The actual fighting betta of the Thais do not have the flowing and easily injured veil fins that have been bred into our decorative bettas. Our fish, changed by selective breeding, no longer fits its behavior. For this reason it is better to perform tests with dummies or mirrors.

The dummies are kneaded from plasticine into approximately the shape of a fighting fish and then painted with waterproof colors: dark blue, red, with gill covers lying flat, and red, with spread gill covers. We can also try to find out whether the fish react to cardboard dummies that are held up against the aquarium glass from the outside. Incidentally, we should not purchase red betta males for these tests, since they often exhibit a changed behavior and court very easily. Keep the fighting fish males each individually in a small aquarium that needs to be

Simple tests can be set up to demonstrate the different responses of a fish to various types of schooling behavior. Using small species of barbs or tetras (schools of one or two species) and simple equipment, you can observe many interesting behaviors.

equipped in only the most spartan manner.

Test 1. Prepare a table with the headings "**Spreading of gill covers,**" "**Fin beating,**" and "**Ramming.**" We now put a mirror along the side glass of the aquarium (best directly in the water). The behavior is registered during the following 20 minutes by marks in the appropriate columns. After every two minutes, draw a horizontal line on the chart so we later can show the dependence of the various actions on time by means of a graphic representation. If possible, this test should be done with different animals and with each in different water temperatures (between 16 and 32°C).

Test 2. How do the fish react to different dummies? Is the motion, the size, the shape, the coloration of the dummy significant?

Learning Behavior of Fighting Fish

Key stimuli may be emitted by members of the same species or by other factors in the surroundings. In an appropriate frame of mind, the animals will react to them instinctively. However, these instinctive actions are by no means rigidly established, particularly if they are connected with extra-specific surroundings. The animals are capable of learning (changing environmental conditions necessitate this).

The following test can be carried out not only with the fighting fish, *Betta splendens*, but also with gouramis, cichlids, and many other fishes. It is important, however, that the subjects are not too timid toward their keeper. The fish should know tubifex from their normal feedings but must be hungry for the test.

A small ball of tubifex is enclosed in a transparent plastic bag and put into the water in front of the fish. The fish will swim toward it and snap at the worms. The worms are offered at regular intervals for a duration of one minute each. During this period the snapping movements of the fish are counted. After each presentation, a rest period of ten minutes is interposed. After one hour (or earlier, if the fish no longer reacts), a rest period of three hours is interposed and then the test is repeated.

If we represent our results graphically, we will get typical curves determined by habit and negative training. The fish learns that the tubifex are unreachable. Similar tests can be made with fish that spit at their prey. Archer fishes (*Toxotes*) and *Colisa* species are able to flush their prey from the airspace into the water by means of drops or streams of water skillfully spit from the water level. This also can be done with dry food. *Colisa lalia* is particularly well suited for this experiment. However, these experiments are not as easy as the ones previously described, since not all fish exhibit the spitting behavior under aquarium environments.

The notoriously aggressive males of the Siamese fighting fish, *Betta splendens*, are easily adapted to a variety of experiments to show behavioral traits of the fighting fishes.

THE SPECIALIZED AQUARIUM

Facing page:
The very stylized courting and nesting behavior of the three-spined stickleback has long made it a favorite with fish behaviorists.

There are animals that are not suitable for a community aquarium but which, nevertheless, are so interesting that it is worthwhile establishing a separate aquarium for them. To be exact, even the mini-tank is a specialized aquarium, but the fish mentioned next will grow bigger and need aquaria with side dimensions of not less than 70 cm.

The Stickleback Tank

Without exaggeration, sticklebacks are fascinating and at the same time beautiful fish. Each aquarist who lives in an area where they occur should try to get some sticklebacks one fine spring day. Since they are rarely offered in pet shops, we have to catch them ourselves. After observation, the fish must be returned to freedom at the place of capture!

The three-spined stickleback (*Gasterosteus aculeatus*) and the nine-spined stickleback (*Pungitius pungitius*) are both common Eurasian and North American species. Although in the wild both species occur together on occasion, they are, as close relatives, competitors and should not be kept together in the aquarium under any circumstances. The nine-spined stickleback, equipped with weaker spines, often lives in narrow, plant-rich ditches, while the three-spined stickleback occurs in broad ditches or flowing waters. Its spines make it appear unattractive to pikes and other fish-eaters, although they do not protect it

from being chased. Both species are often found in brackish water.

The Three-spined Stickleback

The males of this species of stickleback are as beautifully colored in spring as any tropical fish: the underside is bright red, while the upper side and the eyes shine a bright green-blue in the sunlight! In an aquarium 80 cm long there is unfortunately only enough room for one male (the vanquished fish of the same sex are constantly chased by the dominant male). It is best if we put into a 70-80 cm aquarium one male and two or three females ready to spawn and of about the same size. However, we should not choose the largest animals for our tank. Medium-sized sticklebacks represent the majority of the sexually mature fish. They are only two years old, and many of them die at the end of the reproduction period. Only a few sticklebacks — most of them females — reach an age of three years.

The stickleback aquarium should be put into a cool spot. The water temperature should not exceed 20°C, and the water must not be too soft! If our fish stay at the water surface, breathing heavily, we must aerate. If we want to breed the fish indoors, we must see to it that they are kept under conditions simulating a long day, because they will not spawn during periods with few

hours of light. During a daily light period more than 16 hours in duration, however, the fish should spawn even in fall and winter. If there is room, the aquarium may also be placed in the garden or on a balcony. If it is put against a north wall, it remains cool, yet during spring and early summer it gets enough direct sunlight in the late afternoon and evening that the males can be seen displayed in their full splendor.

Plant the aquarium densely. We also must arrange for possible hiding places for the female. In the foreground, a sandy expanse should remain unplanted because it will be selected by the male as the nesting place. As building material, it must be offered plants such as *Fontinalis, Vesicularia, Utricularia,* filamentous algae, or peat fibers. As a substitute, it may even accept yarn thread.

Sticklebacks need much food. Artificial food is unsuitable, but frozen food is accepted. The best food is mosquito larvae, but brine shrimp, tubifex, and small earthworms are also eaten.

In the wild, sticklebacks are ready to spawn from April to June. At that time the male makes a nest on the bottom using plant fibers. Again and again he glides above the fibers, excreting a hardening kidney secretion that glues the plant particles together. At the end, the male tunnels through the plant heap by forcibly digging through it, thus forming an entrance and an exit. Now the male tries to guide a female toward the nest by jerky guidance swimming. He shows her the entrance to the nest, and if the female is in a matching mood, she swims in and spawns. The male immediately glides across the spawn, fertilizing it. After laying the eggs, the female is no longer tolerted near the nest. She is best removed and returned to her place of capture. Frequently the male will then also spawn with the other females (they, too, will have to be released).

The father is extremely busy caring for the brood. He remains constantly at the nest to fan fresh water to the brood with strong strokes of his pectoral fins. Even when the young hatch after 5-14 days (depending on the temperature) and swim free at last, the father remains busy with the brood for a while longer. However, since he will soon confuse the young with food, he, too, will have to be removed.

Young sticklebacks may be raised with brine shrimp nauplii. Normally, however, we will not do this, but instead return the young to the place where their parents were caught!

The Nine-spined Stickleback

This species is also called the dwarf stickleback, although its size of 6 cm

Nine-spined sticklebacks, *Pungitius pungitius,* at their nest. In this species the males may turn entirely black.

approaches that of the three-spined stickleback. However, it is much more delicate than its more robust relative. The number of rays in the dorsal fin that have been transformed into small spines varies between 7 and 12.

If the aquarium is well planted, we can put into a 60-80 cm tank two males of the same size and three or four females. The care of the nine-spined stickleback is similar to that of the three-spined, but the nine-spine may even be somewhat less demanding.

If we have two males in the aquarium, we may observe the interesting territorial behavior of the males, which now sometimes turn velvety black. For instance, they build their nests, which are usually 4 cm in size and made from peat fibers, filamentous algae, or other materials, hanging in the water plants if possible. They differ in other details of behavior from their three-spined relatives.

An Aquarium for Bitterlings and Mussels

If we want to gain an insight into their interesting reproductive behavior, we need mussels for a bitterling aquarium. However, I must mention right at the outset that in keeping bitterlings and mussels we may make interesting observations, but that the entire course of breeding from the laying of eggs to the young bitterlings swimming free can only be observed with some luck. This depends on not only the bitterlings, but — as we are about to see — also on the mussels.

For the breeding of bitterlings (*Rhodeus*), all European freshwater mussels should be suitable, even the wandering mussel (*Dreissena polymorpha*), but the best is the pond mussel, *Anodonta*. River mussels of the genus *Unio* also

Early steps in spawning of the bitterling. First the male (top two figures) approaches the mussel and releases a cloud of sperm that is inhaled into the mussel. Next the female, with her long ovipositor hanging free, approaches the mussel.

Above: A bitterling, *Rhodeus sericeus.* Photo by K. Paysan. *Below:* Completion of egg-laying in the bitterling. The female positions herself over the mussel and eventually sticks her ovipositor into the mussel's inhalant siphon. There her eggs are released to be fertilized by the sperm present in the mussel already.

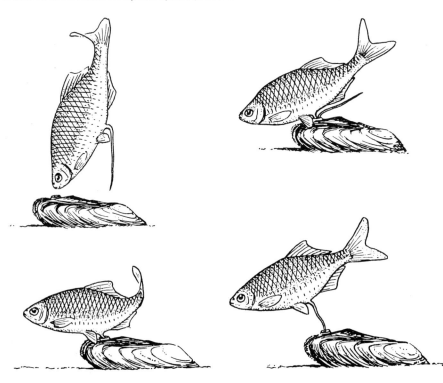

are ideal, but they require more oxygen. We will not be able to do without a slight aeration of the aquarium, anyway!

The breeding successes with bitterlings depend mostly on the good condition of the mussels. As filterers of the smallest plankton, we cannot keep the mussels in the aquarium long, but we can try to slow down the decline of their strength with dissolved dry food carefully placed with an eyedropper at the mussel's intake opening.

In the latitude of Germany, bitterlings are ready to spawn from the end of April to the middle of May. In their mating display the males are ornamented with subdued violet, steel-blue, and reddish colors. In spring, they have a gleaming white "spawning rash" on the front of their heads. These are actually groups of small "nuptial tubercles."

For a pair of bitterlings and three mussels, we should use at least a 40-liter aquarium. In a 50- to 60-liter aquarium we may put two males, two or three females, and a correspondingly larger number of mussels.

About the equipment of the aquarium — As a substrate, we had best use fine sand that we add to about 10 cm in depth. A rock barrier placed obliquely across the tank divides an anterior unplanted sandy part from the back part that is planted. The area in front is the "sandbox" for our mussels, which will be prevented by the rock barrier from digging up the plants. For planting we

Two excellent specimens of the archerfish *Toxotes chatareus*. Although no species of archerfish can be said to be truly common in the aquarium hobby, this is one of the two species occasionally imported. Given the proper care in a properly set up aquarium, archerfishes can provide many marvelous shows of their "shooting" ability.

use bunch plants. The planted area may also be provided with coarse gravel. The water should be not too soft, with the temperature ranging between 16 and 22°C. In consideration of the mussels, we must not use a filter under any circumstances. But we do need an aerator.

If possible, we should establish the bitterling aquarium a month before the spawning period, about at the end of March. For the first three weeks, we populate it with daphnia and cyclops only, then add the mussels, and only after another week do we add the bitterlings.

Soon after the addition of the fish we will see that they are beginning to exhibit an intense interest in the mussels. In the females the laying tube (ovipositor) lengthens to 3-5 cm, then one day later the fish usually spawn. With a lightning- quick movement the female puts her laying tube into the outflow opening (excurrent siphon) of the mussel and thus deposits her egg. Little later, the male gives off its semen over the influx opening (incurrent siphon). The eggs, 3 mm in diameter, are thus fertilized in the interior of the mussel. Here, in the gill cavity of the "wet nurse" the well-sheltered brood develops.

After about two weeks the young fish are already remarkably large and leave their mussel as independent little fish. No doubt the mussels — in the wild also — are damaged by this behavior of the bitterlings. On the other hand, in their own propagation they depend on fish, too, since the mussel larvae (glochidia) must develop parasitically in the skin of fish before they can take up their life in the muck and sand on the bottom of the water. It is unlikely that we can ever observe the development of mussels in the aquarium, since the mussels — regarding their special method of feeding — cannot be kept strong for very long in ·a normal aquarium.

Archerfishes in the Aquarium

Because of their behavior — using jets of water shot with sure aim to wash land insects into the water — archerfishes are especially interesting. Unfortunately, they are often said to be difficult to keep. This is wrong: neither their feeding requirements nor their water requirements mark them as difficult fishes!

At present, five or six species of archerfishes are known. Among them are species that grow to more than half a meter in size. Most of them are vertically striped, but some are completely unmarked.

We are interested only in the regularly available species *Toxotes jaculator* and *T. chatareus*. Both species originate in southeastern Asia but normally do not occur together: *T. jaculator* inhabits the brackish regions of rivers, while *T. chatareus* is only found in fresh water. The pet shops often do not differentiate between these two species, yet this is important, since *T. chatareus* is, by far, more suitable for our freshwater aquarium.

T. jaculator and *T. chatareus* are easy to tell apart. In addition to differences in the body structure (body shape, relative size of the eyes, number of spines in the dorsal fin), there is one characteristic mark which enables even a layman to pick out *T. chatereus* at a glance — the "*chatareus* spot," a small blotch always found between the first and second large body bars.

If we have a choice, we should select a *Toxotes* that is not too darkly colored.

The black coloration is the night dress of the fish, but at the same time also the coloration of oppressed fish. Such fish may be completely healthy, but they are weaker than the dominant ones and, since they find it more difficult to get to the food, they may also be more delicate.

As a glance at the tank in the pet shop shows, archerfish often do not get along. This means that either we select five or more fish for a large aquarium (1.50 m or longer), decorating it with roots reaching to the surface in such a manner that several separate territories as well as hiding places are offered to the fish, or we are satisfied with keeping only a single fish in the community aquarium.

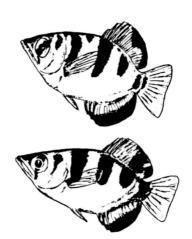

The two most common archerfishes are very similar in pattern. Notice the small spot in front of the second body bar of *T. chatareus* (top), absent in *T. jaculator.*

Keeping one in a community aquarium is absolutely charming — however, we should not choose small fishes as companions for our *Toxotes*. If we feed it well, it can grow to 15 cm and its mouth becomes enormous! It is some comfort that by its nature it is not a fish-eater; it instead lies in wait for flying food. We will see that it is constantly on the move, yet always remaining near the surface. In the middle and lower water layers even small fishes are not in danger. Nevertheless, large archerfish should not be combined with zebras, cardinals, and neons.

The aquarium should have a fairly large plant-free space — especially at the water surface — to meet the fishes's need for swimming. The water temperature may range between 23 and 28°C. When changing the water or transferring into another aquarium, we must be careful: if the fish "flops over" in the new water, it must immediately be put back into the old water! As far as their food is concerned, archerfishes are not very demanding, but the food must be sufficiently large. Small archers will eat flake food without fuss; larger ones, however, are no longer satisfied by this. As long as they are not yet adapted, they may be given lots of mosquito larvae. In addition, mealworms, waxmoth larvae, or grasshoppers may be put on the surface. They do not like tubifex. Once a *Toxotes* is adapted, its feeding is no longer a problem: it will eat fish (raw or cooked), shrimp, raw beef, and even cooked ham. It should be given all this in portions of suitable size. The fish will immediately shoot toward the food and snap for it. Feeding an archerfish is a lot of fun — but be careful not to overfeed! Especially when feeding the meat of mammals, some restraint should be exercised. With proper care, archerfishes live for several years. In time they can become virtually tame, taking food from the aquarist's hand.

The archerfishes have become known and famous for their ability to shoot down prey with water. However,

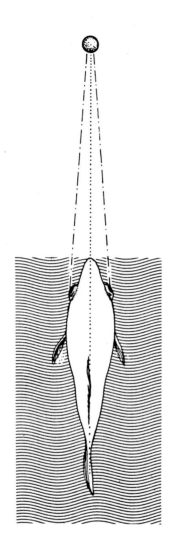

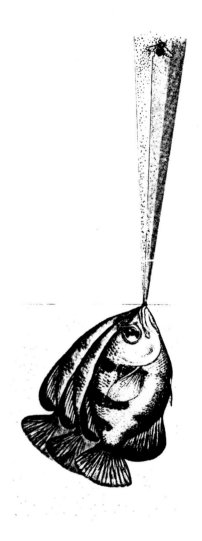

Left: Binocular aiming in *Toxotes.* If the fish can see the prey with both eyes simultaneously, it cannot miss it in a side-to-side direction. *Right:* Aiming in *Toxotes,* viewed from the side. During the expulsion of the water stream, the fish assumes a more upright position. Since the angle between the longitudinal axis of the body and the stream of water does not change, the stream sweeps over the prey.

they cannot hit flying insects because the aiming mechanism takes several seconds. First the fish positions itself at the surface in such a manner that it can see its prey equally well with both eyes. The longitudinal axis of its body is lined up with the prey and with it the spitting groove, which lies in the upper jaw of the fish and acts like a rifle barrel. Even though the fish now cannot miss its aim sideways, it still is complicated to find the correct spitting angle.

A very specialized tank set up to duplicate as closely as possible the mangrove estuary habitat. Mangrove struts have been placed in a sand bottom and even covered with oyster spat. The tank supports healthy populations of *Toxotes*, *Scatophagus*, and even a puffer or two. In such a tank the archerfishes will be able to successfully display their odd style of hunting when insects are introduced to the branches above the water. Photo by Dr. Herbert R. Axelrod at Steinhart Aquarium.

Because of physical laws, light rays are refracted when falling at an angle where the water meets the air. Thus, the target must seem higher to the fish than it really is. The fish corrects this flaw by positioning itself as steeply as possible under its prey. The remaining difference is taken care of by a trick: the fish spits not just one drop, but a virtual stream at its prey. During the spitting, it sweeps the stream lengthwise by changing the position of its body. To put it in human terms: to be "sure," the fish spits at the same time a little too high and a little too low.

To observe the shooting, either the water surface of the community aquarium must be lowered to about 15 cm below the upper frame or a paludarium (aquarium-terrarium) must be established. It also is sensible to "work" only with well adapted, somewhat tame fish. At first, feed them sparingly with delicacies such as bloodworms. Then attach some bloodworms to the glass about 2-5 cm above the water level. This should be done at the feeding place known to the fish. If the fish does not notice the bloodworms, throw one or two directly into the water. Usually, the fish will first try jumping to reach the food sticking to the glass. Stick the next helping of food some centimeters higher up on the glass. With a lot of patience, this method will sooner or later get the archerfish to spit. The initial triggering of the water spitting is the hardest; later it will become increasingly easy to trigger this behavior.

If we keep archerfish together with *Colisa lalia* and *C. labiosa*, we sometimes can observe a regular spitting contest. *Colisa* species are also known to spit water drops at their prey, but they spit their drops only about 5 cm into the air and are thus not serious competition for the archerfishes.

Archerfishes can also be kept in a paludarium with a water depth of 15-20 cm. For this *Toxotes chatareus* again is suitable and in the paludarium can well be combined with *Trichogaster leerii*. In that case, the water should be soft to medium hard, and the temperature should lie around 27°C.

A Paludarium for Mudskippers

The droll mudskippers are attractions in every show aquarium. If you see mudskippers for sale in your pet shop and happen to have a fairly large tank (at least 1.20 m long) at home, you should take some of these fish with you. With their eyes protruding far beyond their heads, they are reminiscent of frogs; however, they are real fish, gobies belonging to several species in the genera *Periophthalmus*, *Periophthalmodon*, and *Boleophthalmus*, among others. Most frequently imported is probably *Periophthalmus barbarus*, originating at the coasts of eastern Africa, Asia, and Australia.

Mudskippers live in the sandy and slimy tidal areas of river estuaries and lagoons. The tropical shallows here are overgrown with mangroves and low palms. Sometimes the fish climb up their air roots in order to look around. Usually, however, they crawl around in the mud on their pectoral fins, which are almost shaped like legs, looking for food. When in danger, they can flee with lightning- fast jumps. Because they are real fishes, they have to visit the water occasionally to keep the skin and gills moist.

Diagrammatic view from above of a possible way to put together a paludarium for mudskippers. The plants include *Cyperus* rushes at the corner and *Hygrophila* toward the middle of the land area. Keep the setup simple and easy to clean for best results.

For breeding, mudskippers establish territories that they defend jealously against others of the same species. The eggs lie in deep mud holes that they the gobies have dug by themselves. Based on this description, it is evident why breeding these fish in the aquarium has not yet been successful.

An aquarium for mudskippers with a bottom of 120 x 40 cm is suitable for five or six fish. It may be quite flat, but it is important that it has a tight-fitting lid — or else the fish, which are good climbers, may easily get away! Above all, the fish require a high moisture content of the air, which can only be maintained in a covered aquarium. The temperature should lie between 25 and 30°C.

Since mudskippers live in the tidal regions of rivers, they are tolerant in regard to the water composition. All species can tolerate fresh water occasionally, but most are grateful for the addition of some salt (1 tablespoon per liter) to their water.

The aquarium (paludarium) must be equipped with a sizable land portion. With flat rocks placed sideways, build a terrace that is left largely without plants, although it may have some areas with *Cryptocoryne affinis* or *C. wendtii*. The lower part of our paludarium becomes the water section. It is provided with some large pieces of rock that should stick partly out of the water, offering the animals additional resting places. A large root sticking far out of the water completes the decorations. The free water space is planted only with a large aquatic fern in one corner. Perhaps we can also guide a decorative philodendron root into the tank.

The mudskipper paludarium as seen from the front. Such a simple but attractive design allows the fish ease of access to both their preferred habitats and makes them feel at home. Contented fish live longer and happier lives than stressed fish.

In the lowest part, the substrate needs to be only 2-5 cm deep; in the land part, however, we require a depth of 10-15 cm. It should consist, if possible, of fine sand. Fill the tank with water so that the land part remains uncovered. We will probably notice that one or more of the mudskippers will dig a shallow ditch here an additional bathing place. The average water level will be about 10 cm.

Mudskippers will eat flake food but are not satisfied by them. Smaller species may be fed with water fleas (they also like mosquito larvae!), which they take without hesitiation from the water. Small earthworms and insects are removed from the water with quick jumps and eaten on land. Well-adapted mudskippers will become quite tame and will take the delicacies from tweez-

ers in the aquarist's fingers. For this thawed frozen food such as mussels, fish, and crabs is especially suitable. ‑

According to species and the area of origin, the fish may react quite variably to an occasional or regular addition of salt and which foods they prefer. However, they are all very grateful for a regular water change.

As fishes that will bring life to the water part of the paludarium, the eleotrid gobies *Batanga lebretonis*, *Mogurnda mogurnda*, and *Eleotris* species are suitable. We may also combine the mudskippers with archerfishes.

Above: If the water section of your mudskipper paludarium looks rather barren to you, it is not difficult to find fishes that will live in it. One such fish is the purple sleeper, *Mogurnda* species, shown here. These fishes are very tolerant of hard waters and quite colorful as well. Photo by G. Schmida.

Below left: If you can find one at your local pet shop, mudskippers make good and interesting, not to mention oddball, pets. *Below right:* Blind cave tetras are common fish in pet shops and never fail to have an appreciative audience as they go through their daily routines of feeding and living just as though they had functional eyes. Photos by J. Vierke.

Blind Cave Tetras in the Aquarium

In 1936, in central Mexico near Ciudad Valles, in the limestone cave system of Cueva Chica, a completely blind species of fish, the blind cave tetra *(Anoptichthys jordani)* was discovered. The eyes of this fish have become atrophied in the everlasting darkness of the caves, and its skin pigments are lacking. The blood vessels that shine through make this fish appear rosy and somehow naked. This species of tetra is closely related to the pigmented and eyed *Astyanax fasciatus mexicanus*, and most current authors consider it to be a local variety of this subspecies. In fact, in some caves the fully eyed and pigmented fish outside the cave gradually became less pigmented and smaller-eyed the further inside the cave they occur.

When first hatched the young cave tetras have fully functioning eyes, which become atrophied with increasing age. Although their eyes have grown completely closed, even the adult fish still can notice some light.

Blind cave tetras do not feel comfortable under the usual aquarium conditions. For their complete well-being they need dim light. This in turn excludes planting the tank. Still, the aquarium need not look bare. With pieces of oddly formed limestone their cave biotope can be very well imitated. If we find suitable rocks we can make the aquarium even dimmer by forming a ceiling.

In contrast to other tetras and the majority of other tropical fishes, the cave tetra does not mind the use of the decorative limestone in the aquarium. The fish actually requires medium-hard to hard water. In addition, it needs temperatures from 15-28°C, unusually high for a cave animal. The pH of the water should lie between 7.5-8.0 and thus be alkaline. If we use limestone for the decorations and do without roots that would enrich the water with humic acids, these water values will establish themselves automatically in normal tapwater.

The entire tank should be illuminated only with a weak bulb, producing a somewhat mysterious effect. Placed in a dark corner of the living room, it has a peculiar charm, especially in the evening.

Dwarf Cichlids

Dwarfs generally remain below 10 cm in length and are not destroyers of plants. They originate in South America and Africa. These colorful fishes offer a pronounced enrichment for the community aquarium and form a pleasant contrast to the usual schooling fishes in their behavior. Occasionally they may be observed caring for their brood even in the community aquarium.

We may generalize and say that the South American dwarf cichlids prefer softer water, while the Africans, on the other hand (with the exception of the *Nanochromis* species) like medium-hard to hard water.

Medium-sized and Large Cichlids

Medium-sized and especially large cichlids sometimes cause problems since they occasionally destroy the plants in the aquarium. Some dig up the plants with their grubbing activities, others even eat them. If the plants are properly surrounded with rocks or, preferably, if they are planted in separate pots even the large diggers have no chance — however, this does not help against the plant-eaters. The South American species of the genera *Aequidens*, *Cichlasoma*, and *Geophagus* will usually leave hard-leaved plants (*Echinodorus*, *Sagittaria*, giant *Vallisneria*) alone.

In a tank of about 1.50 m side length, we can keep about three of the larger cichlid species from South America — preferably in pairs. For example: one pair *Cichlasoma meeki*; one pair *Aequidens pulcher*; two to four *G. steindachneri*. As fishes that lay their eggs freely on rocks and roots (open breeders), *C. meeki* and *A. pulcher* will defend a large breeding territory that remains off limits for other fishes. The mouthbrooding *Geophagus*, on the other hand, require territories only for a very short time (for spawning). The female will then carry the eggs around in her mouth until the young are released after about 20 days.

If such a cichlid tank is stocked with too many cichlids, everything may go along quite peacefully but the open-breeders are not able to form territories and thus cannot show us their interesting breeding behavior. In moderately stocked tanks, on the other hand, we may with some luck observe several pairs caring for their broods simultaneously.

As a substrate use coarse gravel, but there also should be some sand in spots. Put the sand mainly in the foreground; this will be the "sandbox" for the *Geophagus*, which will chew through the sand in their search for something edible. Several large pieces of rocks and a massive, gnarled root reaching to the water's surface will complete the decorations. In the background plant some hardy plants such as *Echinodorus* or *Vallisneria*, which should have at least a week to take root before we add the fishes. Rocks placed next to the plants will make it more difficult for the fish to dig them up. On the root, fasten some Java fern and use water sprite as a plant. For the running of the aquarium, we also need a good filter. Cichlids are often "dirty" fishes.

When stocking the fish, you may use another species of *Geophagus* instead of *Geophagus steindachneri*; instead of *Cichlasoma meeki* use *C. nigrofasciatum*, *C. spilurum*, or *C. severum*; and instead of *Aequidens pulcher* use the peaceful *A. maroni*.

The ram, *Microgeophagus ramirezi*, has a tangled taxonomic history involving the use of three generic names, but it is still an excellent small cichlid for the community tank or for a single-species aquarium. Photo by B. Kahl.

Those who put no value on a geographically correct combination may also keep the decorative combtail, *Belontia signata,* with these larger South American cichlid species. Of course, small fishes are not comfortable (or safe) with large cichlids!

The large cichlids listed here as examples are relatively harmless, but we still must be careful in the beginning, because animals that do not get along with each other may fight terribly.

Other cichlid species such as the beautiful but quite large Texas cichlid, *Cichlasoma cyanoguttatum;* the Jack Dempsey, *Cichlasoma octofasciatum;*

The firemouth cichlid, *Cichlasoma meeki,* is a moderately large Mexican cichlid that adapts very well to larger community tanks. Although it is rather aggressive, it is not a killer and tends to mind its own business when with fishes of its own size. This is often one of the first cichlids kept by beginning aquarists. Photo by B. Kahl.

Closeup of a firemouth cichlid with gill membranes flared. Photo by H.J. Richter.

especially large *Oscars, Astronotus ocellatus;* and the agressive pike cichlids, *Crenicichla* species, are better suited for the dedicated single-species aquarium.

Because of their often different water requirements and especially their different behavior, American and African species should not be kept together if possible. Here, too, there are fishes that belong in the single-species tank because of their agressiveness, such as *Hemichromis fasciatus.*

The usually very colorful mbuna cichlids from Lake Malawi are occasionally called the "coral fishes of the fresh waters." They are relatively easy to combine with each other, since as mouthbrooders they have no pronounced territorial requirements. In a tank with a bottom of 100 x 40 cm, we may keep two or three species of

Large oscars, *Astronotus ocellatus,* are highly favored among aquarists who like a large fish with a personality. Although an oscar must be kept in its own tank when it gets larger, it has a reputation for soon learning to recognize its keeper and even for liking to be petted or stroked on the head. New color varieties have also changed a basically brownish or grayish fish into a reddish one with the same character traits.

Pseudotropheus, Melanochromis, and *Labeotropheus.* Of each species it is best to keep only one male with about three females. The fish usually are easily propagated, although there are some exceptions.

Mbunas need hard, alkaline water (such as flows from most water faucets). For this reason, we may decorate their tank with oddly shaped pieces of limestone and dolomite. Whether these fishes will tolerate plants or will consider them as food supplements will have to be seen in each case.

147

Because of their very unusual water quality demands — very hard and alkaline — Malawi and Tanganyika cichlids are usually kept in special tanks. Shown above is a species of *Pseudotropheus* from Lake Malawi. Photo by Andre Roth. *Below:* The angelfish, *Pterophyllum scalare,* is one of the most popular cichlids. It can be kept with sedate fishes in a community tank or given its own tank if you expect to spawn it successfully. Photo by J. Vierke.

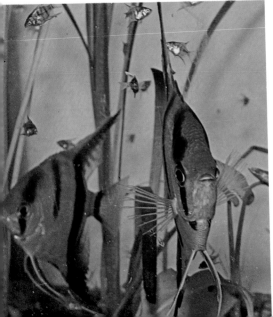

Basically, we may state that the larger the aquarium and the better they are divided by means of decorative elements, the fewer the difficulties in the combination of cichlids.

Angelfish (*Pterophyllum scalare*) are large and especially decorative cichlids that can be found in many community aquaria. These majestically calm, unusually long-finned fish are indeed an ornament for the community aquarium. They are undemanding and do not eat plants, and they are available in many different varieties such as veil fins, marbled, silver, albino, etc. I personally consider the natural form, sometimes slighted as being "common," more attractive than the fancy varieties, especially specimens with beautiful, high fins.

Angels need well-planted tanks of at least 1 m side length. They have no

The discus fishes, *Symphysodon,* are without doubt the royalty of the aquarium. The two species occur in a great many color varieties and hybrid forms ranging from brown to brilliant blue to green to bright red. Although discus are not considered to be impossible to breed any longer, they still require very special techniques for raising the fry, which feed off the parents' slime in nature. Discus are still very expensive fishes and should be kept in their own tank. Photo by B. Kahl.

special requirements but should occasionally be given live food. If they are combined with too small fishes, it may happen that a fully grown angelfish will eat its small companions. They particularly like to chase small neons; this often seen combination comes undone at the moment the angels have grown large enough and have discovered their

Headstanders, such as these brilliantly accented *Anostomus anostomus,* are usually considered to be peaceful although rather large tetras. They are thus often kept in community aquaria, which is fine under most circumstances. For some reason, however, they have an attraction to the slime of angelfish and perhaps other cichlids and may develop a habit of literally "pasturing" on the sides of the fish, eventually killing them. Photo by Dr. Herbert R. Axelrod.

taste for neons. Another popular combination is equally dangerous: angels and *Anostomus* (headstanders), since the *Anostomus* sometimes discover that the skin mucus of the angels tastes extremely good. They will begin to virtually pasture on the angels, which are not skillful at maneuvering. The headstanders may injure their skin to such a degree that the angels will die from it. Other than this, the angels can be combined with larger livebearers with excellent results.

A pair of angels ready to spawn must be in a well-planted tank without fellow inhabitants. The water should be soft (to 10°DH) and slightly acid.

Adult angels will often spawn even in the community aquarium. The eggs may be stuck on a large leaf, a rock, or a root. The eggs commonly are trans-ferred to a separate tank where they are allowed to hatch and the young are raised away from the parents. However, it is much more beautiful to observe the natural development and risk the young being eaten by the parents. Unfortunately, few of our aquarium angels satisfactorily care for their brood, so that the experience of observing a beautiful pair with its young is rare. There are many books on breeding aquarium fishes that give details of breeding these and hundreds of other species.

Snakeheads are large, aggressively carnovorous fishes that are certainly not suitable for most aquarium conditions. However, young *Channa micropeltes* (above) are colorful fish that are often imported and hard to resist. If given their own large aquarium right from the start they make interesting and long-lived fish that may even develop a personality. Photo by Dr. D. Terver, Nancy Aquarium, France.

The saucer-shaped, often splendidly colored discus (*Symphysodon aequifasciata* and *S. discus*) are known to be especially desirable. They are by far more demanding animals than most previously mentioned cichlids, but even discus are suited for the community aquarium if we have a good filter and provide soft, acid water and occasional live food. Fully grown discus are most effective in an aquarium that has been especially equipped for them with roots and beautiful plant growth. Here their special requirements can be best met.

For breeding discus, select a sterile tank of at least 80-90 cm in length. For reasons of better hygiene, we will do without substrate and plants. For spawning, flowerpots or clay urns placed upside down have proven themselves. The fish now must have a variety of live foods, including if possible mosquito and other aquatic insect larvae. The water must be soft and have a pH value of 5.5 to 6.

After they become free-swimming, the young depend on their parents, since for the first days they feed exclusively on the skin mucus of the parents. Only after about ten days will they begin to eat brine shrimp nauplii.

An Aquarium for Snakeheads

From time to time, snakeheads (*Channa*) are offered in the trade. If a separate aquarium about 80 cm long is available, this opportunity should be seized and the fish purchased. This is one way of bringing into the home a really carnivorous fish that is easy to care for and quickly becomes quite trusting. Because of the sometimes not inconsiderable size of the snakeheads, we can establish a totally different relationship with them than with a small fish. Since the snakeheads are relatively sedentary, we can make do with a comparatively small tank. The substrate of an aquarium for snakeheads should consist of coarse gravel. For planting, choose some robust species such as *Vallisneria, Crinum*, or — although it does not fit in geographically — Amazon swordplants. Well-suited as a floating plant is water sprite, *Ceratopteris thalictroides*. For safety's sake we can set the plants into small flowerpots that are buried in the gravel in such a manner that the pots are not visible. The fish now will not be able to free the roots of the plants. Since the snakeheads regularly take in atmospheric air, we do not need an aerator. If we always want to have clear water, however, we will not be able to do without a strong filter. Set the heater thermostat for about 27°C.

The feeding of a snakehead makes for no great difficulties. Quite the opposite: everything of a meaty nature will be devoured — however, the food (pieces of cooked and raw fish and mammal meat) should not be too fatty! Pelleted foods are also welcome. If you wish, food tablets may be purchased in a pet shop.

An aquarium for a snakehead should be proportioned to the expected adult size of the fish, not to the small juveniles usually purchased. Snakeheads usually do not bother plants, so both floating plants and rooted species can be used.

152

Our snakeheads can do entirely without live or freshly killed food fish; nevertheless, they are grateful for offerings of guppies or other small fishes from time to time. We also should occasionally throw earthworms and mealworms into the tank. Some species, such as the little snakehead, also like to eat water snails.

The snakehead most recommended for the aquarium is probably the little snakehead, *Channa orientalis*, which is found throughout tropical Asia. In the course of about two years, it grows to just about 20 cm in length, which makes it the smallest of the known species of snakeheads. It is attractively colored, totally undemanding, and will become so tame that it allows itself to be stroked!

In an 80-cm tank, we may keep two adult *Channa orientalis*. If these animals initially should not get along, we must try separating them with a pane of glass. So far, this species has not been bred in the aquarium, but it should not be too difficult.

Channa striata, a "lovable bandit" suitable for the moderately large aquarium. Photo by J. Vierke.

Most other Asiatic snakeheads become quite large and grow quickly into the "large aquarium stage." If we want to care for them even as adult fish, we must prepare a tank 1.20 m length for them. These fish are even more lively than *Channa orientalis* and remain attractive even in old age because of their often unusual markings and their snake-like appearance. This holds true especially for the Africans among them (*C. obscura, C. africana, C. insignis*) which only grow to barely 35 cm in length. To keep a pair of these species, an 80-cm tank is sufficient. African Snakeheads have been bred in the aquarium.

In a sufficiently large aquarium we can combine snakeheads with other robust fishes. Especially suitable are the climbing perch (*Anabas testudineus*) combtails (*Belontia*), and large ctenopomas such as *Ctenopoma kingsleyi*. Larger cichlids are also suitable.

153

FROM THE
VIRGIN
FOREST TO THE
LIVING ROOM

Who does not dream occasionally of the tropical home of our decorative fishes as he sits in front of his living room aquarium: of the mysterious darkness caused by the vine-covered forest giants, filled with many voices; of the small rivers, rich in fishes, which often are almost covered with the corpses of trees and with leaves; of the light-filled, lukewarm ponds and river coves, which are partially covered with floating plants blooming violet-purple and bright red.

It is true that very many aquarium fishes come from the breeding basement of our fish breeders or from the open-air ponds and tanks of the many breeders in Asia, but many have really known the tropical rain forest. Of course, the individual circumstances are very different, but we will try to trace here the ways in which our chocolate gouramis, pearl gouramis, loaches, and spiny eels have come from their homes in the wild.

In their homes in Malaysia and Indonesia, they live in clear rivers and the beds of streams in the virgin forests, waters that have been tinted slightly brown with humus. The water here is usually acid, with a pH value of 5-6, and a conductivity that lies below 30 microSiemens. Measuring the water hardness here with the usual aquarium reagents would be useless, since the result would always be zero. The water temperatures usually lie between 24 and 26°C, but where the sun can shine unimpeded on standing coves and lakes, it may rise to 30°C and more.

In the jungles of southern Malaysia, some Asli tribes occupy themselves with the catching of decorative fishes. The Asli are a tribe of short people, actually the original inhabitants of the peninsula, who have retreated from the immigrant Malayans into the impenetrable rain forests. Here they live in isolation according to their old customs, with their own language and a nature religion, spending their lives as fishermen and hunters who still go out to hunt with the blowpipe and poisoned arrows. The small, loosely grouped huts stand on pilings near the rivers. Someone visiting these friendly and amiable people would notice that oxygen bottles and plastic bags are almost the only attributes of western civilization here — important utensils for the transport of live decorative fishes! With large fixed nets and small handnets, the fish are caught here, the large ones for the food market, the small ones for the exporters of aquarium fishes in far-away Singapore. At regular intervals on predetermined dates, Chinese come to the Aslis. Their ancestors had immigrated as workers on the rubber plantations and the tin mines. Most of them are now tradespeople in the cities, as are the purchasers of fishes from the Aslis. They provide the collectors with clothes and metal utensils

and in turn take the fishes with them to the nearest large city. These include live snakeheads, catfishes, and more rarely water turtles. The animals must be alive, because dead animals bring only half the price — in the humid, hot climate, they might already be spoiled, at least as far as the purchaser is concerned.

The aquarium fishes are brought to some of the large aquaria that a trader has standing in the open air market. Here also swim zebras, swordtails, and goldfish. This is the pet shop for the local population. Evidently the demand there is no less than in Western pet shops. For this reason there are angels, goldfish, and armored catfishes. The prophet is of no account in his own land! Neither the local aquarists nor the pet shop dealer and his collectors care that in the ditches nearby there are

Girls of the Asli tribe leaving to capture aquarium fishes in a Malayan river. Along the banks of this river through the virgin forest of the Malayan peninsula live many popular aquarium fishes, including chocolate gouramis, tiger barbs, many species of *Rasbora,* and other aquarium favorites. Photo by J. Vierke.

rarities greatly desired by many European experts. A single fish or even ten have no value for the wholesaler; there have to be at least 50 or 100.

The Chinese are extremely conscientious; that is why the "tag-alongs and oddballs" so much in demand by many are found in exports from South America, but not in shipments from Southeast Asia. Carefully sorted according to species, the trader takes a weekly trip to Singapore to resell the fishes to the exporter, another Chinese. The catch-

On this fish farm in Singapore are bred many thousands of aquarium fishes. They are kept in concrete tanks and in aquaria until ready for export to Europe and the United States for final sale to the fish-buying public. Photo by J. Vierke.

ers and intermediate dealers on the Malayan peninsula on Borneo and Sumatra work on his orders. However, there are many other Chinese dealers in Singapore. Their fish are furnished to Japan, America, and all European countries.

Mr. Choo, an exporter in Singapore, has a large area with several open-air ponds for keeping the fish; in addition there are far more than 50 concrete tanks (3 x 2.4 m), and for special rarities he uses large aquaria. All this is outdoors, protected merely by corrugated roofs against the bright sunlight and its heat and against the tropical cloudbursts. In addition, the concrete tanks are protected against heating up too much by a layer of floating plants (water hyacinths). The water temperatures lie around 26-29°C all year long — there are no real seasons here.

Here in Singapore, breeding also takes place not only on the fish farm itself but in many private homes. The breeders usually furnish their fish half-grown to the exporter, who finishes raising them. The fish bred are largely South American fishes (angels, platies, guppies, tetras), but also fighting fish. This fish farm alone stocks 7000-8000 male fighting fish at any given time! Each of them lives in a separate glass container. Water plants are also raised in great numbers in Singapore, both submersed and emersed.

The fully air conditioned office in Singapore constantly receives telephone calls and orders via telex. In the covered warehouse, Chinese are busy packing fishes into large plastic bags, providing them with additional oxygen, and placing them in large styrofoam boxes. Then they go to the airport. Seventeen hours later the freight is in Frankfurt, Germany. Here it is either picked up directly or forwarded to another airport. The large importers pick up their freight and store it in their warehouses.

If you ever visit an importer, you will be overwhelmed on your first visit by the number of aquaria, the number of fishes in the tanks (generally sorted by species), and the abundance of rare fishes that are never seen in some pet shops. These importers get their fish not only from Singapore but also from Bangkok, Hong Kong, and who knows where.

The pet shop dealers (retailers) now select their stock from the large importer, either in person or from lists. The travels of our tropical pets into our tropical aquariums are known to every aquarium dealer. For the majority of the fishes, this path is a dead-end or a one-way street. It is great if an amateur succeeds in the propagation of a species, but this is usually not easy, since as a rule the fish have certain requirements which must be met by the breeder. If one succeeds in breeding some fish which can then be brought back to the pet shop, one may be assured that the fish were kept under good conditions and that one is more than just a consumer of tropical fishes!

The Amazon basin of Peru, Colombia, and especially Brazil produces a great many of the most commonly seen tropical fishes for sale in your local pet shop. The innumerable rivers, streams, and lakes of the region produce an astounding diversity of tetras, catfishes, and dwarf cichlids, among other types of fishes, many of which have become staples of the aquarium hobby. Photo of the Rio Abacaxis by Dr. Herbert R. Axelrod.

FISHES FOR
THE AQUARIUM

Aquarium technique, water chemistry, and knowledge of nutrition have the purpose of providing optimal living conditions for the fishes in the aquarium. However, the fishes are the main thing — so the greater part of this book should be devoted to them. Only a fraction of the many species that have been kept in amateur aquaria so far regularly reach the trade. The permanent stock of a dealer includes only about 100 species.

In the discussions of the genera and species of our decorative pets I have tried to provide the reader with an inclusive overview on the one hand and to point out important and interesting characteristics of the fishes on the other. The more frequently available species of fishes have been taken into special consideration.

Purchasing New Fish

Many pet dealers are willing to fill special orders for rarer fishes for their clients — as long as they are enumerated on the lists of the large importers. Some rare species can be obtained by advertising in hobby magazines or, better yet, in the publications of specialized interest groups.

When purchasing, one should make sure, of course, to get healthy fish. We should not accept fishes with nibbled or pinched fins or that are otherwise obviously sick.

We are also advised again and again not to put newly acquired fish directly into the community aquarium, but to keep them separated for about one week in the quarantine tank. Illnesses that may appear can be more easily treated here, but, above all, our other fishes are not infected! On the other hand, in many instances these diseases will appear in such a tank, which is frequently too small! I personally do without quarantine in principle for the new aquisitions — and I have only rarely been sorry!

Customarily, the salesman will pack the fishes into plastic bags. However, we should not transfer the new aquisitions directly from the transport bag into the aquarium. In order to let the water temperatures adjust, put the bag on the water surface of the aquarium for about 15 minutes. Panic-stricken specimens that constantly try to get out of the bag should be freed sooner, since otherwise they may suffer serious damage! Even when the temperatures in the transport water and the aquarium water are the same, we should not transfer the fish directly. Instead slowly fill the transport bag with aquarium water until the aquarium water predominates. In this manner the fish are accustomed gradually to the new water conditions.

Every new fish that comes into a previously stocked tank is at first subject to harassment from the others, even though normally it might be the strongest. It is intimidated by its new surroundings and it first has to adapt to the new water conditions. But even though initially it may be chased by the other fishes, it will normally soon find its own social position in the tank.

Basically, we must inform ourselves before each purchase of fish about the requirements of the fish, whether they can be met, and whether these requirements agree with those of their fellow pets. The following pages will serve this purpose.

For extensive information, the reader should not only check the entry under the name of the species but should also read what is written in the descriptions of the genus and the family to which it belongs!

A small group of swordtails, *Xiphophorus helleri,* to give an idea of the amount of variation found in a single species. Photo by B. Kahl.

Relationships of Fishes and Classification

Scientists order animals and plants according to different categories (families, genera, species, etc) that reflect relationships. For scientists as well as for laymen, this is practical for various reasons. For one, this method provides a generally valid and clear sequence. In addition, the animals placed in a certain group resemble each other, since their common traits in looks, behavior, and requirements come from a common ancestor. However, the advan-

tages are accompanied by disadvantages.

If new research shows that a previously made grouping is not in accordance with the actual descent, it has to be corrected. This is the reason for the frequent changes in scientific nomenclature. If it turns out that a name considered valid thus far is merely the second description of an earlier description overlooked thus far, the name must be changed. Here rules the right of the older name (the rule of priority) even though the other name may have become well established.

A scientific name consists of at least two parts, the name of the genus and, following it, the name of the species. If the species has to be subdivided, the name of a subspecies may be added as a third component. It is also important to know the name of the person who initially described it and the year of the initial description. Both are often listed after the scientific name, as is the case with the fishes described on the following pages. If these indications are in parentheses, it means that the author in question described the original species under a different generic name than the now valid generic name. The scientific names are important, even though we don't have to remember them. On the other hand, in the jargon of the advanced aquarist many species are called only by this name! Whether difficult or easy to learn, the scientific names are unique and internationally binding. If you want to carefully identify fishes or plants you should also use the scientific names.

Explanation of the Symbols

17cm Maximum overall length (tip of the mouth to the end of the tail fin) in usual aquarium conditions. In the wild or in particularly large tanks this value is often considerably exceeded (this is noted separately in the text, if applicable).

23°C Average temperature required. This value can vary by ±2°C.

G Suitable for the community aquarium (prerequisites are fellow inhabitants of suitable size and matching requirements for care).

A Dedicated tank indicated or necessary.

S School fish or very social fish. Must be kept in groups.

H Prefers hard and slightly alkaline water.

W Prefers soft and slightly acidic water.

N Should be kept in medium-hard or slightly harder water (9 - 15°DH).

( ) Indications in parentheses mean reservations. More can be found in the text.

DESCRIPTION OF THE FAMILIES, GENERA, AND SPECIES

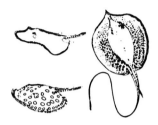

CLASS CHONDRICHTHYES

(SHARKS AND RAYS)

Dasyatidae (Stingrays)

Occasionally, a few freshwater species from South America (*Potamotrygon laticeps*, *Potamotrygon motoro*) and southeastern Asia (*Dasyatis* species) are imported. Because of their dangerous tail spines, these animals must be handled with extreme care. Accidents may lead to serious, very painful wounds!

These lively bottom fishes all grow quite large. Even in the smallest species, the disk-like body grows up to 30 cm in width. Stingrays are usually friendly toward their fellow inhabitants.

Care: Stingrays need sufficient room for swimming and a fine, sandy substrate into which they will often almost disappear. By nature, they are mollusc and crab-eaters, but in the aquarium they also accept earthworms, tubifex, fish, meat, and food pellets.

CLASS OSTEICHTHYES (BONY FISHES)

Lepidosirenidae (Lung fishes)

In this family are the South American lungfish, *Lepidosiren paradoxa*, and the four African species of the genus *Protopterus;* all five species have two functional lungs. The four species of *Protopterus* survive the dry season in a hardened mud cocoon, estivating in a

A freshwater stingray, *Potamotrygon reticulatus*. Photo by Dr. Herbert R. Axelrod.

deep sleep lasting several months. In this encysted state the animals may be shipped completely dry. Through very careful additions of water (lung breathers may suffocate!) we wake them up again.

Care: Lungfishes are in every way undemanding fishes that must be kept individually because of their inability to get along. Use a substrate of coarse gravel, robust plants, and a temperature of 26 -30°C. Meaty food (raw or cooked meat or fish) or food pellets.

Ceratodidae (Australian Lungfish)

A lungfish with only one lung. The only Recent species, *Neoceratodus fosteri*, is strictly protected and is unlikely to get to either America or Europe at this time!

SUBCLASS ACTINOPTERYGII (RAY-FINNED FISHES)
Polypteridae (Bichirs)

These African fishes have an elongated body and are distinguished, above all, by the many rays of the dorsal fin.

Care: These lazy, twilight-active but ravenous animals are suitable for the dedicated aquarium. Care and keeping otherwise as for the snakeheads and the lungfishes.

Polypterus (Bichirs)
This genus has several species, of which occasionally the colorful *Polypterus ornatipinnis* and *Polypterus delhezi* are available. Both species grow up to 35 cm in length. They may also be raised in the aquarium. The fry undergo a larval stage with external gills.

Erpetoichthys calabaricus
SMITH (Reed Fish, Rope Fish)
This eel-like fish is also suitable for the large fish community aquarium. Smaller fish are eaten! They grow up to 90 cm in length. The sexes may be differentiated by the number of the anal fin rays: the males have 12 - 14, the females 9 - 12.

Polypterus weeksii, a bichir. Photo courtesy Midori Shobo, *Fish Magazine*, Japan.

Acipenseridae (Sturgeons)

Acipenser ruthenus LINNE, 1758 (Sterlet) — 20 cm, 17°C, H - G

Acipenser sp., one of the several very similar short-nosed sturgeons. Photo by Dr. Herbert R. Axelrod.

20 cm	17°C	H-G	

Hungarian fish breeding stations occasionally furnish young fish for the aquarium trade that are still colored almost black. Sterlets originate in the rivers feeding the Black and Caspian Seas and are thus pure freshwater fish that prefer lower temperatures, however. In open waters they may grow to 1 m in length.

Care: Sterlets are constantly on the move and consequently need a lot of open swimming space (the aquarium must not be too small!). They like to dig their food (tubifex, whiteworms, snails, pieces of meat) from the soft, sandy ground. Do not use coarse gravel or decorative items with rough edges, since the fish are likely to injure their long snout! Despite the shark-like appearance they are completely peaceful toward other fishes as long as these are not too small.

Amiidae

Amia calva LINNE, 1766 (Bowfin) 70 cm, 3 - 20°C, A - H - (N)

70 cm	3–20°C	A-H-(N)	

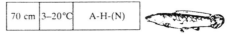

Ravenous nocturnal fish from North America. The fish can breathe atmospheric air and can remain alive for quite some time out of the water. The males have an eye spot in the upper tail root.

Interesting care for the brood by the male. Breeding in the aquarium unknown thus far.

Care: Keeping in pairs only possible in large display aquaria. Very voracious (fish, snails, earthworms, meat).

Lepisosteidae (Gars)

Carnivorous large fishes that are suitable only for the display tank. In addition to gill breathing, the fishes also breathe atmospheric air with the help of the swim bladder.

Lepisosteus osseus (LINNE, 1758) (Long- nosed Gar)

100 cm, 18°C, A - H - (N)

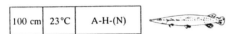

100 cm	18°C	A-H-(N)	

Home: Central and southern U.S.A.

Because of its elongated shape (especially the snout) and its markings, it is very decorative for display aquariums.

Care: Young will eat mealworms and coarse pond food.

Lepisosteus tristoechus BLOCH AND SCNEIDER, 1801 (Tropical Alligator Gar)

100 cm, 23°C, A - H - (N)

100 cm	23°C	A-H-(N)	

Home: Central America.

In open water, it will grow to 3.5 m long and 90 kg in weight. In the wild, will also go into sea water.

Esocidae (Pikes)

Esox lucius LINNE, 1758 (Northern Pike)

80 cm, 5 - 20°C, A - H - (N)

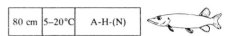

80 cm	5–20°C	A-H-(N)	

Care: Plant and aerate aquaria well. Frequent water changes necessary. Initially pond food, later small fishes.

Umbridae (Mudminnows)

14 cm, 19°C, W - N

14 cm	19°C	W-N	

Few species (*Umbra krameri* from southeastern Europe; two *Umbra* from North America; one *Novumbra*) that with cool care are well suited for keeping in an aquarium, since they are hardy animals. The males of *Umbra limi* turn yellow to orange-red in the spring. They care for their brood.

Care: Dense planting, slightly peaty, soft water. Live food!

Umbra pygmaea, the eastern mudminnow of the U.S.. Photo courtesy Dr. D. Terver, Nancy Aquarium, France.

The Asian arowana, *Scleropages formosus*.
Photo by A. Norman.

Osteoglossidae (Arowanas)

Of the eight or nine species known, only a few regularly reach private hands, though most are imported on rare occasions.

Care: Very large tanks (according to the size of the fish and to their desire for swimming). Like to jump, so tank must be covered securely! Smaller specimens are fed with mealworms, small fish, and pellets; larger fishes eat mice, rats, pork, and beef, and of course other fishes such as goldfish.

Scleropages formosus MUELLER AND SCHLEGEL, 1829 (Asian Arowana)
  90 cm, 27°C, W - A - (G)

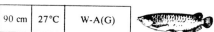

90 cm	27°C	W-A(G)

Very decorative, large-scaled fish that has been imported repeatedly by way of Singapore. A food fish in its southeast Asian home. A mouthbrooder (female).

Care: Needs soft water (not more than 14°DH).

Osteoglossum bicirrhosum VANDELLI, 1829 (Common Arowana)
  60 cm, 26°C, W - A - (G)

60 cm	26°C	W-A(G)

Home: South America.

Is said to be mouthbrooder (male). Other remarks as for *Scleropages formosus*. Breeding in captivity has been successful.

Osteoglossum ferreira KANAZAWA, 1966 (Black Arowana)
  60 cm, 26°C, W - A - (G)

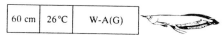

60 cm	26°C	W-A(G)

Resembles *O. bicirrhosum* in appearance and requirements for care, but young fish have darker fins and two dark lengthwise bands.

Arapaima gigas CUVIER, 1829 (Arapaima)
120 cm, 26°C, W - A

120 cm	26°C	W-A

Decorative giant fish from the Amazon region that are only suitable for very large display aquaria. Is said to reach 3 m in the wild! Food fish.

Pantodontidae (Butterfly Fish)
12 cm, 28°C, A - W

12 cm	28°C	A-W

Pantodon buchholzi, the butterfly fish, is the only representative of this family. The bizarrely shaped, twilight-active fish is at home in tropical West Africa and lives there mainly on insects falling on the water. It is capable of a gliding flight over several meters.

The sexes can be recognized by the different anal fin shapes. Its rear edge is notched barely at all in the female, deeply in the male. Has been bred in aquaria.

Care: In the community aquarium there are feeding problems! Sometimes, small fish are eaten there. It is best kept in a paludarium or shallow dedicated tank. Peaceful with each other. Food (mealworms, crickets, flies, as well as dry food) is only taken directly from the surface. Processed food alone is not sufficient in the long run. Will also eat dead insects, which may be stored in the freezer. Water warm, acid, soft (to 12° DH).

Notopteridae (Old World Knife Fishes)
This family includes nocturnal ravenous fish that grow quite large. Their body shape, which is pointedly attenuated towards the rear, is distinctive. The long anal fin is grown together with the tail fin and forms a continuous fin edge, whose rhythmical, wavy movements allow the fish to swim forward and backward. With the help of a swim bladder, they can breathe atmospheric air. The breeding of one spe-

Pantodon buchholzi, the African butterfly fish. Photo by J. Vierke.

Notopterus chitala, the clown knife fish. Photo by Dr. Herbert R. Axelrod at the Berlin Aquarium.

cies in the aquarium has been successful. They care for their brood.

Care: Rock and root hiding places are necessary not only for breeding!

Notopterus chitala (HAMILTON- BUCHANAN, 1822) (Clown Knife Fish)

40 cm, 27°C, W - A - (G)

40 cm	27°C	W-A(G)

This species, found from India to Malaysia and Sumatra, grows to more than 1 m. Color markings variable with age; there are often several circular spots lined up on the rear part of the body.

Care: The fish prefer soft water and will eat dry food. Larger specimens need fish and meat.

Notopterus notopterus (PALLAS, 1780)

35 cm, 26°C, W - A - (G)

35 cm	26°C	W-A(G)

This uniformly dark-colored species is at home in India.

Care: Smaller than the previous species, thus better suited for the amateur.

Notopterus afer GUENTHER, 1868 (African Featherfin)

60 cm, 26°C, W - A - G

60 cm	26°C	W-A-G

This species (also called *Papyrocranus afer*) originates in the waters of tropical West Africa. The young are attractively marbled on a brown-red ground. Adults are uniformly violet-brown. Often quarrelsome.

Care: Soft, slightly acid water. Eats only live food.

Xenomystus nigri (GUENTHER, 1868) (African Knife fish)

20 cm, 26°C, W - A - G

20 cm	26°C	W-A-G

In contrast to the *Notopterus* species, *Xenomystus* lacks the dorsal fin. This

167

species is capable of uttering short, barking sounds.

Care: Smaller and thus easier to keep. Prefers live food and soft, slightly acid water. Fearful of light, so needs root cover.

Mormyridae (Elephant-noses)

Easily 130 different species belong to this African fish family. They are seldom colorful but are often interesting in other regards. Their shape is often bizarre.

One interesting aspect that should be mentioned here is the special formation of the brain. This is perhaps the cause of the pronouned play instinct that has not been observed in other fish. For instance, it is possible for them to occupy themselves for hours on end with a leaf or a piece of wood.

Most elephant-noses have a weak electrical organ in the caudal peduncle that, together with special sensory organs situated in the head area, allows them to orient themselves even in murky waters. In addition, their constantly emitted impulses also serve to determine the borders of their territories. We cannot notice their electrical signals directly, but their fellow inhabitants in the aquarium can. Initially they will be irritated, but they will soon become accustomed to them.

Care: Usually do not get along with each other and should, therefore, be kept singly or in twos (animals of similar strength). On the other hand, they are completely peaceful toward other, even much smaller, inhabitants. They need cavernous hiding places and, if possible, quite high temperatures. Otherwise, the water values are of little significance. Many of them have a trunk that they use to dig with in the bottom for insect larvae, tubifex, and similar things. Some fish will only accept dry food. Since they are twilight-active, feed only in the evening.

Gnathonemus petersi (GUENTHER, 1862) (Peter's Elephant-nose)

22 cm, 26°C, G - A

22 cm	26°C	G-A

Peter's elephant-nose, *Gnathonemus petersi.* Photo by B. Kahl.

Probably the most frequently kept species. The "trunk" is formed only by the elongated lower lip. Animals dark blue-gray, with a large, light-edged spot between the fins.

Care: Sex differences unknown. Breeding successes unknown thus far. Combination with others of its species problematic, even in large tanks. However, completely peaceful toward other inhabitants.

In contrast to G. *petersi*, the species *G. elphas* and relatives have a real trunk, their mouth opening lying at the end of elongated upper and lower jaws.

Gnathonemus schilthuisae BOULENGER, 1899.

10 cm, 25°C, G - N

| 0 cm | 25°C | G-N |  |

Species which remains small, reminiscent in body shape and markings of *G. petersi*, has instead of a trunk only a bulbous protruding chin. Easier to keep in company with animals of the same species; pronounced play instinct.

Care: Like G. *petersi*.

Mormyrus kannume FORSKAL, 1775

50 cm, 25°C, G! - N

| 50 cm | 25°C | G!-N | |

Differs from the *Gnathonemus* species by the much longer dorsal fin. They are occasionally traded as young animals. However, all species of *Mormyrus* grow so big that they cannot be considered as fishes for the usual community aquarium. On the other hand, *Haplochromis* species and other larger cichlids are suitable as companion fish. The similar species *M. tapirus* is called the tapir fish.

Cypriniformes

Most aquarium fishes belong to this order. The carp-like fishes are distinguished by having the Weberian apparatus, transformed anterior vertebrae that form a sound-conducting connection between the swim bladder and the inner ear. Functionally, this may be compared to the stapes and anvil in the middle ear of humans. The fish hear better, and at the same time they are informed by means of the swim bladder about variations in water pressure.

Characidae (True American Tetras)

This family, rich in species, furnishes a very great number of beautifully colored decorative fishes of small size. They are all schooling fishes that should be kept in groups of at least six, but if possible in even larger numbers. All tetras lay eggs. Internal fertilization takes place only in a few genera (*e.g.*, *Boehlkea*). Some tetras disperse their eggs freely in the water or among finely articulated plants, while others fasten them to leaves. There are also species that care more intensively for the brood, but they are exceptions. The larvae hatch one to three days after fertilization. With the adhesive glands on their heads they adhere to rocks or plants until they have used up their yolk sacs. After about five days they swim to the surface, fill their swim bladders with air, and begin to look for food by swimming on their own.

Care: According to their origins, these fishes, with few exceptions, prefer soft and acid water. However, most adults can be kept in the aquarium without difficulties in water of up to 15°DH. For spawning and for the development of the eggs and the early larvae, however, optimal water conditions are required.

Aphyocharax

Slender, typical tetras. Of the about 20 species, only one has really become established in the aquarium.

Aphyocharax anisitsi EIGENMANN and KENNEDY, 1903 (Bloodfin)

5.5 cm, 24°C, W - S - G

5.5 cm	24 °C	W-S-G

Aphyocharax anisitsi, the bloodfin. Photo by Dr. Herbert R. Axelrod.

Home: Rio Parana and Argentina.

Silvery, faintly blue-shimmering little fish, colored reddish at the basse of the belly fins. Only the pectoral fins are colorless. Males slenderer and more strongly colored at spawning time.

The designations *"A. affinis"* and *"A. rubripinnis"* are synonyms, therefore invalid second descriptions of this species.

Care: For breeding, placed in pairs into soft, slightly acid water. Raise temperature by 2°C, add delicate water plants. Low water level advantageous. Use spawning grid, since they are pronounced egg-eaters.

Astyanax fasciatus CUVIER, 1819 (Silvery Tetra)

9 cm, 21°C, N - H - S - A - (G)

9 cm	21°C	N-H-S-A(G)	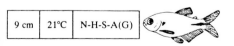

About 70 species are counted in the genus *Astyanax*. All are quite colorless and, therefore, are rarely imported. However, the fish are hardy and their

An albino silvery tetra, *Astyanax fasciatus*, showing the bright red eye typical of albinistic fishes. Photo by H. J. Richter.

breeding is not difficult. The blind cave tetra, which usually still is called *Anoptichthys jordani*, is only a cave-dwelling morph *A. fasciatus*.

Boehlkea

Elongated tetras which resemble the genus *Glandulocauda*. Undemanding fishes which like to swim. Internal fertilization. After fertilization, the females lay their eggs on plant leaves, without the male being present.

Boehlkea fredcochui GERY, 1966 (Blue Tetra)

5 cm, 25°C, W - S - G

5 cm	25°C	W-S-G	

Home: Rio Maranon from Iquitos to Leticia.

The sides of these fish are bright blue; in the males, shimmering splen-

171

didly violet. Formerly, the species was erroneously designated as *Microbrycon cochui*.

Charax

These ravenous tetras have a high back, sometimes a veritable hunchback. Especially noticeable is the long anal fin. They like to stand quietly in the water with their small heads pointing obliquely downward.

Charax gibbosus LINNE, 1758 (Glass Headstander)

15 cm, 23°C, W - (G) - S

| 15 cm | 23°C | W-(G)-S |  |

Home: Guyana, central and lower Amazon, Rio Paraguay.

These soft yellowish brown, somewhat transparent fish are sometimes also called "glass tetras." Behind the gill cover they have an elongated dark shoulder spot. On one hand, it is characterized as a fish- eating tetra with needle-sharp teeth, while on the other it is reported to be peaceful toward its tankmates. Males are slenderer and smaller than females.

This species is sometimes mistaken for *Roeboides guatemalensis*, which has a similar appearance and care requirements. The Guatemala glass tetra has smaller scales.

Care: Densely planted aquaria. For breeding use a large aquarium with plants. Soft water! Spawning at dusk.

Cheirodon

For the cardinal tetra and neon tetra see *Paracheirodon*.

Coelurichthys

This genus is closely related to the genera *Glandulocauda* and *Mimagoniates*. Their systematic positions have not yet been clarified conclusively.

Coelurichthys microlepis (STEINDACHNER, 1876)

7 cm, 23°C, W - G - S

| 7 cm | 23°C | W-G-S |  |

Home: Clear-water rivers and streams of Brazil, from Rio de Janeiro to the Rio Itapocu. Color not particularly in-

Roeboides species, a glass headstander. Photo by Dr. Herbert R. Axelrod.

teresting. Body shape similar to *Danio*. The lower half of the body is shimmering bluish, the upper part yellowish-brown. Reproductive behavior like *Coelurichthys tenuis*.

Coelurichthys microlepis, a croaking tetra. Photo by E. C. Taylor.

Coelurichthys tenuis NICHOLS, 1913 (Tenuis Tetra)
    4.5 cm, 23°C, W - G - S

4,5 cm	23°C	W-G-S	

On top bluish-silver with a wide, deep blue lengthwise band directly below the center line, the band extending to the end of the tail fin and ends there in the upper part of the lower half. Elongated fish with fins placed far to the back, reminiscent of *Danio*. For a long time this species was known under the erroneous name *Mimagoniates barberi* — an existing species, which, however, has not yet made an appearance in the aquarium trade. Internal fertilization is preceded by peculiar courting dances on the part of the male. The deposition of eggs may follow within days or weeks. The female fastens the eggs to the underside of the leaves of water plants. The larvae hatch after 24 to 30 hours.

Care: Lively species that requires soft water. Somewhat sensitive.

Corynopoma

This genus contains only one species, which is often incorrectly called *Stevardia*.

Corynopoma riisei GILL, 1858 (Swordtailed Characin)
    7 cm, 25°C, W - G - S

7 cm	25°C	W-G-S	

Not especially colorful and for this reason not often offered for sale. On the other hand, the males are distinguished by beautifully elongated dorsal and tail fins. Their reproductive behavior merits special attention. The males open their gill covers wide, thereby extending a long, spoon-shaped attachment of the gill covers. The end of this "spoon" becomes colored darkly. The females fall for this dummy, trembling in the open water: it considers it as prey and snaps at it. This positions its swimming parallel to the courting male, which uses the opportunity for copulating with the female. Internal fertilization takes place. The female stores the sperm packets in her body. A one-time fertilization may ensure a life-long laying of ferilized eggs by the female. In earlier times this species was thought to be parthenogenic when it was observed that the females could lay fertilized eggs without the presence of males.

Care: An undemanding species. Especially recommended for keeping by aquarists with biological interests. Breeding simple.

Ctenobrycon

The following species of this genus is occasionally found in aquaria.

Ctenobrycon spilurus (VALENCIENNES, 1849) (Silver Tetra)

8 cm, 25°C, W - G - S

8 cm	25 °C	W-G-S	

Home: Northern South America.

Females with stronger body, usually paler in color. Breeding easy. After a furious chase, the eggs are laid in plant thickets. Brood grows rapidly.

Care: The undemanding fish like moderately large aquaria with some densely planted spots.

A spawning pair of sword-tailed characins, *Corynopoma riisei*. Photo by H. J. Richter.

Exodon

This genus has only one species.
Exodon paradoxus MUELLER and TROSCHEL, 1844 (Bucktoothed Tetra)
15 cm, 26°C, W - (G) - S

The bucktoothed tetra, *Exodon paradoxus.*
Photo by Dr. Herbert R. Axelrod.

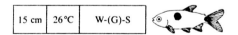

15 cm	26°C	W-(G)-S

Home: Northeastern South America.

The fish is distinguished by the strong lip teeth. Two large, deep-black spots, one on the base of the tail and the other in the shoulder area, characterize the young fish; later on, the spots fade. The females are heavier at spawning time. Breeding is possible, but raising of young is very difficult.

Care: Suitable only with reservations for keeping in aquarium. Do not combine with small tetras. Even larger tetras might be molested, since *Exodon* often tries to eat the scales of its companions. Combination with catfishes and loaches possible. Sometimes bothers plants, too. In tanks that are too small there is a possibility of their biting one another. They should nevertheless be kept in schools in well-planted tanks (hardy plants) with hiding places. Frequent feedings of live food are important. The aquarium must be covered because they jump. Water not too hard and slightly acid.

Gephyrocharax

The species of this genus are distinguished by, among other things, a dorsal fin set far to the back and a long anal fin. The sexes are easily differentiated by the lowest fin ray of the tail fin: in the male, it is free. Internal fertilization.

Gephyrocharax atricaudata (MEEK and HILDEBRAND, 1916)
    6 cm, 25°C, W - G - S

6 cm	25° C	W-G-S	

Home: Panama.

Basic body color soft green and bluish. Lengthwise body stripe that becomes more marked toward the rear, broadening in the root of the tail fin and enclosing here a strongly shimmering green-blue spot.

Occasionally, a second, similar species may be imported: *Gephyrocharax valencia.* However, it lacks the beautiful markings on the base of the tail fin.

Care: Lively, undemanding, and peaceful species that, however, should occasionally be given live food in addition to dry food. Larger, well planted aquaria with partial floating plant cover advantageous.

Glandulocauda

Typical of males of this genus is a gland-like scale-covered structure at the base of the tail fin that apparently secretes chemicals that attract females. This helps make possible sperm packet fertilization, which appears here as in the related genera *Corynopoma* and *Gephyrocharax.*

Glandulocauda inequalis EIGENMANN, 1911 (Croaking Tetra)
    6 cm, 22°C, W - G - S

6 cm	22°C	W-G-S	

Home: Uruguay, Southern Brazil.

Females smaller, males with asymmetrical tail fin (lower part broader). Nicely colored.

Breeding not difficult, but not particularly productive (at most 70 eggs during one spawning). Fertilization of the eggs internally in the ovaries of the female. Eggs are laid mostly on the undersides of leaves of water plants.

It is remarkable that this tetra has the ability to breathe atmospheric air. When it expels the air, a long drawn-out chirping sound can be heard.

Care: Undemanding and lively fish. Eats dry food, but needs live food often for its well-being. Larger, well-planted aquarium.

Gymnocorymbus

Compact little fishes with strongly formed dorsal and anal fins reminiscent of *Megalamphodus* species.

Gymnocorymbus ternetzi
(BOULENGER, 1895) (Black Tetra)
6 cm, 25°C, W - N - G - S

6 cm	25 °C	W-N-G-S	

Home: Mato Grosso area, Parana, Brazil.

Popular aquarium fish that is also bred in long-finned form. Rearward part of the body black, in older animals gray. Males somewhat smaller, with white tips on the tail fin. In transmitted light it can be seen that the translucent body cavity of the male runs into a point toward the rear, but in the females it is rounded in the rear. Breeding possible even for beginners.

Care: Variety of live food, frequent water changes. Stocking in groups with slightly greater number of males advantageous. Water slightly acid, soft (not above 8°DH). Parents must be removed after spawning, as they will eat eggs. The young grow quickly.

The black tetra, *Gymnocorymbus ternetzi*. Photo by B. Kahl.

Hemigrammus

A very large part of the small, colorful tetras in our aquaria belong to this genus of fishes from Central and South America. The sexes are not always easy to differentiate, since they differ not at all or only very little in coloration. In many instances the males are markedly slimmer and more strongly colored. If this method of differentiation does not work, we hold the animals in a glass in front of a light and observe the shape of the swim bladder as well as its position in the body cavity. In females, the swim bladder is narrow and appears to end at the genital pore. In the males, on the other hand, its end is rounded and it is positioned much higher. In addition, there usually is a free space between the swim bladder and the other internal organs in the male. In the female this space is filled by the ovaries.

Care: These fishes are all very peaceful and undemanding. Nevertheless, some guidelines should be followed in order to observe their most beautiful colors and liveliest behavior. In any case, the fish should be kept by species in schools (at least six). The aquarium should contain at least 30 liters, if possible more, of course. Use soft, crystal-clear water between 5 and 15°DH. It is best to increase acidity by means of peat extract. In addition to a sufficient swimming space in the open, the fish also like a lot of plants. They look most effective above a dark substrate. Occasional feedings of live food have a positive effect on coloration and behavior.

For breeding, which is not difficult if some rules are observed, small 10-liter plastic tanks are suitable.

Hemigrammus caudovittatus AHL, 1923 (Buenos Aires Tetra)

12 cm, 23°C, W - G - S

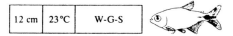

12 cm	23°C	W-G-S	

The long-finned black tetra. Photo by Andre Roth.

Home: La Plata River region.

Typical for this species is the light lengthwise stripe and the black diamond- shaped spot at the base of the tail fin.

Care: This very beautiful tetra needs relatively much food, otherwise it will attack the soft plants. Give lettuce or frozen spinach as additional food! Plant aquarium only with hardy plants *(Echinodorus, Vallisneria)*. Relative to its size, it needs a fairly large aquarium. Do not keep with much smaller fishes, since it is sometimes aggressive. Undemanding regarding the water quality. Easy to breed.

Hemigrammus erythrozonus DURBIN, 1909 (Glowlight Tetra)
    4.5 cm, 25°C, W - G - S

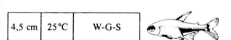

4,5 cm	25°C	W-G-S

Home: Guyana.

One of the most beautiful tetras, with a red-glowing lengthwise band that extends from the mouth to the tail fin. Especially effective in larger schools.

Hemigrammus erythrozonus, the glowlight tetra. Photo by R. Zukal.

There is also a golden-colored mutation. These forms are to be kept and bred like the normal form.

Care: For breeding, add peat extract and keep the carbonate hardness at most 1°DH. Breeding temperature 28°C. Add water plants (Java moss). Spawns readily. Young fish will take freshly hatched brine shrimp nauplii immediately after they become free-swimming.

Hemigrammus hyanuary DURBIN, 1918 (January Tetra)
    4 cm, 25°C, W - G - S

4 cm	25°C	W-G-S

Home: Central Amazon River region. Named after Lake Hyanuary near Manaus.

Very lively fish that occasionally may be shy, however.

179

Care: Dense planting and company of other lively fish. Spawns in twilight. Breeding is not always easy.

Hemigrammus marginatus ELLIS, 1911 (Bassam Tetra)

8 cm, 26°C. W - G - S

8 cm	26°C	W-G-S

This formerly popular species has been replaced in the aquarium by more colorful forms.

Care: An undemanding fish in every respect, whose breeding, however, may sometimes be problematic.

Hemigrammus nanus LUETKEN, 1874 (Silver-tip Tetra)

5 cm, 24°C, W - G - S

5 cm	24°C	W-G-S

Home: Rio San Francisco in eastern Brazil.

Colored yellow-brown with white fin tips. A black lengthwise stripe begins in the middle of the body and ends in the tail fin. During the spawning season, the male's coloration turns a beautiful brown- red. This species often lacks the typical adipose fin that lies between the dorsal and tail fins. This species spawns in the evening, best in faint artificial light. Formerly known by the synonym *Hasemania marginata* and *Hasemania nana*.

Hemigrammus ocellifer STEINDACHNER, 1882 (Head and Tail Light Tetra)

4.5 cm, 25°C, W - N - G - S

4,5 cm	25°C	W-N-G-S

Home: Amazon River region and Guyana.

Silver-tip tetras, *Hemigrammus nanus*. Photo by B. Kahl.

Attractive in not too bright aquaria because of its luminous red spots in the upper iris and in front of the dark tail spot. The subspecies *H. ocellifer falsus*, of usually more slender build, has this spot only sketchily developed or it is lacking entirely.

Care: Makes low demands regarding the water quality and is also unproblematic for breeding. However, it is effective only in a dark tank. Partially cover the surface with floating plants!

Hemigrammus pulcher LADIGES, 1938 (Garnet Tetra)

5 cm, 26°C, W - G - S

5 cm	26 °C	W-G-S	

Home: Peruvian part of the Amazon.

Beautiful, quiet species of markedly stocky build. Two subspecies are differentiated: the nominate form, *H. pulcher pulcher*, and *H. pulcher haraldi*. The latter is distinguished by a consid-

Garnet tetras, *Hemigrammus pulcher*. Photo by D. Kahl.

erably shorter lengthwise band on the lower half of the caudal peduncle. The front part of the anal fin is white in the males.

Care: Aquarium not too bright. A partial cover of floating plants is favorable. Breeding is not easy. A larger plastic aquarium (30-50 liters) is needed because the male chases furiously. Females that are not ready to spawn are chased to death.

Hemigrammus rhodostomus AHL, 1924 (Rummy-nosed Tetra)

4.5 cm, 24°C, W - G - S

4,5 cm	24 °C	W-G-S	

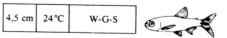

Home: Lower Amazon.

The red snout and three striking spots stripes on the tail fin are characteristic.

This species is often confused with the very similar *Petitella georgiae*, and differentiation is possible almost only by direct comparison, unless dentition and other characteristics not accessible to the aquarist are considered. In *H. rhodostomus* the black tail fin spots are located more closely together and the outer stripes extend less closely to the tail fin ends. The red color of the head often extends in a wedge along the sides of the body almost to the beginning of the dorsal fin. Like many other tetras, the males are easily recognized by the fact that they become entangled in the net because of the little hooks on their anal fin rays.

Care: These lively fish need clear, soft water, whose pH value should lie in the slightly acid range.

Hemigrammus rodwayi DURBIN, 1909
(Gold Tetra)
5.5 cm, 25°C, W - G - S

5.5 cm	25°C	W-G-S	

Home: Lower Amazon and Guyana.
Beautiful, but only rarely imported. Characteristic for this species is a circular black spot at the base of the tail that is edged in cherry-red in the males. A pathological variety of this species (according to Gery) is the solid gold "*H. armstrongi*". This variety when caught

The gold tetra, *Hemigrammus rodwayi*. Photo by A. Norman.

in the wild has a gorgeous golden sheen, which unfortunately is lacking in their offspring. The golden coloration is said to be caused by a parasitic worm that in the aquarium cannot infest the animals of succeeding generations because of the absence of intermediate hosts!

Hemigrammus ulreyi (BOULENGER, 1895) (Pennant Tetra)

5 cm, 25°C, W - G - S

5 cm	25°C	W-G-S

Home: Mato Grosso region and Paraguay River.

A rarely imported fish, not to be confused with the more common "false ulrey," *Hyphessobrycon heterorhabdus.* The fish are colored an unobtrusive light green and have a narrow, whitish lengthwise band, occasionally with a

Rummy-nosed tetras, *Hemigrammus rhodostomus.* Photo by Dr. D. Terver, Nancy Aquarium, France.

reddish tinge, that begins at the edge of the upper gill cover and ends in the base of the tail fin. This stripe lies on another darker band.

Hemigrammus unilineatus (GILL, 1858) (Feather-fin Tetra)

5 cm, 25°C, G - S

5 cm	25°C	G-S

Home: Small bodies of water in Trinidad and northern South America.

Its uncommon status in aquaria is explained by its relatively dull coloration. The fish is translucent greenish gray with an often barely noticeable gold-colored lengthwise line.

Care: Peaceful fish that is problem-free in care and breeding.

Hyphessobrycon

Includes a large number of popular aquarium fishes. The fishes of this genus strongly resemble those of the genus *Hemigrammus* described above. The differences include the scaling of the tail fin base, which is lacking in this genus in contrast to *Hemigrammus*, and the dentition.

The differences in the distinction of the sexes are often clearer in this genus than in *Hemigrammus*, and occasionally a marked sexual dimorphism is found. There are differences also in the behavior. The males of this genus open their courtship with a typical fluttering dance that is completely lacking in *Hemigrammus*.

There are no differences between these two most important aquarium genera of tetras in their requirements. I refer here to what has been written about the genus *Hemigrammus*.

Care: The ideal tetra aquarium has large dark areas that are covered over with roots and floating plants and also free spaces flooded with light.

Of the many species belonging to this genus, only those of greatest importance can be addressed separately.

Hyphessobrycon bifasciatus ELLIS, 1911 (Yellow Tetra)

5 cm, 22°C, W - G - S

5 cm	22°C	W-G-S	

Home: Coastal regions of southeastern Brazil.

The fish is colored a softly translucent yellow and distinguished by two vertically elongated dark shoulder spots. Fins of young fish are reddish, but this color fades with increasing age.

Hyphessobrycon serpae, or at least the fish called this in the hobby. See the photo of *H. callistus* on the facing page. Photo by R. Zukal.

Callistus tetras, *Hyphessobrycon callistus*, one of the serpae tetras of the aquarium hobby. Photo by B. Kahl.

The male is more slender and has a larger, convex anal fin. The anal fin of the female is concave.

Care: Very undemanding schooling fish that occasionally can tolerate lower water temperatures to 16°C. For breeding, raise temperature to around 24°C. Breeding is very easy.

Hyphessobrycon callistus
(BOULENGER, 1900)
(Callistus Tetra)
    4 cm, 25°C, W - G - S

4 cm	25°C	W-G-S

Home: Paraguay basin.

Lively, sometimes territorial. The animals then stand under plants, their heads bent slightly downward, and attack those fishes which approach too closely. This often leads to damage to the fins of other small tetras. Beautiful and popular aquarium fish.

This often bright red fish is often confused with externally very similar ones of other species. It is distinguished by a marked shoulder spot and by a black marked anal fin. It is differentiated from the similarly marked *serpae* tetra mainly by the larger shoulder spot and the much larger black portion of the dorsal fin. The species does not exhibit any sexual dimorphism, but the females are plumper at spawning time.

Care: For breeding 27°C; peat extract.

Hyphessobrycon erythrostigma (FOWLER, 1943) (Bleeding Heart Tetra)
  12 cm, 26°C, G - S

12 cm	26°C	G-S	

Home: Colombia.

This species was long known by the synonym *H. rubrostigma*. It is especially notable for its large size in this otherwise rather small-sized genus. The males have a sickle-shaped elongated dorsal fin and are larger than the females. In spite of their size, the fish are peaceful and harmless toward each other, although the males may threaten each other for hours with spread fins. Unfortunately, the breeding of this beautiful species rarely succeeds.

Hyphessobrycon flammeus MYERS, 1924 (Flame Tetra, Tetra from Rio)
  4.5 cm, 22°C, W - N - G - S

4,5 cm	22°C	W-N-G-S	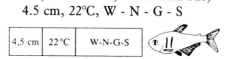

Home: Surroundings of Rio de Janeiro.

Beautifully colored and peaceful fish that is very hardy and completely undemanding. Sex differences: male with uninterruptedly black-edged anal fin.

Care: Surely the most easily bred species of tetra; for this reason, beginners should give it a try. Select beautiful parents for breeding! Needed is a well cleaned aquarium of about 20 liters. Add finely branched plants. It is best to cover the bottom with a spawning grid or coarse gravel, since the par-

A bleeding heart tetra, *Hyphessobrycon erythrostigma.* Photo by J. Vierke.

ents are great spawn eaters. The best
water is somewhat acid and soft (4 -
6°DH); however, breeding is also possible in medium-hard water. The normal water temperature is raised by
about 2°C. The fish spawn in pairs or
in a school. Remove adults after
spawning. Eggs are transparent. Young
hatch after one to one and a half days,
and after another five days will swim
free. Feed with minute live food. Success in raising young may also be had
with finely powdered dry food that
sinks to the bottom. Do not forget frequent partial water changes!

Hyphessobrycon georgettae GERY, 1961
   3 cm, 27°C, W - S - (G)

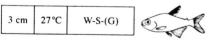

3 cm	27°C	W-S-(G)	

Home: Southern Surinam, where it
is reported to occur in overgrown
ponds in the Paru savanna.

Care: These small, very peaceful little fish are demanding in regards to water temperature; the other water values
are less important. Most fully colored

Hyphessobrycon griemi. Photo by R. Zukal.

in the dedicated tank or in the company of other fishes that remain small
and will not disturb them, such as *Corydoras pygmaeus*. Then they may assume a strong red coloration. Frequent
water changes!

The breeding tank should be no less
than 10 liters. Add many plants to
spawn on and, for violently chasing
males, a second female.

Hyphessobrycon griemi HOEDEMAN,
1957
   4 cm, 25°C, W - G - S

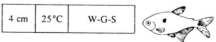

4 cm	25°C	W-G-S	

Home: Brazil.

Resembles *H. flammeus*, but is less
red, the shoulder spot smaller, and
with white fin tips on abdominal and
anal fins.

187

Care: Almost as undemanding as *H. flammeus* and accordingly easy to breed.

Hyphessobrycon herbertaxelrodi GERY, 1961 (Black Neon)
   4 cm, 25°C, W - G - S

4 cm	25°C	W-G-S

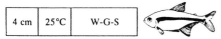

Home: In the Rio Taquary near Coxim in Brazil.

Lively, vigorous schooling fish. Peaceful. The fish has a black band below its center line that may be of different widths in different individuals. A very popular species.

Care: For breeding, slightly acid, soft water (non-carbonate hardness to 4°, carbonate hardness O°). Young fish grow quickly.

Hyphessobrycon heterorhabdus (ULREY, 1864) (False Ulrey, Flag Tetra)
   5 cm, 25°C, W - G - S

5 cm	25°C	W-G-S

Home: Lower Amazon, Rio Tocantins.

A frequently kept schooling fish which has a tricolored lengthwise band extending from the gill covers to the beginning of the tail fin. The upper part of the band is red, followed by a narrow, pure white zone. At the bottom, the band is black.

A hardy and peaceful species. Females are larger and plumper. Breeding is not always easy.

Hyphessobrycon ornatus AHL, 1934 (Jewel Tetra)
   6 cm, 25°C, W - G - S

6 cm	25°C	W-G-S

Home: Distribution from the lands of Guyana to the lower Amazon. Probably a synonym of *H. bentosi*.

Jewel tetras, *Hyphessobrycon ornatus*. Photo by B. Kahl.

The stunning black neon, *Hyphessobrycon herbertaxelrodi*. Photo by R. Zukal.

A beautiful red-tinged species, hardy and peaceable, therefore excellently suited for the community tank. The males have a pennant-like attenuated dorsal fin. No shoulder spot!

Care: Breeding is not difficult for people with experience if adequate water conditions are provided: 28°C, carbonate hardness as low as possible, addition of peat extract, pH neutral or only slightly acid. Immediately after swimming free, the young eat newly hatched *artemia*. Frequent water changes are important, since the young are very sensitive to nitrites.

Hyphessobrycon pulchripinnis AHL, 1937 (Lemon Tetra)

5 cm, 25°C, W - G - S

5 cm	25°C	W-G-S

Home: Central Brazil.

Faintly yellowish fish with beautifully colored red iris and tail markings in dorsal and anal fins. Leading edge of anal and abdominal fins as well as parts of the dorsal fin yellow. Anal fin in the female only weakly or not at all dark-edged; in the male, marked, black edge.

Care: Peaceful fish for the community aquarium. Breeding not always easy.

Hyphessobrycon rosaceus DURBIN, 1909

4 cm, 25°C, W - G - S

4 cm	25°C	W-G-S

Home: Western Guyana.

Closely related to *H. ornatus;* often confused with *H. serpae.*

Care and Breeding: Like *H. ornatus.*

189

Hyphessobrycon serpae DURBIN, 1908
(Serpae Tetra)
5 cm, 25°C, W - G - S

Black phantom tetras, *Megalamphodus megalopterus* (male on left, female on right). Photos by J. Vierke.

| 5 cm | 25°C | W-G-S | |

Home: Amazon basin.
Often confused with the *H. callistus*. There are blood-red aquarium forms which aquarist erroneously call *"H. minor."* Females more pale in coloration than males.

Markania

This genus contains two species, one of which occasionally reaches our aquaria. The fishes have a relatively small head and a small, asymmetrical tail fin whose upper lobe extends to a point, while the lower is rounded.

Markania nigripinnis (PERUGIA, 1891)
(Orange-finned Tetra)
15 cm, 25°C, W - G - S

| 15 cm | 26°C | W-G-S | |

Home: Region of the upper Paraguay, Parana.

The fish has a dark shoulder spot as well as a spot at the beginning of the tail fin. With increasing age, these spots pale. Robust fish, they will occasionally attack water plants. Fins reddish in the males; in the females with a more yellowish tinge.

Care: Large aquaria with hardy plants. Occasional additions of blanched lettuce or frozen spinach. Breeding not difficult.

Megalamphodus

This genus was established on the basis of anatomical distinctions that are not obvious to the aquarist. It is closely related to *Hyphessobrycon*, and the care is similar. The males with their streamer-like fins are reminiscent of *H. ornatus* and its relatives. Hybridization of *Megalamphodus megalopterus* with *Hyphessobrycon ornatus* has · been successful.

Megalamphodus megalopterus EIGEN-MANN, 1915 (Black Phantom Tetra)
4.5 cm, 24°C, W - G - S

| 4,5 cm | 24°C | W-G-S | |

Home: Rio Guapore in the Mato Grosso highlands.

Lively, hardy schooling fish that prefers to stay in thee lower water layers. Pronounced light-edged black shoulder spot and very large, dark-tinted fins. Dorsal fin of the male high, widely fanned; female with smaller fins, less gray in coloration, often more reddish.

Care: Likes dense planting and dark zones in the aquarium. Requires soft water for its care. Breeding as for the *Hyphessobrycon* species. Spawn-eater; eggs light-sensitive!

Megalamphodus sweglesi GERY, 1961 (Red Phantom)
4 cm, 22°C, W - G - S

4 cm	22 °C	W-G-S

Home: Upper Rio Meta in Colombia.

Resembles in body shape and markings (shoulder spot) the black phantom tetra, but instead of the gray tones it has a beautiful red coloration. The red dorsal fin of the male is larger than that of the female, but not as fan-shaped and large as that of the black phantom. The dorsal fin of the female is more colorful; the leading edge is red at its base, followed by a deep black zone; the tip is white.

Care: Best in a somewhat dusky tank in not too hard water. For breeding, especially soft, slightly acid water is needed. Breeding is more difficult than with the black phantom tetra.

Moenkhausia

A genus including about 40 species. The tail fin is covered at its base with small scales. The spawning behavior resembles that of the genus *Hyphessobrycon* as far as the fluttering dances of the males are concerned.

Moenkhausia pittieri EIGENMANN, 1920 (Diamond Tetra)
6 cm, 26°C, W - G - S

6 cm	26°C	W-G-S

Home: Venezuela.

High-backed animals with sickle-like elongated dorsal fin in the males. Col-

Diamond tetras, *Moenkhausia pittieri.* Photo by B. Kahl.

oration uninteresting (blue-grey), but with strikingly shiny scales. Peaceful, lively fish.

Moenkhausia sanctaefilomenae STEIN-DACHNER, 1907 (Yellow-banded Moenkhausia)

7 cm, 23°C, W - G - S

7 cm	23°C	W-G-S

Home: Region of the Rio Paraguay.

The large body scales are dark-edged, so that the flanks appear to be covered with a net. The upper edge of the iris is bright red, the basal part of the tail fin deep black. Will in rare cases attack tender water plants. Females larger and plumper than males.

Care: For breeding needs soft, slightly acid water. Aquarium for breeding should not be too small.

Nematobrycon

This genus includes two species that are distinguished by pointed tail fin lobes as well as a thread-like elongation of the central fin rays that is more pronounced in the males. Adipose fin lacking in these tetras. Both species are strikingly attractive but need extremely soft water for their care (1 - 4°DH) and a slightly acid pH value, so they are not fish for everyone.

Nematobrycon lacortei WEITZMAN and FINK, 1971 (Rainbow Tetra)

6 cm, 25°C, W - G - S

6 cm	25°C	W-G-S

Home: Colombia.

Differs from the better-known emperor tetra by the fact that its lengthwise band dissolves into single spots at its upper edge and by its bright red iris. Not a popular fish and probably a tank-raised hybrid that may not exist in nature.

Care: Like the emperor tetra.

The yellow-banded moenkhausia, *Moenkhausia sanctaefilomenae.* Photo by J. Elias.

Nematobrycon palmeri EIGENMANN, 1911 (Emperor Tetra)
6 cm, 25°C, W - G - S

Emperor tetras, *Nematobrycon palmeri.*
Photo by B. Kahl.

6 cm	25°C	W-G-S	

Home: Rio San Juan and its tributaries (Colombia).

Striking because of its body shape and coloration. Below the center of the body is a deep black lengthwise band that extends into the elongated central caudal rays. Above this line is a beautiful shimmering bluish area. Iris iridescent blue-green. Lively and peaceful.

Care: Dense plantings with sufficient swimming room. Older males occasionally form territories and fight harmless battles with each other. Breeding difficult. Very soft, acid water needed. Keep in pairs.

Paracheirodon

Some peculiarities of dentition led to the establishment of this genus, and it has recently been expanded to include all the blue and red small tetras — *Paracheirodon innesi, Cheirodon axelrodi,* and *Hyphessobrycon simulans.*

Paracheirodon axelrodi (SCHULTZ, 1956) (Cardinal Tetra)
5 cm, 26C, S - G

5 cm	26°C	S-G	

Home: Tributaries of the Rio Negro, Brazil and Colombia.

The water values here are so extreme

that they cannot even be approximated in the community aquarium: pH 5, hardness below 1°DH, conductivity below 10 microSiemens. The water temperatures in nature lie around 26-28°C. These are schooling fish that are especially effective in a somewhat darker tank (floating plants, rear wall!) above a dark substrate.

The cardinal tetra may well be the most strikingly colored and most highly demanded species of tetra. Named to honor its discoverer, Dr. Herbert R. Axelrod. Its name has been changed again by Dr. Stanley Weitzman to *Paracheirodon*. Previously it was called both *Hyphessobrycon* and *Cheirodon*.

Care: Peaceful and easy to care for. Cardinals demand by no means the same water values as at home. For breeding, however, we should try to approximate them! Breeding problematic. Soft, acid water (pH 5-5.5) of about 2°DH (carbonate hardness at most 1°) is a prerequisite. Spawning in open water or near finely branched plants late in the evening or at night.

The cardinal tetra, *Paracheirodon axelrodi.* Photo by B. Kahl.

Eggs and brood must be protected from light. At 27-29°C, the larvae will hatch after 18-20 hours and swim free after about five days.

Paracheirodon innesi (MYERS, 1936) (Neon Tetra)
    4 cm, 22°C, W - G - S

4 cm	22 °C	W-G-S

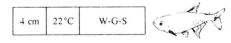

Home: Upper course of the Amazon in Peru and other parts of the Amazon basin; discovered by Dr. Axelrod in Rio Purus, Brazil, too.

One of the best-known aquarium fish. Splendidly shimmering with blue and red. In contrast to the much more colorful cardinal tetra, the red coloration is only on the rear half of the body. Females markedly stouter.

Care: Less demanding than the cardinal, but most not be kept too warm! For breeding, use fish that are not too old. Keep them separated by sex in 18 - 22°C and feed well on bloodworms and mosquito larvae . Stop feeding one day before transfer into breeding tank! Transfer into about 23°C in a well-cleaned 10-liter all- glass tank, pH between 6.3 and 6.8, soft water (1 - 2° non-carbonate hardness, no carbonate hardness). Add fine-leaved spawning plants that previously were disinfected briefly in potassium permanganate. Darken the basin, since they are twilight spawners. Larvae hatch after 24 hours. When the fry are free- swimming, feed with infusoria, later with *Artemia* nauplii. By observing all these rules, breeding is no longer too problematic.

Paracheirodon simulans (GERY, 1963) (False Neon)
3.5 cm, 23°C, W - G - S

3,5 cm	23°C	W-G-S

Home: Rio Iufaris, a tributary of the Rio Negro, Brazil.

Splendidly colored little fish that because of its similarity to the even more strongly colored neon tetra will always remain in its shadow. Female larger and stouter. Breeding difficult.

Petitella georgiae GERY and BOUTIERE, 1964
6 cm, 25°C, W - G - S

6 cm	25°C	W-G-S

Home: Upper course of the Amazon.

Only representative of this genus. It

Neon tetras, *Paracheirodon innesi*. Photo by H. J. Richter.

strongly resembles *Hemigrammus rhodostomus* and is often confused with it. Females larger and stouter.

Care: Breeding in soft, slightly acid water. Keep in pairs.

Poptella

Includes some disc-shaped fishes that formerly were called *Ephippicharax*. The appearance of these and other closely related fish such as the members of the genus *Stethaprion* are excellently described by the common name "silver dollar" fishes.

Poptella orbicularis VALENCIENNES, 1849

12 cm, 25°C, W - G - S

12 cm	25°C	W-G-S

Home: Large areas of tropical South America.

A lively, hardy fish that needs a larger aquarium. Body shape rounded. They are quite dull silvery, but iridescent in color when light strikes them at a favorable angle. Breeding has been successful in several instances.

Prionobrama filigera (COPE, 1870) (Glass Bloodfin)

6.5 cm, 25°C, W - G - S

6.5 cm	25°C	W-G-S

Home: Rio Madeira.

Lively, glassy transparent fish with red tail. Flanks often bluish iridescent. The first rays of the anal fin are whitish and frequently thread-like.

Care: Lively fish for roomier aquaria that like to stay near the surface. Prefer soft, slightly acid water.

Pristella

This genus, which includes only two species, is to be placed between the genera *Hemigrammus* and *Hyphessobrycon* as regards morphology and behavior.

Petitella georgiae, the false rummy-nose. Photo by H. J. Richter.

Pristella maxillaris (ULREY, 1894) (Pristella)
   4.5 cm, 24°C, W - N - G - S

The pristella, *Pristella maxillaris*. Photo by H. J. Richter.

4,5 cm	24 °C	W-N-G-S

Home: Venezuela, Guyana, and in rivers and small savanna creeks in the lower Amazon region.

Better known under its former name, *P. riddlei*. Its black-white-yellow dorsal and anal fins and red tail fin are its main colors. Males smaller, slimmer. Sexually mature males and females cannot be combined at will for breeding.

Care: Hardy fish that can be bred in harder water. Its natural habitat in South America extends in many places to include brackish water zones. Tank not too bright, dark substrate. Occasionally shy. It is best if the pairs find each other in the school. Shade breeding tank and protect it against disturbances. Add fine-leaved plants as spawning substrate. Very productive, breeding not difficult.

Pseudocorynopoma

Related to the genus *Corynopoma*, but without internal fertilization.

Pseudocorynopoma doriae PERUGIA, 1891 (Dragonfin Tetra)
   8 cm, 22°C, W - G - S

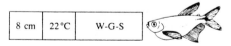

8 cm	22 °C	W-G-S

Home: Southern Brazil and the La Plata region.

The common name refers to the strongly extended dorsal and anal fins of the males. Not particularly attractive in color.

Care: Undemanding. Good jumper, cover aquarium well. Breeding productive (up to 1000 eggs).

197

Thayeria (Penguins or Hockeysticks)

The fish of this genus are distinguished by their resting position, with the head pointing obliquely upward. This behavior is emphasized by an elongated lower tail fin lobe and a black body stripe ending there.

Care: like *Hemigrammus*.

Thayeria boehlkei WEITZMAN, 1957 (Boehlke's Penguin)

6 cm 24°C, W - G - S

Home: Upper Maranon, Brazil.

The most frequently imported species of this genus, it is usually erroneously called *T. obliqua*. Lengthwise body band begins at the upper edge of the gill cover. Sexes are marked identically, but sexually mature females are plumper. The sexes can also be differentiated by the shape of the swim bladder as in *Hemigrammus*.

Care: Lively species that needs sufficient open swimming space. The fish also like to stay quietly near the surface under plant leaves. Good jumpers, aquarium must be carefully covered. Breeds in tanks that are not too small. Water about 3 - 5°DH, no carbonate hardness. Optimal breeding temperature 26°C. Most favorable combination: three to five females and one or two males. Spawning in the open water. Until the hatching of the young, the pH value must not drop below 7.0, else the embryos die. After swimming free, feed initially with infusoria and later with brine shrimp nauplii.

Thayeria obliqua EIGENMANN, 1908 (Short-striped Penguin)

8 cm, 25°C, W - G - S

Home: Amazon.

Often confused with *Thayeria boehlkei*. In this species, however, the black band is distinct only in the tail and be-

Boehlke's penguin, *Thayeria boehlkei*. Photo by J. Vierke.

gins indistinctly about at the level of the adipose fin, occasionally somewhat earlier.

Care: Like *T. boehlkei.*

Other species: *T. ifati* (band begins shortly before the start of the dorsal fin).

Triportheus

This genus presently includes nine species widely distributed in the rivers throughout South America. They have strongly convex bellies and long pectoral fins. With the aid of their pectoral fins, the *Triportheus* species are said to be able to fly, but at present nothing further is known about the escape flight of these species.

Triportheus elongatus (GUENTHER, 1864) (False Hatchetfish)
20 cm, 25°C, W - G - S

20 cm	25°C	W-G-S	

Home: Widely distributed in the Amazon and in the river regions to the north.

Silvery, green iridescent above. Rarely kept because of their size and

Triportheus angulatus, a false hatchetfish. Photo by A. Norman.

generally unattractive coloring. Probably not yet bred.

Care: Suited only for larger aquaria. Very undemanding here.

Alestidae (African Tetras)

The Africa and South America tetras still are kept in one common group by many scientists, and there is little doubt that the families are closely related. Most imported species reach a length of 10 cm and more.

Alestes

These are without exception colorless small-headed species that inhabit larger rivers and whose body shape is reminiscent of herrings. With the exception of tail fins, which occasionally are colored red, the animals are solid silvery and without distinctive markings. Some species formerly numbered

199

in this genus now belong to the genera *Brycinus, Micralestes,* and *Phenacogrammus.*

Care: Since the fishes of this genus become quite large (up to 45 cm!) and are, in addition, very lively, they can be kept only in larger aquaria.

Brycinus

Genus rich in species with relatively large scales. A spot at the base of the tail fin that extends to the central tail fin rays is a typical marking.

Brycinus bimaculatus (BOULENGER, 1899)

15 cm, 23°C, W - G - S

Home: Upper Congo.

In front of the typical tail spot is a body spot on the side shortly behind the dorsal fin.

Similarly formed is *Brycinus nurse,* which grows to 25 cm in length and whose indistinct body spot is placed far to the front, obliquely above the base of the pectoral fin.

Care: Both species are decorative fish for large, well-planted tanks.

Brycinus longipinnis (GUENTHER, 1864) (Long-finned African Tetra) 15 cm, 23°C, W - G - S

Home: Tropical West Africa in rapidly flowing waters.

Lively, decorative schooling fish. The male has a pennant-like, elongated dorsal fin and a large, convex anal fin with a whitish edge. The female remains somewhat smaller than the male, with a straight or somewhat concave anal fin.

Care: Live food is given preference, especially insects and insect larvae. Soft water for breeding. Eggs 2.5 mm. Brood hatches after about six days, immediately eats brine shrimp nauplii.

Arnoldichthys spilopterus. Photo by D. Terver.

This species resembles *B. chaperi*, also imported from West Africa, so strongly that the fish usually are not distinguished (*B. longipinnis* has 26 - 27 scales in a lateral line; *B. chaperi*, in contrast, 28 -30).

Arnoldichthys

This genus contains only one species. It is spindle-shaped, elongated, with strikingly large scales on the flanks and the upper side of the body, and smaller scales lower on the body.

Arnoldichthys spilopterus
(BOULENGER, 1909) (Red-eyed Characin)
7 cm, 25°C, W - G - S

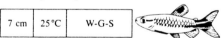

7 cm	25 °C	W-G-S	

Home: Nigeria and Cameroons.

Rapidly swimming, lively species. Said to grow up to 12 cm in the wild. Dorsal and anal fins with black, light-edged markings.

Care: Need much open swimming space, but also denser plant stands in which they can hide. Occasionally like to jump, so cover aquarium well.

Phenacogrammus interruptus.

Breeding successful only in a few instances.

Micralestes

Thus far 14 species are known, of which only a few have been kept in aquaria. The species are all very much alike and difficult to differentiate even for specialists. All species remain comparatively small and have a pale band below a darker lengthwise band. Otherwise, they are quite colorless.

Phenacogrammus

These fishes, closely related to *Micralestes*, live exclusively in the Congo basin.

Phenacogrammus interruptus
(BOULENGER, 1899) (Congo Tetra)
10 cm, 24°C, W - G - S

A very decorative species whose males may get very beautiful, elongated fins (exception: pectoral fins) at matu-

10 cm	24 °C	W-G-S	

rity. Especially the dorsal and tail fins may be veil-like.

Care: For full fin development, roomy, well-planted tanks are needed, as are frequent feedings with insects and their larvae and regular water changes. The fish require slightly acid, not too hard water (to 10°DH). Stocking in schools necessary!

Breeding is successful only with optimally kept animals. It requires a large aquarium of at least 50 liters content. Young fish hatch after six to seven days and immediately need food.

Hemigrammopetersius

A genus of African tetras which includes about 15 species. Most frequently kept is the following species, formerly called *Petersius caudalis:*

Hemigrammopetersius caudalis BOULENGER, 1899 (Yellow-tailed African Characin)

7 cm, 23°C, W - G - S

The males have a yellowish tinged body and yellow dorsal and tail fins.

Central tail fin rays dark and somewhat elongated. Anal fin of male with broad white edge.

Care and Breeding: Like Congo tetra.

Serrasalmidae (Piranhas and Pacus)

Deep-bodied, occasionally even disc-shaped, fishes from South America that are distinguished by their abdominal keel that extend forward from the beginning of the anal fin. Their abdominal fins are small. The jaws are furnished with large, sometimes very sharp teeth. Sexual differences are only minor. All species grow quite large.

We distinguish three subfamilies. The subfamily Myleinae, with the genera *Colossoma*, *Mylossoma*, and *Metynnis*, are fishes that eat leaves and fruit that fall into the water, as well as water plants. They have strong but not very sharp teeth. In some parts of South America they are protected, since they

Hemigrammopetersius caudalis. Photo by Gene Wolfsheimer.

Colossoma oculus. Photo by A. Norman.

keep the rivers free of undesirable floating plants. The subfamily Serrasalminae includes the piranhas, which are adapted for a carnivorous diet and can tear the meat from fish and mammals with their sharp teeth. The third subfamily, Catoprioninae, consists only of the species *Catoprion mento*, which in the wild is said to feed partly on the scales of other fishes.

Colossoma

These large tetras, called "pacus" in their home, are known as excellent food fish. Aquaristically, they are without significance, though in display aquaria they are sometimes impressive because of their bullish shape and size. *Colossoma brachypomium* grows to 60 cm in length. Pacus are pure vegetarians.

Metynnis

Differ from the other, similarly built large tetras by their strikingly large adipose fin. The determination of the species is extremely difficult, since all species are very similar. Even scientists do not agree. Their estimates of the number of species in this genus vary from twenty to six.

Care: All *Metynnis* are predominantly vegetarians. They are suitable for tanks in which we forego all planting from the start. Instead, they can be decorated with bizarre roots and large rocks. For food, we give many different leaves and fruit. Head lettuce is especially welcome. The amounts needed are enormous! Occasionally we should also offer live food.

Metynnis argenteus AHL, 1924
    14 cm, 26°C, W - A - S

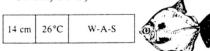

14 cm	26°C	W-A-S	

Home: Guyana and eastern Amazon basin.

Species which remains small; effective only in a large school. Sometimes provided with faintly marked dots on the upper half of the body, otherwise silvery.

203

Metynnis hypsauchen (MUELLER and TROSCHEL, 1844) (Plain Metynnis) 14 cm, 26°C, W - A - S

14 cm	26 °C	W-A-S

Home: Virtually all of tropical South America, in standing, strongly overgrown waters. Often in enormous schools.

Silvery, fins occasionally yellowish. Depending on origin, with a more or less clearly defined shoulder spot. Sometimes erroneously called *M. schreitmuelleri*. Has been bred on occasion. Spawns in open water. Very productive (to 2000 non- sticky eggs). Does not eat spawn.

Metynnis maculatus (KNER, 1859) (Spotted Metynnis) 12 cm, 25°C, W - A - S

12 cm	25°C	W-A-S

Home: Basin of the Rio Madeira, a southern tributary of the central Amazon.

Distinguished by a body with many black spots about equal in size to the diameter of the pupil or a little larger. Otherwise silver colored. Males with black-edged tail fin, reddish interior edge. Females markedly plumper at spawning time.

Care: Spawns in tufts of *Myriophyllum*. Young will eat medium-sized cyclops nauplii immediately after swimming free on the fourth or fifth day.

Very similar in appearance is *M. lippincottianus*, which also originates in the Amazon basin. Both species sometimes are wrongly called *M. roosevelti*.

Mylossoma

Large plant-eating tetras with a broadly extended chest line. The particularly flattened back after the beginning of the dorsal fin is characteristic.

Mylossoma aureum. Photo by Gene Wolfsheimer.

Care: Like *Metynnis,* but more problematic inasmuch as they all grow to about 25 cm, in length and require correspondingly large aquaria.

Myleus rubripinne. Photo by Dr. Herbert R. Axelrod.

Myleus

Large plant-eating tetras. Only suitable for the display aquarium! Quite attractive. *M. schomburgki,* whose males have dark fins and a broad black stripe that extends from the beginning of the dorsal fin across the body to the anal opening.

Serrasalmus (Piranhas)

Sharp teeth and very strong chewing muscles allow these fishes to tear meat from the bodies of larger animals. Concerted attacks by swarms of piranhas in the rivers of South America have repeatedly led to human deaths. However, many travelogues are exaggerated. Normally piranhas are fish-eaters that hunt fishes of their own size. Protected, by reason of instinct, are fish of a round body shape. This prevents them — at least in the open waters — from attacking each other. Because of this, the plant- eating Metynnis species are also protected.

To be kept only with others of the same species in the aquarium. Old piranhas of the species *S. rhombeus, S. striolatus,* and *S. hollandi* are reported to be loners that will immediately attack others of their species. At least in old age, they are to be kept individually only. Better suited for being kept in the aquarium are the schooling piranhas of the species *S. nattereri,, S. spilopleura,* and *S. piraya,* the especially feared species from the Rio San Francisco in eastern Brazil. Despite their instinctive inhibitions, they will immediately attack ill or weakened (thus behaving unnaturally) animals of their own species. On the other hand, keeping them in the company of other fishes is sometimes successful.

In the U.S.A., it is usually prohibited by the states to keep piranhas! Indeed, they are not without danger. Utmost care is indicated, especially when removing the fish from a net! Adult piranhas will occasionally jump for the fingers of their keepers. On the other hand, I know piranha-keepers who for years handled the cleaning of the glass with their bare hands in the water...but one of them now has a large scar on his hand!

Serrasalmus nattereri (KNER, 1859)
(Red-bellied Piranha)
30 cm, 25°C, W - S - A

30 cm	25°C	W-S-A

Home: Amazon basin and Orinoco system.

Base color gray, the throat and the pectoral, abdominal, and anal fins bright red. Protruding lower jaw. This species of piranha is the one that is probably most often kept in aquaria.

Care: To be kept with several others. Young animals will take all live foods. Old fish react differently, and will also take worms, meat, and dead fish. Large aquarium!

Breeding in large display aquaria has frequently been successful. The animals like to spawn in the roots of water hyacinths.

Serrasalmus rhombeus (LINNE, 1766)
(White Piranha, Spotted Piranha)
38 cm, 25°C, W - A

38 cm	25°C	W-A

Home: Amazon basin and farther north to the Guianas.

Young animals diamond-shaped, silvery with dark dots, becoming much more compact, almost disc-shaped, with age. At that stage, as loners, they can no longer be kept in groups. They then turn almost black, frequently being called "*S. niger*" in error. They then often have deep-red throats and gill covers.

Catoprion

This genus consists only of the following very attractive and harmless species.

Serrasalmus nattereri. Photo by J. Vierke.

Catoprion mento MUELLER and TRO-
SCHEL, 1844 (Wimple Piranha)
18 cm, 25°C, W - S - (G)

Catoprion mento. Photo by Dr. Herbert
R. Axelrod.

18 cm	25 °C	W-S-(G)

Home: Guianas and Amazon basin.

Striking, very beautiful, non-danger-
ous species (however, is reported to
sometimes eat the scales of fellow tank
inhabitants). The pennant-like elongated anterior rays in the dorsal and
anal fins are characteristic. Jutting
lower jaw. Body color silvery. Orange-
red spot on gill cove, anal fin orange-
colored. Base of tail root and outer tailfin rays black. Unfortunately, it is
rarely imported.

Care: The fish is said to be hardy
and to accept live food of all kinds.

Gasteropelecidae (Hatchetfish)

Distinguished by their body shape
which is tailored entirely for their escape flights. They have an almost
straight back line with a dorsal fin that
begins far to the rear. The abdominal
line forms a semicircular arc. This is
formed by a comparatively gigantic
shoulder girdle from which springs the
mightily developed pectoral fin muscu-
lature. The pectoral fins are extended,
wing-like, and in resting position proj-
ect upward far beyond the line of the
back. With whirling beats of the pectoral fins, the fish are able to penetrate
the surface and fly through the air for
several yards. When in danger, they
thus can escape their enemies by flying. The abdominal keel is so sharp
that it splits the surface of the water on
landing, so that the fish can elegantly
submerge again.

Care: The living environment for the hatchetfishes is exclusively the water's surface. It should not be restricted by too many floating plants or leaves drifting on the surface. On the other hand, they also need an opportunity for staying directly at the surface in the protection of leaves. It goes without saying that the aquarium must be covered very well. The temperature requirments are quite high. Dried food is accepted, but live food is better. It is taken preferably directly from the surface. If water fleas, wingless fruit flies, and mosquito larvae are allowed to dry in the air for a short time, they will stay on the surface. Otherwise, the animals are kept like *Hemigrammus*.
Carnegiella

Hatchetfishes that remain small; no adipose fin. Thus far, three species are known.
Carnegiella marthae MYERS, 1927 (Black-winged Hatchetfish)

    3.5 cm, 27°C, W - (G) - S

Carnegiella strigata. This is the *C. strigata strigata* subspecies because of the short-handled "Y" stripe in the middle of the keel.

Home: Northern and central South America.

Silvery fish whose chest and abdominal keels are black-edged. A dark stripe runs from the gill cover to the tail fin, which is bordered with gold or silver toward the top.
Care: Water to 12°DH. A sensitive species that has been propagated in captivity. Delicate fish!
Carnegiella myersi FERNANDEZ- YE-PEZ, 1950

    2.5 cm, 27°C, W - (G) - S

Home: Upper Amazon.

The smallest hatchetfish, without special markings.

Care: Keep only with small, harmless fish. Very delicate, but not as sensitive as *C. marthae*.

Carnegiella strigata GUENTHER, 1864 (Marbled Hatchetfish)

4.5 cm, 27°C, W - G - S

Home: Small forest rivers near the Amazon and in Guyana.

Silvery, with coarser or finer marbling, depending on origin. Likes shade. Harmless and hardy. Said to spawn near the surface in fine plants. Raise like the *Hemigrammus* species.

Gasteropelecus

All three species of this genus have adipose fins.

Gasteropelecus maculatus STEINDACHNER, 1879 (Spotted Hatchetfish)

9 cm, 27°C, W - G - S

Home: Extreme northwestern South America and Panama.

Below a lengthwise body stripe are several vertical bands composed of dots. Dorsal fin dark-edged.

Marbled hatchetfish, *Carnegiella strigata fasciata,* the subjects with the long-handled "Y" stripe. Photo by B. Kahl.

Gasteropelecus sternicla (LINNE, 1758)
(Silver Hatchetfish)
  6 cm, 27°C, G - S

6 cm	27°C	G-S	

Home: Tropical South America.
Barely distinguishable from *G. levis*. Both species are quite hardy. Body silvery, unmarked except for black lateral band.

Thoracocharax

Hatchetfishes with especially deep bodies, anteriorly with an almost vertical outline. Anal fin beginning far to the rear. Markedly larger scales than the other genera. An adipose fin is present.

Thoracocharax securis (FILIPPI, 1853)
(Black-tipped Giant Hatchetfish)
  9 cm, 26°C, W - G - S

9 cm	26°C	W-G-S	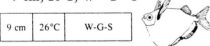

Home: Central South America.
In old specimens, the body is almost as tall as it is long (without tail fin). Silvery, shimmering, with dark lengthwise body band that iridesces blue or green, depending on the angle of light. Tip of dorsal fin dark. Unfortunately, not very often available.

Thoracocharax stellatus (KNER, 1859)
(Black-based Giant Hatchetfish)
  7 cm, 24°C, W - G - S

7 cm	24°C	W-G-S	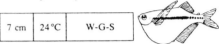

Home: Calm rivers in central Brazil to Argentina.
Less disc-like than the previous species. A blackish spot in the base of the dorsal fin.

Silver hatchetfish, *Gasteropelecus sternicla*. Photo by B. Kahl.

Erythrinidae (Trahiras)

Large tetras. They are striking because of their shape, which is totally atypical for tetras. They are elongated fishes with a rounded tail fin, short anal fin, and lacking an adipose fin. With their needle- sharp teeth they can hold and kill their prey. However, they cannot tear chunks of meat from their victims like piranhas. Some species grow very large and are given to biting in an unbelievable degree. A supplemental breathing organ allows them to survive even in water that is very low in oxygen. In the dry season they often remain in drying creeks and rivers.

Not recommended as typical aquarium fishes, they are interesting for display aquariums or for lovers of vicious fishes.

Hoplias

This genus includes three or four species that grow to 25 - 100 cm. Extremely predaceous and aggressive! The fish jump! Do not reach into the aquarium!

Thoracocharax stellatus, the black-based giant hatchetfish. Photo by Dr. Herbert R. Axelrod.

Hoplias malabaricus (BLOCH, 1794)
(Tiger Fish, Trahira)
60 cm, 25°, W

60 cm	25 °C	W	

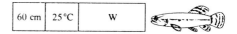

Home: Throughout all of tropical South America in slow-flowing standing water.

Young are occasionally imported; they are reddish brown on the back, more yellowish toward the abdomen, with red bands across the head and a greenish band along the sides. Adults are dirty green with irregular dark markings. All fins with dark, line-like spotted markings.

211

Care: Keep individually! Likes to hide between plants and roots. Feeds on live fishes, large worms, perhaps scavenges. Makes no special demands regarding the water composition.

Breeding probably possible only in large display aquaria. Spawns in shallow, overgrown pools. Builds a nest and guards the young.

Erythrinus

This genus has only the following species:

Erythrinus erythrinus (SCHNEIDER, 1801) (Short-finned Trahira)

   25 cm, 25 °C, (A) - W

25 cm	25 °C	(A)-W	
			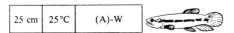

Home: South America and Trinidad.

Varying in coloration, often with light spots on the sides. Dorsal and anal fins often spotted. Dark lengthwise body band. Dorsal fin elongated in the male. Twilight animal.

Care: In large aquaria may possibly be kept with similar-sized fish of the same species, since considerably less vicious than *Hoplias*. Food includes live fishes and large worms.

Closely related to this species is *Hoplerythrinus unitaeniatus,* which grows to 30 cm in length. The fishes look quite similar, but in *H. unitaeniatus* both sexes have a short dorsal fin. Care is similar to that for *E. erythrinus.*

Ctenoluciidae (Pike Tetras)

Pike-shaped predaceous tetras from South America with an adipose fin and elongated jaws, the lower jaw shorter than the upper and the upper with a fleshy flap. 20 - 100 cm long, depending on the species. They belong to the genera *Boulengerella* and *Ctenolucius.*

The short-finned trahira, *Erythrinus erythrinus.* Photo by A. Norman.

Care: Temperatures around 25 °C. Since the fish are timid and easily frightened, they need large, well planted aquaria. Their snouts are easily injured otherwise. Not to be combined with the usual decorative fishes! Will eat predominantly live fish and, after acclimatization, larger invertebrates.

Ctenolucius hujeta has been bred. The 14 - 15 cm breeders produced 1000 -3000 eggs per spawning.

Chalceidae

Rather elongated, large-scaled tetras from South America that are reminiscent of *Arnoldichthys* in shape and scaling.

Chalceus

Of this genus, two species are known. These lively schooling fishes grow up to 35 cm in length and need, therefore, very large tanks and the appropriate diet (earthworms, pieces of meat). Voracious eaters.

Crenuchidae

South American tetras with a long dorsal fin and somewhat reminiscent in shape of killifishes. With pronounced sexual dimorphism.

Crenuchus spilurus GUENTHER, 1863 (Sailfin Tetra)

6 cm, 26 °C, W - S - G

6 cm	26 °C	W-S-G	

Home: Western Guyana and central Amazon.

Magnificent, peaceful fish whose large mouth is indicative of predaceous habits. The dorsal fin of larger males is elongated and flag-like. Their anal fin also is larger than in females. Characteristic of the species is an eye-sized round, black spot on the lower part of the caudal peduncle.

The red-spotted copeina, *Copeina guttata*. Photo by Dr. Herbert R. Axelrod.

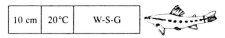

10 cm	20°C	W-S-G

Home: Tropical South America.

With a dark, lengthwise body band and several vertical bands. Sexual differences: males considerably slimmer, often with fine brown dots at the base of the dorsal fin. Peaceful, hardy schooling fish. Likes to stay near the bottom or on larger rocks. Also likes rocks as hiding place. When searching for food, moves jerkily above the bottom.

Care: No special water requirements. However, likes clean, fresh water. Eggs are deposited between plants. Hatching after 30 - 40 hours.

Lebiasinidae

Elongated tetras that are widely distributed throughout South America. They are grouped into two subfamilies: Lebiasininae and Pyrrhulininae. All the fishes of interest to the aquarist belong to the latter group.
Copeina

At present, only two species are included in this genus, and it has not yet been determined whether they are subspecies of the same species. Adipose fin lacking. No sexual dimorphism. Body more compact than in *Copella*. Tail fin totally or almost symmetrical.
Copeina guttata (STEINDACHNER, 1875) (Red-spotted Copeina)
    15 cm, 25 °C, W - G - S

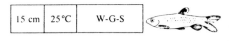

15 cm	25°C	W-G-S

Home: Central Amazon region and its tributaries.

Peaceful, hardy fish, but sometimes shy. Reddish silvery coloration with bluish iridescence. Large-scaled. On each scale along the flanks is a red spot. Unpaired fins and abdominal fins reddish. Often a black spot in the dorsal fin. The sexes are almost impossible to distinguish. During the spawning season the female has a more pronounced abdominal bulge. Frequently, the male is somewhat more strongly dotted or its upper tail fin lobe is a tiny bit longer. Males fan a nest cavity, where they spawn (up to 2000 eggs!). Occasionally they spawn on flat rocks or on leaves. After spawning, remove the female. The male guards the eggs andd provides a constant flow of fresh water by fanning. He continues to guard the hatched young for some time.

Care: Good jumper, so carefully cover the tank. An attractive species if kept in schools in larger aquaria.

Copella

A not very uniform genus with several species whose determination in many instances confounds even the experts. Elongated fishes without an adipose fin. Tail fin in both sexes with extended upper lobe. Sexual dimorphism: males with elongated fins.

Care: All species prefer soft, slightly acid water. Occasionally shy. Add floating plants! Cover aquaria well, since all *Copella* species are good jumpers.
Copella arnoldi (REGAN, 1912) (Splash Tetra)
8 cm, 23 °C, W - G - S

| 8 cm | 23 °C | W-G-S |  |

The splash tetra, *Copella arnoldi.* Photo by B. Kahl.

Home: Lower Amazon region, in the Rio Para and in Guyana.

A peaceful, elegant fish with reddish fins, especially in the males. Dark spot in the central part of the dorsal fin. Does not tolerate high temperatures. Has an especially interesting care for the brood. The fish spawn out of the water on the aquarium cover or on leaves hanging over the water. For this purpose, both partners repeatedly jump out of the water while closely pressed together in order to stick the eggs to a surface and to fertilize them. After spawning, the male guards the spawning site. In addition, he tries to constantly keep the eggs damp. To do this, he splashes the eggs with his tail fin. The brood hatches after 24 - 36 hours and falls.

Copella metae (EIGENMANN, 1914) (Zigzag Copella)

6 cm, 25 °C, W - G - S

| 6 cm | 25 °C | W-G-S |  |

Home: Rio Meta in Columbia.

A clearly marked zigzag band extends from the mouth through the eye to the tail base. In the male, the upper tail fin lobe is clearly elongated. The fish spawn on the upper side of large leaves of water plants that previousiy have been meticulously cleaned by the male. The care of the brood is the exclusive job of the father, who guards and fans the eggs. *Copella nattereri* (STEINDACHNER, 1875)

5 cm, 25 °C, W - G - S

| 5 cm | 25 °C | W-G-S |  |

Home: Central Amazon.

An elongated species that remains small and resembles in coloration and shape *C. arnoldi*. A large black spot in the center of

Copella vilmae, a colorful but rarely seen species. Photo by H. Schultz.

the dorsal fin, often reddish below it. Reproduction like *C. metae.*

A similar marking in the dorsal fin is displayed by the close relative *C. vilmae,* whose body, especially on the underside, is colored a strong reddish shade.

Nannobrycon (Oblique Pencilfishes)

A genus consisting of only two species. The adipose fin is lacking. The animals swim in an obliquely upward body position. They are distinguished by a dark lengthwise band that continues into the equally black lower tail fin lobe.

Nannobrycon eques (STEINDACHNER, 1876) (Brown-tailed Pencilfish)

5 cm, 25 °C, W - G - S

5 cm	25 °C	W-G-S

Home: Central Amazon.

A popular species. Forms schools among the water plants near the banks. Likes dense planting in the aquarium, too. Floating plants! Easy to keep in the community tank with peaceful fishes. Becomes really lively only in the twilight. The species is characterized by two parallel stripes positioned closely together

Nannobrycon eques, the brown-tailed pencilfish. Photo by S. Frank.

in the lower half of the body. Night coloration diagonally striped.

Females plumper; abdominal fins transparent. Abdominal fins in the males with light edge and milky-white tips.

Care: Breeding easy in 10-liter aquarium (without substrate!). Water soft, pH about neutral or slightly acid. Not very sensitive. Fasten *Cryptocoryne* to the bottom with a rock. The eggs are deposited under the leaves. Hatching after 24 - 36 hours; after another five to six days, the fry swim free. From the start they swim with their heads obliquely upward. Will immediately eat *Artemia* nauplii.

Nannobrycon unifasciatus (STEINDACHNER, 1876) (One-lined Pencilfish)

6.5 cm, 25 °C, W - G - S

6,5 cm	25 °C	W-G-S

217

Home: Central Amazon, Rio Negro, Orinoco, Guyana.

In contrast to *N. eques,* there is only one lengthwise band. In one variation there is an eye-spot in the central area of the tail fin; it formerly was called *"N. ocellatus."* This species also has been repeatedly bred.

Nannostomus (Horizontal Pencilfishes)

South American fishes closely related to *Nannobrycon* but swimming horizontally. With or without an adipose fin. Spindle-shaped, elongated body. Sexual differences: females plumper at spawning time, anal fin straight. Anal fin rounded in the male. About seven species. They have very small mouths.

Care: They will eat live as well as artificial food. The company of overactive fishes makes them timid and keeps them from being effectively displayed. The water hardness should not exceed 15°DH; considerably softer for breeding (5°DH or less).

Nannostomus beckfordi GUENTHER, 1872 (Beckford's Pencilfish)
7 cm, 25°C, W - G - S

7 cm	25°C	W-G-S	

Home: Northern South America

A broad black horizontal band extends from the mouth to the lower part of the caudal peduncle. The tail fin itself is light, half red. In one variety courting males may turn a lively red all over their bodies.

Care: Like all decorative tetras, they need densely planted aquaria with floating plants. Young sometimes will grow up even in the community tank.

The popular Beckford's pencilfish, *Nannostomus beckfordi.* Photo by H. J. Richter.

Breeding tank not too bright. As a spawning substrate, plants are required. However, the eggs do not always adhere. The parents are spawn-eaters. The eggs hatch after about 30 hours. After another three days, the young swim free. Feed initially with infusoria, later with *Artemia* nauplii.

Nannostomus bifasciatus HOEDEMAN, 1954 (Two-striped Pencilfish)
  6 cm, 25 °C, W - G - S

Home: Guianas.
Colored similarly to the previous species, but with another much finer band that runs parallel to it. No red tint on the body; all fins transparent.

Nannostomus espei (MEINKEN, 1956) (Barred Pencilfish)
  3.5 cm, 25 °C, W - G - S

Nannostomus harrisoni, a rarely imported species of pencilfish. Photo by H. J. Richter.

Home: Guyana.
Small pencilfish that is distinguished by five dark diagonal bands pointing toward the front.

Care and Breeding: Like *N. beckfordi*. Despite its delicateness, a relatively hardy fish. Combine with not too large or lively species.

Nannostomus harrisoni (EIGENMANN, 1909)
  6 cm, 25 °C, W - G - S

Home: Guyana and central Amazon.
Snout considerably longer than in the other species of this genus. Dark black horizontal band from mouth to the lower tail fin lobe, where it ends in a reddish area.

Care: Like *N. beckfordi.*
Nannostomus marginatus EIGEN-MANN, 1909 (Dwarf Pencilfish)
4 cm, 25 °C, W - G - S

4 cm	25 °C	W-G-S	

Home: Northern part of South America.

Markedly more compact than the other species of *Nannostomus.* Two horizontal bands, of which the upper is often narrower, extend into the tail fin. On the lower side is a third and weaker black stripe that turns into a black anal fin edge. Dorsal, abdominal, and anal fins with reddish areas. Black leading edge of the dorsal fin. The males have a greater amount of red in their abdominal fins.

Care: Breeding successful even in small spawning tanks of 3 liters and up. It is best to allow the fish to spawn on fine-leaved plants. The breeders must be removed immediately after spawning, since they are terrible spawn-eaters! Immediately after becoming free-swimming, the young may be fed with *Artemia* nauplii. Quite hardy species.

Nannostomus trifasciatus STEINDACH-NER, 1876 (Three-lined Pencilfish)
6 cm, 25 °C, W - G - S

6 cm	25 °C	W-G-S	

The popular three-lined pencilfish, *Nannostomus trifasciatus.* Photo by B. Kahl.

The dwarf pencilfish, *Nannostomus marginatus*. Photo by H. J. Richter.

Home: Upper Amazon.

A beautiful species resembling in its markings *N. marginatus*, but the lengthwise stripes do not extend to the tail fin. The tail fin is in part red, the dorsal fin without black edge. Abdominal and anal fins with light blue edges. This is one of the sensitive species of *Nannostomus*. Its breeding is considered very difficult.

Pyrrhulina

Differs from the related genera *Copella* and *Copeina* by a different dentition. The fins of the *Pyrrhulina* species, particularly the tail and dorsal fins, are more rounded than those of their relatives. Care and breeding as noted for *Copella* and *Copeina*.

Several species, which sometimes are difficult to differentiate. The following species are the main ones of aquarium significance.

Pyrrhulina rachoviana MYERS, 1926

5 cm, 25 °C, W - G - S

5 cm	25 °C	W-G-S	

Home: Lower Parana and La Plata.

This species is frequently sold. A short band extends through the eye but barely beyond the head. The only other marking is a black spot on the dorsal fin that is preceded by a light edge. In their habits the fish remind one of *Copella arnoldi*.

The females ready for spawning are clearly plumper than the males. The reproductive behavior and breeding are strongly reminiscent of those of *Copeina guttata*.

Pyrrhulina vittata REGAN, 1912 (Banded Pyrrhulina)

7 cm, 25 °C, G - S

7 cm	25 °C	G-S	

Home: Amazon River and Rio Tapajos.

Has an eye line like *P. rachoviana* and, in addition, on a reddish tinted base has

Abramites hypselonotus. Photo by B. Kahl.

three body bands angled slightly toward the rear that sometimes look more like spots than like bands. The males have a somewhat larger upper tail fin lobe.

Care: As a lively, peaceful and hardy fish, it can be recommended for the community aquarium, but it needs live food. Unfortunately a short-lived species. This species has occasionally been known to spawn in the community aquarium. The eggs are guarded and fanned by the male. They are usually on the upper side of a plant leaf. If the leaf with the eggs is transferred into a tank with water of identical composition, we have free-swimming young six days after spawning. They are very small and initially eat one-celled animals, but soon they will also accept cyclops and brine shrimp nauplii.

Similarly colored is *P. spilota*. In contrast to *P. vittata*, this species has another spot that lies on the eye line directly above the start of the pectoral fin.

Anostomidae (Headstanders)

Elongated, torpedo-shaped fishes. Only the genus *Abramites* has some higher-backed species. In the genera *Anostomus, Synaptolaemus,* and *Gnathodolus* the narrow mouth opening points steeply upward. Both jaws are set with strong teeth.

Abramites

This genus contains comparatively high-backed animals. It consists of only two species.

Abramites hypselonotus (GUENTHER, 1868)

13 cm, 25 °C, W - G - S

13 cm	25 °C	W-G-S

Home: Amazon and Guianas, but nowhere very numerous. A subspecies, *A.h. solarii,* lives farther south in the Rio Parana and the Rio Paraguay.

The markings are individually variable. They consist of about eight irregular wide crossbars. The black adipose fin contains a striking yellow spot. They like to stand between plants with their heads pointed downward. Mostly peaceful, but older specimens may turn quarrelsome. Thus far, breeding has not yet been successful. The species was formerly called "*A. microcephalus.*"

The second species, *Abramites eques,* is barely known. It is at home in the Rio Magdalena in Colombia.

Care: All usual foods are readily accepted; they also like to eat lettuce and spinach.

Anostomus

Elongated, almost cylindrical fishes. They like to stand obliquely in the water with their heads pointing downward, but can also shoot away like arrows.

Anostomus anostomus (LINNE, 1758) (Striped Headstander)

18 cm, 25 °C, W - N - G - S

18 cm	25 °C	W-N-G-S

Home: Northern part of South America, Amazon region.

The body is covered with three broad, black lengthwise stripes. In between there are two narrower yellowish zones. Dorsal and tail fins colored reddish. Very hardy species. The sexes can only be differentiated by the greater body diameter of the female. It is reported that in exceptional instances breeding has been successful, but complete reports are lacking.

Care: A very popular species that needs well-planted aquaria decorated with roots. The fish like to scrape algae and other growths from the leaves, roots, and aquarium glass. Will accept all foods, but should occasionally be given frozen spinach and blanched lettuce leaves, since they will otherwise go after the plants. In spite of its size, peaceful toward other fishes and its peers. Combining it with large and sedentary fishes such as discus is risky, however, since *Anostomus* may "graze" on the animals. The injuries may become infected and lead to death.

The striped headstander, *Anostomus anostomus.* Photo by R. Zukal.

Anostomus ternetzi FERNANDEZ-YEPEZ, 1949
12 cm, 25 °C, W - G - S

The unusual mouth of *Anostomus ternetzi.*
Photo by H. Schultz.

12 cm	25 °C	W-G-S

Home: Northeastern part of South America.

Is often confused with *A. anostomus.* The edges of the central dark lengthwise band in the region of the front of the body are smooth, however, not jagged. *A. ternetzi* lacks the beautiful red in the fins that is displayed by *A. anostomus.*

Anostomus trimaculatus (KNER, 1859) (Three-spotted Headstander)
15 cm, 25 °C, W - G - S

15 cm	25 °C	W-G-S

Home: Guyana and lower Amazon.

Slender and with a pointed head, but with puffy, upward-directed lips. Solid greenish gray coloration and three more or less strongly defined body spots (the first is often absent or very small). Fins reddish. In the wild, the fish attains lengths of up to 20 cm.

This species is often confused with *A. gracilis,* a quite similar species that only attains lengths of up to 10 cm.

Leporinus

This genus numbers about 50 - 60 species. Taxonomically, they are not well-known. In order to get some kind of overview, the species are combined into four groups according to Gery's Characoids of the World: 1) with crossbars pattern; 2) with dot pattern; 3) with lengthwise stripes; and 4) without obvious pattern. The rabbit-like mouth of some species led to the naming of the genus *(Leporinus = little hare).* There are species with overshot, undershot, or normal mouths.

This genus includes very beautiful fishes that become too big for the average aquarium but are ideally suited for display aquaria. All species are good jumpers. Cover the aquarium! The two most common species are listed here.

Leporinus fasciatus (BLOCH, 1794)
(Banded Leporinus)
30 cm, 25 °C, W - (G) - S

30 cm	25 °C	W-(G)-S

Home: All over tropical South America.

A really beautiful species that is imported again and again. Sides beautiful yellow with ten deep black corssbands. The adult males are slenderer and often show a reddish throat area.

Care: Tends to become quarrelsome if kept alone. For this reason, it is recommended only for keeping in a school in really big aquaria. The fish need vegetarian food additives (head lettuce, rolled oats) and frequent partial water changes. Unfortunately, many fish will also go after the water plants.

Leporinus striatus KNER, 1859 (Striped Leporinus)
25 cm, 25 °C, (G) - S

25 cm	25 °C	(G)-S

Home: Large areas of tropical South America.

Species provided with three black lengthwise stripes. The basic coloration is silvery beige. Tail and anal fins are reddish, all other fins transparent.

Very similar is *L. arcus* from western Guyana which differs by the fact that its central lengthwise band begins behind the eye; in *L. striatus* it starts at the mouth. Also, its fins are colored a stronger red.

Curimatidae (Curimatas)

In this family, rich in genera and species, there are again true headstanders. Many species live on debris and plant remnants; their mouths are without teeth. Actually, only the following species is of aquarium significance:

The banded leporinus, *Leporinus fasciatus*. Photo by R. Zukal.

Chilodus punctatus MUELLER and TROSCHEL, 1845 (Spotted Headstander)
12 cm, 25°C, W - G - S

| 12 cm | 25 °C | W-G-S |  |

Home: Guyana, Surinam, Loreto region in Peru.

Another headstander! Eye with beautiful red iris. Large scales, each with black dot. Dorsal fin black-dotted, other fins transparent. *Chilodus* is reported to make short crackling noises. The females are larger than the males and at spawning time considerably plumper.

Care: For this lively schooling fish we need large tanks with many roots and rocks. The plant growth does not need to be dense. Vegetable food additions (head lettuce, rolled oats) are gladly taken. A peaceful fish; however, will occasionally chase others of its species. Nevertheless, should be kept in schools! Breeding has been successful on various occasions. Vegetable food and live food important. The fish need faintly acid, soft water. For spawning,

Spotted headstanders, *Chilodus punctatus.* Photo by B. Kahl.

algae tufts, fine-leaved plants, or a web of synthetic fibers fastened to the bottom are used. The young hatch after three to four days and are easy to raise with rotifers and brine shrimp nauplii. The young remain together in a swarm and, like typical headstanders, stand vertically in the water.

The subspecies *C. p. zunevi*, originating in the upper Rio Maroni, lacks the dark lengthwise band of the nominate form.

Hemiodidae

Hemiodids are elegant, torpedo-shaped fishes from South America. They have a large, deeply forked tail. The fish sometimes remind me of *Anostomus* and *Leporinus* species, but they swim straight or with their front end slightly upward. Since they grow relatively large, they are of slight interest in the aquarium. They should be kept in a school to be displayed at their best. For this, the mobile and very fast fish need really large aquaria (300 liters or

A hemiodid, *Hemiodopsis* near *microlepis*, lacking the caudal pattern. Photo by R. Zukal.

more). Toward other fish they are peaceful but will occasionally nibble on plants. Additional vegetable food should be given. Only the two most familiar species are listed here.

Hemiodopsis gracilis (GUENTHER, 1864) (Slender Hemiodus)
16 cm, 24°C, W - S - (G)

16 cm	24 °C	W-S-(G)	

Home: Amazon, Rio Sao Francisco, and Guyana.

A striking black stripe begins with a thickening about halfway between the dorsal and adipose fins and ends in the upper half of the lower lobe of the tail fin. The lower half of the caudal lobe is bright red, and the upper lobe also is sometimes colored red. Otherwise the fish is plain silvery.

227

A similar pattern is shown by *H. semitaeniatus*. However, it lacks the strong red in the tail fin.

Hemiodopsis quadrimaculatus (PELLEGRIN, 1908) (Barred Hemiodus)
10 cm, 25°C, W - S - (G)

10 cm	25°C	W-S-(G)

Young and very colorful specimens of *Distichodus sexfasciatus*. Photo by B. Kahl.

Home: Upper Amazon, Guyana, and Surinam.

Characteristic are three black vertical bands on the body and another at the beginning of the tail fin that continues into the lower lobe of the tail fin. The adipose is often reddish. Similar markings are displayed by the species *H. sterni* and *H. huraulti*.

Citharinidae

This family comprises African tetras of quite unlike shapes that have ctenoid scales and usually have small, moveable teeth. Some small species are well suited for the home aquarium, while the larger ones are beautiful display pieces for public aquaria.

Distichodus

River fishes with a small head and a steeply rising back. They predominantly inhabit the zones near the bottom. They usually grow quite large (up to 70 cm!), but even those species that remain smaller are, as aggressive vegetarians, dangerous in tanks with plants. Some of the larger species, such as *D. sexfasciatus* and *D. lusosso* from the Congo region, are attractive large fishe for display aquaria.

Nannaethiops

This genus, closely related to *Neolebias*, has only one species.

Nannaethiops unitaeniatus GUENTHER, 1871 (One-lined African Tetra)

7 cm, 26°C, W - A - (G) - S

| 7 cm | 26°C | W-A(G)-S |  |

Home: All of equatorial Africa.

Silvery with one dark horizontal body stripe that accompanies a golden stripe lying directly above it. Males slimmer. At spawning, the front part of the tail fin and the upper tail fin lobe become blood-red.

Care: This peaceful schooling fish is undemanding but prefers to eat live food. In company it is often shy and easily frightened, but hardy. They are most effectively displayed in a planted tank with fine sand substrate. For breeding use a larger tank (40 - 50 liters) with fine sand bottom (previously scalded!) and a tuft of plants. Soft water. Very productive, spawning most often in the morning sun. Spawn-eaters. Young fish swim free after six days.

Nannocharax

Originating in western and equatorial Africa, with several species.

Nannocharax parvus PELLEGRIN, 1906 (Least African Darter)

5 cm, 24°C, W - G - S

| 5 cm | 24°C | W-G-S |  |

Home: Upper Niger region, in the rivers of Senegal, Gambia, Guinea, and Sierra Leone. Found in slow flowing and standing waters.

Distinguished from other members of this genus by a body shape reminiscent of headstanders. However, the mouth is undershot. A broad, dark lengthwise band leads from the tip of the snout to the tail fin root. *N. ansorgei* is a familiar synonym.

Nannocharax gracilis, one of the African darters. Photo by E. C. Taylor.

Care: Prefers shady, well-planted tanks with sandy substrate. No special requirements concerning the water composition.
Nannocharax fasciatus GUENTHER, 1867 (Banded African Darter)
7.5 cm, 23°C, W - (G) - A - S

The African darters all look very much alike. This is *Nannocharax fasciatus,* the banded African darter. Photo by B. Kahl.

7.5 cm	23°C	W-(G)A-S	

Home: Liberia to the Congo estuary.

Western African bottom fish easily confused with the South American *Characidium fasciatum* but recognizable by its preferred posture. While the South American *C. fasciatum* stands on its pectoral and abdominal fins, the African darter supports itself on its abdominal, anal, and tail fins. The pectoral fins are raised. During quiet swimming the body always remains pointed with the head upward.

The species has an undershot mouth, a straight lateral line, and several irregular crossbars. In Africa there are a great number of similar species of *Nannocharax* that are not always easy to distinguish.

Care: These peaceful animals can be housed in a community tank. Only live food (tubifex, cyclops) is taken directly from the bottom! No requirements concerning the water composition.
Neolebias

This African genus presently consists of seven species. The two species most frequently seen in aquaria are described here.

Neolebias ansorgii BOULENGER, 1912
(Ansorge's Neolebias)
  3.5 cm, 23°C, W - A (G)

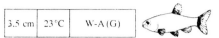

3.5 cm	23°C	W-A (G)

Home: Forest regions of lower Congo and Cameroon.

Body beautifully green shimmering, fins red. At spawning time, entire underside red in males. Usually the fish displays a dark lengthwise body stripe and a vertical line at the base of the tail fin. This beautiful species is often shy and remains hidden on the bottom. Females stockier, males larger.

Care: Must have hiding places. Frequent feedings of live food are necessary. It is best to keep the fish in pairs in a dedicated aquarium. Breeding similar to *Nannaethiops unitaeniata*. Hardness to about 8°DH. Feed the brood first with infusoria protozoans, rotifers, then after one week brine shrimp nauplii.

The better-known form comes from the Cameroons. A less colorful variation from the Congo region has been named *N. landgrafi*.

Neolebias trilineatus BOULENGER, 1899 (Three-lined Neolebias)
  4 cm, 23°C, W - (G)

4 cm	23°C	W-(G)

Home: Congo basin.

Silvery with three lengthwise body stripes. Similarly colored are *N. trewavasae* and *N. unifasciatus*, but their basic coloration is said to be more yellowish.

Care and Breeding: Like *N. ansorgii*.

A breeding male *Neolebias ansorgii*. Photo by H. J. Richter.

Phago (African Pike Tetras)

This includes three or four species from tropical West Africa that grow to about 15 cm in length and specialize in biting pieces of fins off other fishes and feeding on the pieces. They have long, beak-like jaws that are furnished with strong teeth.

Care: Dedicated tank! Food: small fishes, water insects, and insect larvae. They need good hiding places (plants, roots) and temperatures around 27°C. They have no special requirements concerning the composition of the water.

The species *P. maculatus* is the one most frequently available.

GYMNOTOIDEI
Gymnotidae, Rhamphichthyidae, Apteronotidae (American Knife Fishes)
South American fishes with long anal fins whose wave-like motion allows forward and backward swimming. The anal opening is placed far forward.

Care: These fishes often grow very large and are most suitable for the amateur only as young. In addition to live food, they also eat pieces of meat. Larger fish are suitable only for combining with other species as they hardly ever tolerate others of the same species in the aquarium. As twilight animals, they need dark hiding places where they can retreat.

Eigenmannia virescens (VALENCIENNES, 1847) (Green Knife Fish)
3 cm, 25°C, **W** - **A** - (G)

30 cm	25 °C	W-A(G)	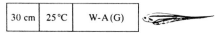

Slow-growing species that can attain lengths of up to 45 cm. The anal fin runs together with the caudal peduncle into a whip-like tip. Tail fin, dorsal fin, and abdominal fins missing. More or less transparent and bluish or greenish iridescent. Young often with irregular vertical stripes.

Phago maculatus, an African pike tetra. Photo by K. Paysan.

Gymnotus carapo LINNE, 1758 (Banded Knife Fish) 60 cm, 25°C,, W - A - (G)

The green knife fish, *Eigenmannia virescens*. Photo by H. J. Richter.

60 cm	25 °C	W-A (G)

Home: Central and South America.

Undemanding twilight animal that in its youth is suited for the aquarium. Built somewhat similarly to the preceding species, but with banded pattern.

The considerably smaller, but more aggressive species *Steatogenys elegans* is of very similar appearance.

Sternarchella schottii STEINDACHNER, 1868 (Flagfin Knife Fish) 22 cm, 25°C, W - (G)

22 cm	25 °C	W-(G)

Home: Upper Amazon, Rio San Francisco.

Has a pennant-like extended dorsal fin that can be laid into a furrow in the center of the back. Anal and tail fins do not run one into another. Softly clay-colored to brownish.

Similarly shaped is the *Apteronotus albifrons*, The ghost knife fish, growing to 50 cm in length. It is solid black, sometimes with two ivory-colored vertical bands on the caudal peduncle.

Electrophoridae (Electric eels)

The electric eel, *Electrophorus electricus* (LINNE, 1766), is familiar from display aquaria. The almost featureless eel-like fish grows to 2.5 m in length. It lives throughout large areas of South America in small rivers, ditches, and creeks. Electric eels have an electric organ of modified muscle fibers that can develop a charge of up to 800 volts.

233

The electrical shocks kill or paralyze their prey and repel stronger opponents.

Care: In aquaria, electric eels may be fed lean warm-blooded animal or fish meat. They require soft or medium-hard water with temperatures around 25°C.

CYPRINOIDEI (CARP-LIKE FISHES)
Cyprinidae (Minnows, Barbs, and Carps)

Distributed almost world wide (except tropical America and Australia-New Zealand) this fish family is very rich in species, with about 1250 described. Characteristic of these fishes are heavy pharyngeal teeth attached to the inner base of the gill arch supports, plus a Weberian apparatus like that of the tetras and catfishes.

To facilitate an overview over this large family, it is grouped into sub-families. The subfamilies of Cyprininae and Rasborinae in particular furnish many popular aquarium fishes. Their feeding poses no problem, since they will eat artificial as well as live foods. Their breeding also is usually not difficult.

Abraminae

These are typically inhabitants of temperate latitudes. Of aquarium interest are especially the Southeast Asian species of the genus *Chela*.
Chela

Fishes with relatively straight back line and a keeled, wide breast and convex belly line. Surface fishes reminiscent in general appearance of the South American hatchetfish.

The electric eel, *Electrophorus electricus*. Photo by K. Paysan.

Chela laubuca (HAMILTON-BU-CHANAN, 1822) (Indian Hatchetfish)
6 cm, 25°C, W - N - G - S

The Indian hatchetfish, *Chela laubuca*. Photo by B. Kahl.

6 cm	25°C	W-N-G-S

Home: Southeast Asia. Widely distributed in standing and running waters. Peaceful, lively, delicately transparent fish. Good jumpers!

Care: Will accept all foods, but only near the surface. For breeding, medium-hard water is sufficient. Twilight-spawner. Brood initially takes infusoria, but also finely ground dry food.

Other *Chela* species are occasionally imported that are to be kept in a similar manner.

Leucaspius

This genus includes a plain-looking little fish whose reproductive behavior is of particular interest:

Leucaspius delineatus (HECKEL, 1843)
8 cm, 19°C, N - H - S

8 cm	19°C	N-H-S

Home: Central and eastern Europe. Schooling fish in lakes and small rivers.

In the wild rarely grows up to 12 cm in length. Silvery iridescent with pronounced bluish iridescent lengthwise band. Distinguished from the similar looking *Alburnus alburnus* by the much shorter anal fin. Males slenderer and somewhat smaller than females.

Care: Peaceful, lively coldwater fish. Needs sufficient space for swimming about, but plant the sides of the aquar-

ium well! Accepts live and dry foods. No special water requirements. If the temperature exceeds 21°C, aeration may become necessary. Breeding fish must be wintered cold! For breeding, use three or four pairs. Put reed stems into the water! Female deposits string of eggs in a spiral around the stems, and the male cares for the brood. He keeps the stems moving by fanning them and covers the eggs with body slime that inhibits the development of bacteria.

The scales were used in the past for the manufacture of artificial pearls.

Cyprininae

Subfamily very rich in species, with fishes of the most different origins. Almost all species are omnivorous and equally unproblematic in their other requirements. The sexes usually can be recognized without difficulty by the sturdier body shape of the females. If sexual dimorphism is present, it is mentioned in the description of the species.

For breeding and raising use soft to medium-hard water. The eggs are dispersed between water plants and receive no care from the parents. Spawn-eaters! The raising of the brood, which swims free after two to four days, succeeds without problems since they usu-

ally eat *Artemia* nauplii or strained small cyclops right from the beginning; many will also accept soaked, finely ground dry food.

Balantiocheilos

This includes only *B. melanopterus,* the bala shark, a species from the flowing waters of Southeast Asia. In the wild it grows to 35 cm in length, so, since it is a fast swimmer, it is only suitable for the really large home aquarium, especially since they should be kept in a school. Otherwise, single fish may annoy other inhabitants of the aquarium. Peaceful and easily satisfied. Attractive because of its simple colors (body gray, fins gray or yellow with black edge). Likes ˙to jump. Cover! In a sufficiently large tank, breeding should be possible.

Barbus

To put some order into the abundance of these species, an attempt has been made to group the fishes of this genus according to the number of their barbels and some other characteristics:

1. *Barbus:* Four barbels on the upper jaw, scales (60 - 70 per lengthwise row);
2. *Barbodes:* Four barbels on the upper jaw, larger scales (25 - 50 per lengthwise row);
3. *Capoeta:* Two barbels on the upper jaw, large scales (fewer than 30 per lengthwise row);
4. *Puntius:* No barbels, large scales (rarely more than 30 per lengthwise row).

According to several modern workers in the group this scheme of genera is neither practical nor does it indicate accurately degrees of relationship. Therefore, we are following the tradition of recognizing a single genus, *Barbus*, especially since the division into four genera is of no help to the aquarist, anyway, as barbels are difficult to count.

The species inhabit predominantly the tropical zones of the Old World. Among them are a multitude of companionable little fishes that are excellently suited for being kept in the aquarium. They should be kept by species in a school, *i.e.*, at least six to eight individuals. Their food and water requirements are usually minimal.

Barbus arulius (JERDON, 1849) (Longfin Barb)
12 cm, 23°C, W - N - G - S

12 cm	23 °C	W-N-G-S

Home: Southern and southeastern India.

Large-scaled fish, beautifully blue-shimmering. Older male with dark red dorsal fin whose rays extend far beyond the edge.

Care: Well suited for planted community tank, but without too delicate plants! Shelters of roots. Males in spawning season with spawning tubercles in the region of the snout (small white pimples). Breeding not very productive.

Barbus barilioides BOULENGER, 1914
6 cm, 21°C, W - G - S

6 cm	21°C	W-G-S

Home: Plant-rich rivers in Angola, Zambia, and southern Zaire.

Barbus arulius, the longfin barb. Photo by H. J. Richter.

The small, elongated fish is rust-red all over its body and its fins, marked with 12-15 dark blue or black vertical lines. Male smaller.

Care: For breeding use neutral, soft water (to 3°DH), temperature 24 - 26°C. Immediately after swimming free, young fish will eat brine shrimp and cyclops nauplii.

Barbus bimaculatus (BLEEKER, 1864)
7 cm, 25°C, W - N - S - G

7 cm	25°C	W-N-S-G	

Home: Rivers in Sri Lanka.

Characteristic are two black spots, one at the base of the dorsal fin, another at the beginning of the tail fin. Male with wide red lengthwise stripe. Large-scaled species.

Care: Well-planted tanks with hiding opportunities. Keep not too bright. Like to swim, often shy. A peaceful fish that occasionally attacks tender water plants. In that case, add blanched lettuce, frozen spinach, or similar items.

Barbus conchonius (HAMILTON- BU-CHANAN, 1822) (Rosy Barb)
8 cm, 22°C, W - N - G - S

8 cm	22°C	W-N-G-S	

Home: Running and standing waters in northern India. Attains lengths of up to 15 cm!

Recognized by a black spot on the forward part of the tail. At spawning time, males bright red on chest and abdomen. Beautiful fish, in addition totally undemanding and peaceful.

Care: Even beginners may succeed with breeding at the first try. Spawning takes place in small tanks stocked with plants. If possible, use a spawning grid or trap since the parents are spawn-eaters. Breeding temperature 23 - 24°C. Remove parents after spawning. Brood

Barbus bimaculatus. Photo by J. Vierke.

swims free after about six days and can be raised with ground tubifex or dry food.

Barbus cumingi (GUENTHER, 1868)
 5 cm, 25°C, W - G - S

| 5 cm | 25°C | W-G-S |  |

Home: Mountain forest rivers in Sri Lanka.

Distinguished by the two black vertical bands, of which the front one is longer. Dorsal fin with delicate black marking.

Care: For breeding use soft water (to 5° noncarbonate hardness, at most 1° carbonate hardness). Young grow rapidly.

Barbus everetti BOULENGER, 1894 (Clown Barb)
 10 cm, 26°C, W - N - G - S

| 10 cm | 26°C | W-N-G-S |  |

Home: Malayan Peninsula, Borneo.

Irregular blue-black spots on its sides, fins red.

A spawning pair of *Barbus conchonius,* the rosy barb. Photo by H. J. Richter.

Care: Lively schooling fish for not too small aquariums. For breeding, larger tanks are necessary. Soft water!

Very similar in habits and care is *B. dunckeri.*

Barbus gelius (HAMILTON-BUCHAN-AN, 1822) (Dwarf Barb)
 4 cm, 21°, W - S - G

| 4 cm | 21°C | W-S-G | |

Home: India.

Schooling fish of over-grown bank zones. Remaining small, with distinctive body spots.

Care: Suitable only for combination with other delicate forms. Stick their adhesive eggs to the undersides of water plant leaves. Use only fully matured fish for breeding. Raising is possible with dampened, ground dry food.

239

Barbus lateristriga CUVIER and VALENCIENNES, 1842 (T-Barb)
  12 cm, 25°C, W - N - S - (G)

| 12 cm | 25°C | W-N-S-(G) |  |

Home: Southeast Asia.

Has one or two vertical bands in the front of the body and on the caudal peduncle has a lengthwise stripe.

Care: A rapidly growing fish that becomes large (in the wild up to 20 cm!), so only suited for really large aquaria and similar fellow inhabitants!

Barbus nigrofasciatus GUENTHER, 1868 (Black Ruby Barb)
  6 cm, 24°C, W - N - S - G

| 6 cm | 24°C | W-N-S-G | |

Home: Sri Lanka.

A deep-bodied barb that is widely known in aquaria. Peaceful, very undemanding schooling fish. At the time of reproduction, the males are bright crimson red in the front, smoky black in the rear, and moss-green on the back.

Care: The tank should not stand in too much light and should be densely planted in part. As hiding places, give floating plants. Breeding not difficult in spring if the fish have been wintered at cool temperatures (15 - 18°C).

Barbus oligolepis (BLEEKER, 1853) (Checker Barb)
  5 cm, 23°C, W - N - S - G

| 5 cm | 23°C | W-N-S-G | 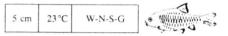 |

Checkered barbs, *Barbus oligolepis*. Photo by B. Kahl.

Home: Sumatra.

Very undemanding, peaceful fish. Male mother-of-pearl colored, shiny, with black fin edges.

Care: Like *B. nigrofasciatus*. Stocked in pairs for breeding. Prefer to spawn on finely branched plants. Raising problem-free.

Barbus pentazona (BOULENGER, 1894) (Five-banded Barb)

5.5 cm, 25 °C, W - N - S - G

5,5 cm	25°C	W-N-S-G	

Home: Southeast Asia.

Several slightly different subspecies. In addition to an eye stripe and a stripe directly at the beginning of the tail fin, they have three black vertical body bands on a reddish body color.

Barbus schwanenfeldi BLEEKER, 1853 (Tinfoil Barb)

20 cm, 24 °C, W - N - S - (G)

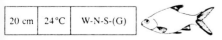

20 cm	24°C	W-N-S-(G)	

Home: Southeast Asia.

High-bodied, attains lengths of up to 35

The tinfoil barb, *Barbus schwanenfeldi*, possible the largest barb kept in the home aquarium. Photo by B. Kahl.

cm in the wild. Usually only young fish are offered for sale. However, they grow very quickly and are, therefore, not suitable for small aquaria. Adults are magnificent show animals, with attractive red fins.

Barbus semifasciolatus GUENTHER, 1868 (Half-striped Barb)

8 cm, 22 °C, N - S - G

8 cm	22°C	N-S-G	

Home: Southeastern China.

Shimmering metallic yellow body with about six not particularly strongly defined vertical bands of differing lengths. Reddish fins.

Care: Very undemanding species. The temperature may vary between 16 and 26 °C. Breeding not difficult if the breeding tank is sufficiently large.

241

The light orange color variety called "*B. schuberti*" is viewed as a mutation of this species. It lacks the vertical bands, instead having several irregular black dots and spots.

Barbus tetrazona (BLEEKER, 1855) (Tiger Barb)

7 cm, 24 °C, S - G

| 7 cm | 24 °C | S-G | 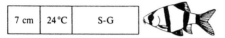 |

Home: Southest Asia.

One of the most popular aquarium fish, often also called the Sumatra barb. There are two subspecies (often considered full species), the nominate form, *B. t. tetrazona*, originates in Sumatra and has, in addition to the eye band and the band at the beginning of the tail fin, two vertical black body bands. The lower half of the dorsal fin is black. Very similarly colored is *B. t. partipentazona* from Thailand, whose dorsal fin markings encroach on the body and show the beginnings of a band anteriorly, not a full band.

There is also an albino color variety with red eyes, an iridescent green color form (the moss-green tiger), and other recently developed color forms.

Care: Lively, sociable fish that have only minimal requirements. They like roomy, well-planted tanks. When combining with other fishes, consider that they occasionally annoy larger, less agile fish very much by fin nipping!

Soft water for breeding.

Barbus ticto (HAMILTON-BUCHANAN, 1822) (Tick-tac-toe Barb)

6 cm, 24 °C, W - N - S - G

| 6 cm | 24 °C | W-N-S-G |  |

Home: India to Burma.

Hardy, lively fish. Grows up to 10 cm in the wild. Characteristics are two black body spots, one directly behind the gill

Odessa barbs, thought by some to be a color variety of *Barbus ticto*. Photo by B. Kahl.

Cherry barbs, *Barbus titteya*. Photo by R. Zukal.

cover and one at the base of the tail. Dorsal fin in the male spotted. There are two races: the nominate *B. t. ticto* originates in Sri Lanka and India and is not very clearly distinguishable from *B. t. stoliczkae* in Burma.

The "Odessa barb" is often considered to be a color form of this species, though the spotted ventral fins make this doubtful. In their display coloration, the male shows a rough-edged wide deep red lateral stripe, the two body spots having faded.

Barbus titteya (DERANIYAGALA, 1929) (Cherry Barb)

5 cm, 24 °C, W - N - S - G

5 cm	24°C	W-N-S-G	

Home: Sri Lanka.

Males at spawning time strong violet-red, females with light black-edged lengthwise body stripe. There are racially caused differences in the degree of the red coloration.

Care and Breeding: Like *B. bimaculatus*. Stocked in pairs, not very productive. Spawn-eaters.

Barilius

Surface-dwelling fishes, seldom seen in the aquarium, which are distinguished by their torpedo-like shape and a very large mouth.

Barilius christyi BOULENGER, 1920 (Copper-nosed minnow)

13 cm, 23 °C, W - S - (G)

13 cm	23°C	W-S-(G)	

Home: Congo region.

Elegant, rapidly swimming schooling fish of almost salmon-like shape. The sides are covered with 10 - 18 narrow vertical lines. The number of lines is supposed to increase with age. On the snout there is a striking copper-red spot.

Care: As a surface fish, it accepts food mostly on the surface. Soft water!

Barilius neglectus STIELER, 1907

7 cm, 22 °C, N - G - S

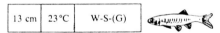

7 cm	22°C	N-G-S	

243

Two of the great many aquarium forms of the goldfish, *Carassius auratus*. Photo by B, Kahl.

Home: Japanese islands.

Undemanding surface fish. More compact than *B. christyi*. Plain colored with shining silvery lengthwise band edged above and below with narrow blue lines.

Care: May be wintered 15 - 18 °C. For breeding, about 23 °C. Very productive.

Caecobarbus

Represented by the Congo blind barb, *C. geertsi*, which lives in the subterranean waters of Thysville in Zaire. This 10 cm long fish is, like the cave tetra, blind and unpigmented. It looks pale silvery-pink, has long barbels, and is easily distinguished from the cave tetra by lacking the adipose fin.

Care: Keep at 21 °C. Has not been imported for a long time!

Carassius (Goldfishes)

A genus closely related to the carps (*Cyprinus*), but distinguished by lacking barbels. Goldfishes are at home in Europe and northern Asia and occur there predominantly in standing or slowly flowing, small waters. Extremely tough and self-sufficient.

Carassius auratus (LINNE, 1758) (Goldfish)

About 20 cm, 18°C, N - S - A

ca. 20cm	18 °C	N-S-A	

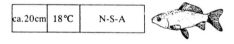

The presumed original form of the goldfish, *C. auratus gibelio*, is widely distributed throughout Europe and Asia. The Chinese have bred and kept goldfish and their varieties for more than 1000 years. Goldfish are less pond fish than are carp, but they, too, were originally bred for being viewed from above, not from the side, as they were kept formerly in clay bowls, wooden buckets, etc.

There are many sometimes very grotesque varieties of goldfish, several with doubled tail and anal fins: veiltails (roundish body, strongly enlarged downward flowing fins); "egg" fish (round body, without dorsal fin, short tail fin); comet (with single, but extremely elongated tail fin); celestials (like egg fish, but with upward directed, ball-like protruding eyes); lionhead (like egg fish, but with blisterlike growths on the head. There are many other color forms. First-rate breeding fish are very valuable, and there are even international guidelines for judging! Animals disadvantaged in swimming or looking for food — this applies to most egg-shaped or long-finned varieties, are best kept separated from more active forms.

Care: Most advantageously kept several specimens in a roomy dedicated tank. "Goldfish bowls" are unsuitable! Coldwater fish that will tolerate higher temperatures. If kept indoors, heating is not necessary even in winter. If kept in ponds, keeping is more or less danger-free in winter only in sufficiently deep ponds (at least 90 cm water depth). It is better to bring the animals into a cool, frost-free room (basement, in tub or vat) for wintering. At temperatures of less than 10°C, the fish will no longer take food, and continued feeding would spoil the water. The egg-shaped and long-finned varieties are not suited for keeping in ponds in cool climates. They are more sensitive and need minimum temperatures of about 15°C.

Breeding occurs in roomy, densely planted tanks in temperatures around 22°C. Spawn-eaters! In commercial breeding farms the eggs and sperm are obtained by milking the parents and artificially fertilizing the eggs. Young initially dark in color. In ponds, breeding often succeeds all by itself. However, sensible breeding is only possible with a careful selection among the often only second- or third-class fish.

Cyprinus (Carp)

This genus contains the common carp and its varieties plus a couple of doubtfully placed poorly known species. They are sociable bottom animals with two pairs of barbels and are active mostly at twilight. The genus is Eurasian in distribution.

Cyprinus carpio LINNE, 1758 (Carp and Koi)

25 cm, 18°C, N - H - S - (A)

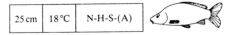

25 cm	18°C	N-H-S-(A)	

Some of the many color patterns of koi, *Cyprinus carpio*. Photo by Dr. Herbert R. Axelrod.

Skin-head barbs, Cyclocheilichthys apogon.
Photo by J. Elias.

Home: Mainly in southeast Europe and central and eastern Asia; in Japan bred for centuries as colorful pond fish.

Modestly useful foodfish that in the wild may attain lengths of 120 cm. Wild carp are elongated but cultivated varieties may be built sturdier and may have reduced but enlarged scales (mirror carp) or almost completely lack scales (leather carp). The original Japanese colored carp, koi, like the wild carp, are relatively long- bodied with regular, complete scaling. Selective breeding in Japan led to the modern koi, of which first-class examples are extremely expensive!

Care: Japanese koi are not aquarium fish! They are bred for decorative ponds, and their beauty is judged by the Japanese connoisseurs from above (in top view). Depending on the breeding goals, a particular type of color is significant. The keeping of koi in ponds in climates colder than that of Japan is difficult inasmuch as the wintering of the fish must take place in separate containers (tubs or such in the basement). A decorative carp pond must not freeze over! The temperatures should remain constant between 16 - 20°C. For keeping in ponds, goldfish are much better suited to cold latitudes. The keeping of decorative carp in aquaria makes sense only in large display aquaria.

Cyclocheilichthys

Of this genus, the skin-head barb (*Cyclocheilichthys apogon*) occasionally turns up in our tanks as young fish. In Southeast Asia and Indonesia it is a popular food fish. They have 10 - 12 rows of black spots on the side and a black spot at the base of the tail, a difference from *Rasborichthys altior*, which is often confused with this species but remains smaller. Grows up to 50 cm long and in the long run is suitable only for large display aquaria.

Labeo (Sharks)

A genus rich in species that are at home in Africa and tropical Asia. The fish are distinguished by large fins often differing in color from the body. The dorsal fin and the deeply forked tail fin usually are strongly developed. The curved back line and the almost straight abdominal profile, as well as the undershot mouth, mark the fish as bottom-feeders. Nevertheless, the fish like to swim. The mouth is surrounded by protruding lips and most often two pairs of barbels, of which a movable pair is in front of the nostril and is often spread toward the front.

Care: Most species grow quite large and are, therefore, only conditionally suited for keeping in the aquarium. All *Labeo* species need larger tanks well provided with hiding places. Smaller specimens usually get along quite well with each other, but with increasing age they may turn into real brawlers. Defeated fish are ceaselessly chased and find no rest. It is best to acquire only a single fish right from the outset. The chances for breeding success with *Labeo* species are only minimal anyway.

Morulius species are closely related to *Labeo*, but their dorsal fin begins farther in front. *M. chrysophekadion* (the black shark) is solid black on the body and fins and are provided with an especially large dorsal fin; it is often offered for sale. Only young are suited for the normal aquarium, since they grow to 60 cm! Rapid growth! Individual care as for *Labeo!*

Labeo ansorgii BOULENGER, 1907
    10 cm, 25°C, W - G

10 cm	25°C	W-G

The magnificent red tailed black shark, *Labeo bicolor.* Photo by B. Kahl.

Home: West Africa.

A rarely imported species with tall, delta-shaped dorsal fin and deeply forked tail fin. Black-brown with shimmering silvery scale edges. Fins colorless.

The other African species sometimes imported grow large. *L. weeksii* thus reaches an overall length of 25 cm, and *L. forskalii* grows to 40 cm in length. These fishes are unsuitable for keeping in the aquarium since, besides being too large and quarrelsome, they are also plainly colored.

Labeo bicolor SMITH, 1931 (Red Tailed Black Shark)

12 cm, 26°C, W - N - G

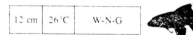

12 cm	26°C	W-N-G

Home: Rivers and lakes of southern Thailand.

Because of its attractive coloration, this is one of the more popular aquarium fishes. When in good health, it is colored velvet-black and has a bright red tail fin. However, not all specimens develop the deep black color.

Care: Usually kept only as individuals, in very large tanks rich in hiding places four to five fish can possibly be kept. In small aquaria many older individuals annoy fishes of other species with constant chases. In very large aquaria they sometimes spawn. However, consistent breeding successes have not been reported thus far.

Labeo erythrurus FOWLER, 1937 (Rainbow Shark)

12 cm, 25°C, W - N - G

12 cm	25°C	W-N-G

Home: Eastern Thailand.

More elongated than *L. bicolor*. The body color may range from light gray-brown to almost black. All fins deep red. Anal fin with broad deep black outside edge. A black spot at the root

The rather mis-named green shark, *Labeo frenatus*. Photo by R. Zukal.

of the red tail fin often extends into the fin. Often confused with *L. frenatus*.

Thus far, breeding successes have not been reported.

Labeo frenatus FOWLER, 1934 (Green Shark)

8 cm, 25°C, W - N - G

8 cm	25°C	W-N-G	

Home: Eastern Thailand.

Smaller than *L. erythrurus*. There is a strong resemblance between the two species, but *L. frenatus* is somewhat more round-bellied and thus appears more compact. The dark edge on the anal fin is only weakly developed. The black spot in the root of the tail fin does not extend into the actual fin, which, by the way, is often very large and deeply split.

Breeding has been successful. The fish deposit the spawn on a previously cleaned spot on the bottom.

Osteochilus

Food fishes distributed throughout

Osteocheilus spilopterus, a hard-lipped barb. Photo by A. Norman.

southeastern Asia that are little suited for the average aquarium because of their size. Occasionally *O. hasselti*, the hard−lipped barb, which grows to 30 cm, can be seen. It is attractively colored when young, every body scale being spotted with brown-red on its base, with a resulting loose row of dots. The fins are yellowish to red and sometimes have dark edges. They are sociable fish that like to move and range along the bottom looking for food. Their lips form a strong scraping apparatus with which they can nibble off algae.

Care: Show animals for large aquaria. Breeding in captivity unsuccessful as yet. Are said to spawn in rapidly flowing rivers in the wild.

Leuciscinae

Mostly elongated Cyprinidae with a short anal fin base (8 - 11 divided rays) that begins behind the dorsal fin; dorsal fin short; no barbels (exception: *Tinca*).

Many of our small native "minnows" such as *Chrosomus* and *Notropis* belong here, as do the European *Leuciscus* and *Phoxinus* species, *Scardinius erythrophthalmus*, and the larger food fishes *Tinca tinca* and *Chondrostomus nasus*. *Chrosomus erythrogaster* is especially recommended.

Leuciscus

A genus widely distributed throughout Eurasia, with small and medium-sized fishes. At aquarium shows in Europe the species frequently found are *L. leuciscus*, *L. rutilus*, and the larger *L. cephalus*. When young, the fish live in schools. However, older specimens tend to remain solitary.

Leuciscus idus (LINNE, 1758) (Chub, Orfe)

40 cm, 18°C, N - S

A European fish that in exceptional circumstances grows to 75 cm in length. An important food fish, especially in eastern Europe. In the wild, xanthistic (yellow) varieties appear occasionally, being called golden orfes. These forms, red-gold on top becoming lighter on the underside, are often used for stocking garden ponds and decorative fountains. An agile fish that likes to swim at the surface. Hardy.

Care: Young are well suited for the unheated room aquarium. Like to jump; well-covered container. Not too small aquarium, since they like to swim! At spawning time, males with spawning tubercles feed on insect larvae, but also other live and artificial foods.

Phoxinus

A genus of small schooling fishes distributed through North America and Europe.

Phoxinus phoxinus (LINNE, 1758) (Dace)

10 cm, 19°C, N - H - S

Home: Running waters and lakes of Europe.

About 15 dark, not sharply edged

Leuciscus idus. Photo by B. Kahl.

vertical stripes on the back. Lively, peaceful fish. Females larger and plumper, males more intensely colored. At spawning time, both sexes show spawning tubercles. Parents are egg-eaters. Raising of young not difficult.

Care: Good for cold-water tank. Undemanding, omnivorous. Needs open swimming space.

Brachydanio albolineatus Photo by B. Kahl

Rhodeinae (Bitterlings)

Eurasian subfamily distinguished by a long, fairly far forward anal fin. Closely related to the rasboras, since experimental crossbreedings resulted in fertile offspring.

Included in this subfamily is the bitterling (*Rhodeus sericeus*), whose home is in Europe and Asia Minor, a most interesting small fish with regard to its behavior but which also is quite attractively colored.

Rasborinae

Slender, often strikingly colored small fishes that are excellently suited for the tropical aquarium. Best-known are the *Brachydanio* and *Rasbora* species.

Brachydanio

Slender schooling fishes originating in southern and southeastern Asia that are always on the move. Very peaceful, but should not be combined with quiet, sedentary species. Undemanding in their care as far as diet and water conditions are concerned. However, need sufficient open swimming space.

Brachydanio albolineatus (BLYTH, 1860) (Pearl Danio)

6 cm, 24°C, W - N - S - G

6 cm	24°C	W-N-S-G	

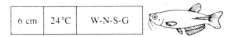

Home: Burma, Thailand, Malaysia, and Sumatra in brightly lit running waters.

251

Body bluish iridescent, with pale orange stripe on the posterior part of body, becoming wider toward the tail fin and edged in blue on both sides. Males colored more intensely, slimmer.

Care: Undemanding. Breeding simple. For spawning, small glass tanks with a water level of about 10 cm and a temperature of 24 - 28°C are sufficient. Put floating water plants into the breeding tank. Remove parent animals after spawning. Young grow rapidly, may be raised even on finely ground dry food.

Brachydanio kerri SMITH, 1931
(Kerr's Danio)
5 cm, 24°C, W - N - S - G

| 5 cm | 24 °C | W-N-S-G |

Home: Jungle rivers on islands off the western coast of southern Thailand.

Depending on the angle of light, iridescent in different bluish shades. One or two delicate orange lateral bands that are especially distinct in the rear half of the body.

Care: Undemanding, lively fish that resembles the pearl danio in care and breeding.

Brachydanio nigrofasciatus (DAY, 1869)
(Spotted Danio)
4 cm, 26°C, W - N - S - G

| 4 cm | 26 °C | W-N-S-G |

Home: Lakes and rivers of Burma.

Very peaceful and undemanding species that remains small. Below a dark blue lateral stripe are several spots of the same color. This species is not always easy to breed and is not very productive. Pronounced spawn-eaters!

Brachydanio rerio (HAMILTON-BUCHANAN , 1822) (Zebra)
6 cm, 22°C, W - N - S - G

| 6 cm | 22 °C | W-N-S-G |

Home: Eastern India and Bangladesh.

The zebra is at the same time the most popular and least problematical aquarium fish that is very effective in a lively school. Distinguished by four dark blue lengthwise bands on a silvery to gold ground extending into the tail fin.

Care: Breeds simply. Egg laying can take place in the fully established tank, all the fish in the school spawning. After spawning, remove breeders, since they are spawn-eaters. To keep from losing too many eggs during spawning, the bottom should be covered with fine-leaved plants or a spawning grid. Course gravel is also very suitable, since the eggs that drop between the pebbles cannot be reached by the adults. Zebras like to spawn after a rise in temperature of several degrees, preferably in the early morning when the sun shines. Productive. Raising of the young possible even with finely ground dry food. Rapid growth.

The leopard danio, *B. frankei*, is characterized by a great number of black spots all over its body. Its status is uncertain. Some authors assume that it is a variety of *B. rerio* or *B. nigrofasciatus*, some a hybrid of *B. nigrofasciatus* and another species, and others believe it to be a valid species. It can be kept and bred much like the zebra.

Danio

In habits and behavior, these Indian fishes strongly resemble *Brachydanio*

Danio aequipinnatus. Photo by B. Kahl.

(some authors have suggested that Brachydanio is a synonym). However, they differ by a larger dorsal fin. While the *Brachydanio* species have only 7 - 9 fin rays, the species of the genus *Danio* usually have 12 - 18 rays in the dorsal fin. In *Danio* the lateral line is complete, while it is incomplete or absent in *Brachydanio*. Generally, the *Danio* species also grow markedly larger.

Danio aequipinnatus (McCLELLAND, 1839) (Giant Danio)

10 cm, 24°C, S - G - W - N

10 cm	24 °C	S-G-W-N

Home: Southwestern coast (Malabar coast) of the Indian subcontinent, in clear, flowing and standing waters.

Resembles in color *D. devario,* but the lengthwise stripes in the rear half of the body begin far in front of the start of the dorsal fin. Markedly slenderer than *D. devario*. In open waters will grow to 15 cm in length. Males slim-

mer than females. Formerly called *D. malabarica*.

Care: Breeding like *D. devario*. Easy.

Danio devario (HAMILTON-BUCHANAN, 1822) (Bengal Danio)

10 cm, 24°C, S - G - W - N

10 cm	24 °C	S-G-W-N

Home: Northwestern provinces of India (Orissa, Bengal, and Assam).

The females are strikingly deep-bodied and thus are reminiscent of *Chela* species. In its markings, the species resembles *D. aequipinnatus* but has duller colors. Behind the gill covers there are indistinct vertical bands that continue below the dorsal fin as two blue lengthwise bands, of which one bends upward and extends into the upper lobe of the tail fin. Males slimmer than females.

Care: Not too small breeding tanks! Temperature for breeding raised by 2 - 3°C. Spawning usually takes place at dawn.

Danio regina (FOWLER, 1934)
10 cm, 24°C, S - G - W - N

10 cm	24°C	S-G-W-N	

Home: Southern Thailand.

Resembles *D. aequipinnatus*, but has no vertical bands on the front of its body, instead having a typical black-blue spot immediately behind the gill covers.

Care and Breeding: As for the other species of *Danio* and *Brachydanio*.

Esomus (Flying Barbs)

Flying barbs have a pair of unusually long barbels that extend rearward as far as the middle of the abdomen. They have large, wing-like pectoral fins by means of which they can actively fly, like hatchetfish. In the air they make an audible humming noise with their whirling pectoral fins. The fish have a *Rasbora*-like shape and a dark lengthwise body stripe that is edged above with a shining yellowish or orange stripe. They must be kept in a tightly covered aquarium.

Esomus danrica (HAMILTON-BUCHANAN, 1822) (Flying Barb)
8 cm, 24°C, G - S - W - N

8 cm	24°C	G-S-W-N	

Home: Surface fish in the ditches and pools of Southeast Asia. Will grow

to 14 cm in length.

Males slenderer, with more vivid coloration.

Care: No demands regarding food. For breeding, use long, low containers partially covered with floating plants. Soft water, slightly acid. Temperature slightly raised. Spawn-eaters. Productive. Larvae hatch after about 16 hours. Young fish swim free after another two to three days.

Similar guidelines apply to the species *E. lineatus*, originating from the region of the Ganges estuary.

Esomus malayensis (MANDEE, 1909) (Malayan Flying Barb)
8 cm, 25°C, G - S - W - N

8 cm	25°C	G-S-W-N	

Home: Thailand, Malayan Peninsula.

Lengthwise band pronounced only in the rear half of the body. It ends in a deep black spot, edged with golden-red, on the base of the tail.

Care and Breeding: Like *Esomus danrica*.

Rasbora (Rasboras)

This fish genus from tropical Asia can be subdivided into two groups. The first group, including such species as *R. daniconus* and *R. borapetensis*, represents a type of slender, very lively fishes that in their home occur predominantly in open, often running waters. In the aquarium they need sufficient open swimming room and prefer soft, slightly acid water. *R. heteromorpha* is rather typical of the other group, to which also belong *R. hengeli*, *R. maculata*, *R. somphongsi*, *R. nigromarginata*, *R. vaterifloris*, among others. They are compact, less rapidly swimming fishes that come mostly from slowly flowing,

254

plant-rich waters of the virgin forest. These fish are more demanding as regards the water quality, especially during reproduction, of course. They like well-planted tanks that include dark areas.

Rasbora argyrotaenia (BLEEKER, 1850)(Silver Rasbora)
10 cm, 24°C, G - S - W - N

Home: Southeast Asia.
Daniconus-type. Shining silvery without further markings. Free edge of the tail fin dark. In the wild, attains lengths of up to 15 cm.
Care: Is only effective in a school in a large tank.

Rasbora borapetensis SMITH, 1934 (Redtailed Rasbora)
5 cm, 25°C, G - S - W - N

Home: Thailand, numerous everywhere in flowing waters.
Silvery, with a light-edged dark lengthwise band; red at the bases of the dorsal and tail fins. Undemanding. Females bigger, plumper than males. *R. sumatrana* looks strikingly similar but has an oblique black stripe in front of the pectoral fin.
Care: Breed in larger, not too bright tank (cover of floating plants). Spawneater. Raising not too difficult.

Rasbora daniconus (HAMILTON- BUCHANAN, 1822) (Golden-striped Rasbora)
15 cm, 25°C, G - S - W - N

Home: Southeast Asia, where it is found as several subspecies.
A particularly slender fish whose appearance resembles *R. borapetensis*, but grows larger and has no red in the fins.
Care: For breeding, stock in large tank at about 8°DH and 26°C. Right after hatching, the young will take brine shrimp nauplii.

Rasbora dorsiocellata DUNCKER, 1904 (Hi-spot Rasbora)
6 cm, 25°C, G - S - W - N

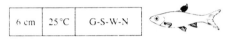

Home: Malaysia and Sumatra.
A species that will stay small. Has a dark white-edged spot in the dorsal fin.
Care: For breeding, the fish need dense tufts of fine-leaved plants.

Rasbora einthovenii (BLEEKER, 1851) (Brilliant Rasbora)
10 cm, 25°C, G - S - W - N

Home: Distributed throughout Southeast Asia and Indonesia.
An elongated, pointed-snout fish with an uninterrupted lengthwise body band from the tip of the snout to the center of the tail fin. Somewhat sensitive.

Rasbora elegans VOLZ, 1903 (Two-spot Rasbora, Elegant Rasbora)
13 cm, 25°C, G - S - W

Home: Southeast Asia, with several subspecies.
In the wild, to 20 cm. Characteristic

are two black spots, one at the beginning of the tail fin and the other in the middle of the body between the dorsal and abdominal fins. A dark stripe at the beginning of the anal fin.

Rasbora hengeli MEINKEN, 1956 (Hengel's Harlequin)
  3 cm, 25°C, G - S - W - N

3 cm	25°C	G-S-W-N	

Home: Sumatra.

Resembles the harlequin, *R. heteromorpha*, but has a smaller dark wedge.

Rasbora heteromorpha DUNCKER, 1904 (Harlequin, The Rasbora)
  4.5 cm, 25°C, G - S - W - N

4.5 cm	25°C	G-S-W-N	
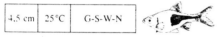

Home: Malayan Peninsula, Sumatra.

Deep-bodied species. A heavy black wedge pointing to the base of the tail fin on a reddish base.

Care: Well-planted aquarium with soft or medium-hard water (the fish live in shady, plant-rich zones of virgin forest rivers and in cultivated land). For breeding soft, slightly acid water and broad- leafed plants. Stocking in pairs. Females plumper. The female attaches its eggs to the underside of the leaves in a supine position while being embraced by the male. Remove parents after spawning. The young hatch after 24 hours, swim free after 5 days. Raising possible with *Artemia* nauplii.

Rasbora kalochroma (BLEEKER, 1850) (Big-spot Rasbora)
  5 cm, 27°C, G - S - W

5 cm	27°C	G-S-W	

Rasbora kalochroma. Photo by B. Kahl.

Rasbora trilineata. Photo by B. Kahl.

Home: Malaysia to Borneo.

An elongated fish colored a beautiful red. Lively without appearing hectic. Two black body spots are characteristic, the first lying obliquely above and behind the base of the pectoral fin, the second above the beginning of the anal fin.

Rasbora maculata DUNCKER, 1904 (Dwarf Rasbora)
2.5 cm, 25°C, (G) - S - W

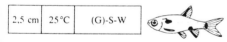

2,5 cm	25°C	(G)-S-W

Home: India to Malaysia and Sumatra.

Body base color red, with three black spots: one in the center of the body, one above the beginning of the anal fin, and one at the base of the tail fin.

Care: Should be kept only with quiet, small fishes. Needs soft, possibly slightly acid water. Spawns above fine-leafed plants. Spawn-eaters! Initial feeding with infusoria. Rapid growth.

Rasbora trilineata STEINDACHNER, 1870 (Scissortailed Rasbora)
12 cm, 24°C, G - S - W - N

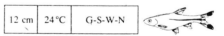

12 cm	24°C	G-S-W-N

Home: Sumatra and Borneo.

Silvery species that is striking because of its prominent tail fin markings: in both lobes, there is a blackish band in the outer third.

Care: For spawning, use a larger tank with fine-leaved plants. Not easy. Young will immediately eat *Artemia* nauplii.

Rasbora vaterifloris DERANIYA-GALA, 1930 (Singhalese Fire Barb)
4 cm, 24°C, G - S - W

4 cm	24°C	G-S-W

Epalzeorhynchus siamensis. Photo by J. Vierke.

is broadly edged with yellow toward the outside. In the White Cloud the dorsal can be edged with red or white. There is also a veil-finned mutation of the White Cloud.

Care: Completely undemanding fish for beginners, but should not be kept too warm! Spawns in plants. Breeding easy. Young will frequently grow up without the help of the keeper.

Home: Sri Lanka.

High-backed fish with relatively large vertical fins. Flanks iridescent, various colors. Males with reddish fins.

Breeding: To a darkened aquarium add fine-leaved plants. Spawn-eaters! Also from Sri Lanka comes *R. nigromarginata*, possibly a synonym.

Tanichthys

Home: Southeast China.

Slender, *Rasbora*-like fish.

Tanichthys albonubes LIN, 1932 (White Cloud Mountain Minnow)

4 cm, 20°C, G - S - N - H

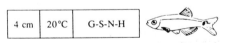

4 cm	20°C	G-S-N-H

Home: Mountain streams in the region around Canton and Hong Kong.

Lively schooling fish with black-brown lengthwise body band that is edged above with shiny gold. *Aphyocypris pooni* is similar, but its dorsal fin

Garrinae

Loach-like elongated carp-like fishes with the mouth area modified into a suction disc. Besides the genera *Discolabeo*, *Garra*, and *Mekongina*, the interesting genus *Epalzeorhynchus* belongs here.

Epalzeorhynchus (Flying Foxes)

Elongated fishes living near the bottom, with undershot mouth. Two species are known in the aquarium. There is nothing known yet about breeding in the aquarium.

Epalzeorhynchus kalopterus BLEEKER, 1850 (Flying Fox)

10 cm, 25°C, G - W - N

10 cm	25°C	G-W-N

Home: Sumatra and Borneo.

Grow up to 16 cm in length. Large-finned, peaceful species. Eats soft algae. Will accept live and dry food. With black- brown sharp-edged lengthwise band that is accompanied by a broad golden-yellow band on top.

Epalzeorhynchus siamensis SMITH, 1931 (Siamese Flying Fox)

10 cm, 24°C, G - W - N

10 cm	24°C	G-W-N

Home: Thailand and Malaysian Peninsula.

Resembles *E. kalopterus*, but lengthwise band with zig-zag edge anteriorly. The accompanying golden band is missing or poorly defined. Excellent algae eater. A peaceful fish that is especially recommended for the community tank.

Gyrinocheilidae (Chinese Algae-eaters)

Only one genus with few species belongs to this family. As an adaptation to the life in rapidly-flowing waters, the mouth area of these fish is transformed into a suction disc and water leaves the gills through a special opening.

Gyrinocheilus aymonieri (TIRANT, 1883) (Chinese Algae-eater)
    10 cm, 24°C, G - N

10 cm	24 °C	G-N

Home: Southeast Asia.
Grows to 25 cm in the wild. Long-lived, very easily satisfied. Young are algae eaters. Older specimens may occasionally annoy other fishes by "grooming," but in general a harmless, recommended species. Breeding as yet unsuccessful. The common name is inappropriate, as the fish does not come from China, but too familiar to change.

Homalopteridae (Hill-Stream Loaches)

Bottom-fishes from rapidly flowing small streams and rivers of the virgin forest rivers of Malaysia and Indonesia to Borneo and China. The often attractively brown-patterned *Homaloptera* species are usually very delicate to keep.

More interesting for the aquarium are the species of *Gastromyzon*, whose bodies are markedly flattened. Their pectoral and abdominal fins have been transformed into suction organs.

A. kuhlii sumatranus Photo by B. Kahl.

Cobitidae (Loaches)

Sociable bottom-fishes with undershot mouths. Distributed throughout Eurasia. Some species are provided with an erectable eye spine that doubtlessly serves as defense against fishes and snakes that want to eat them. The striking colors of many species may be interpreted as a warning signal. Loaches swallow air and absorb it through their intestines.

Acanthophthalmus (Coolie Loaches)

Home: Southeast Asia to Borneo.

Worm-shaped loaches which like to bury themselves in the substrate. The eyes are overgrown with a transparent skin (protection against injuries when digging in the bottom). Active at night and dusk. Eat foods that are found on top of or in the substrate.

Acanthophthalmus kuhlii (CUVIER & VALENCIENNES, 1846) (Coolie Loach)

8 cm, 25°C, G - W

Home: Malayan Peninsula, Borneo, and Sumatra.

This species has black-brown bands on a yellowish ground; the underside is light. A more coarsely patterned form occurs in Sumatra.

Breeding has been successful. Females plumper than males. The greenish eggs are expelled below the surface of the water.

Acanthophthalmus myersi HARRY, 1949 (Myers Coolie Loach, Slimy Myersi)

8 cm, 25°C, G - W

Home: Thailand.

Frequently imported species. The blackish body is covered by about ten narrow yellow or orange vertical bands.

Acanthophthalmus semicinctus FRASER-BRUNNER, 1940 (Half-banded Loach)

8 cm, 25°C, G - W

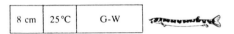

Home: Malaysia.

Upper body half with irregular vertical bands. The bands have the shape of triangles whose points end in the center of the side.

Acanthopsis

Southeast Asian genus with only one species in aquaria.

Acanthopsis choirorhynchus (BLEEKER, 1854) (Horse-faced Loach, Long-nosed Loach)

22 cm, 26C, G - W - N

Home: Southeast Asia to Borneo.

Hardy fish. Elongated, with strikingly long snout. Buries itself regularly into the substrate.

Care: No sharp-edged substrate material, no gravel! Set plants into culture pots. Filter needed! Breeding unknown.

Botia

Twilight-active, usually shy loaches. Usually hidden during the day. Often beautifully marked. Two-pronged spine below the eyes (take care when handling a fish!). Rapidly swimming fishes to be kept in a school. Sometimes quarrelsome. Require frequent water changes.

Botia hymenophysa (BLEEKER, 1852)
(Banded Loach)
   15 cm, 26°C, S - (G) - W - N

15 cm	26°C	S-(G)-W-N

Home: Southern and southeastern Asia.

A striped species that grows to more than 20 cm in the wild. Rather elongated, with deeply forked tailfin.

Botia macracantha (BLEEKER, 1852)
(Clown Loach)
   15 cm, 26°C, S - (G) - W - N

15 cm	26°C	S-(G)-W-N

Home: Sumatra and Borneo (here to 30 cm in length).

Grows slowly. Orange with three

Botia sidthimunki. Photo by J. Vierke

broad black vertical bars. Attractive schooling fish, but often quite shy. Omnivorous. Good-natured.

Botia sidthimunki KLAUSEWITZ, 1959 (Dwarf Loach)
   4 cm, 26C, S - G - W - N

4 cm	26°C	S-G-W-N

Home: Rivers in Thailand.

An attractive species that remains small. Checkerboard-like pattern of round pale spots on the upper side. Peaceful and not shy if kept in a school. Active during the day also.

Most highly recommended loach for the community tank.

Cobitis (Weatherfishes)

The best-known representative of this genus is the Eurasian *C. taenia*. An elongated, blunt-snouted bottom-fish with undershot mouth and barbels. It likes to bury itself in the substrate. Not colorful.

Care: Easy to keep in the cold-water aquarium (15 - 18°C). If in spring we put fully-grown fish into the aquarium, they will usually spawn.

Very similar in appearance are the Southeast Asian *Lepidocephalus* species as well as the Eurasian loach *Noemacheilus barbatus*, which also can be brought to spawning in a similar manner. The tropical Asian *Noemacheilus* species resemble in appearance and care the *Botia* species.

Siluriformes (Catfishes)

Catfishes are usually nocturnal or dusk feeders that live at the bottom. Of the almost 2000 known species, many are excellently suited for being kept in the aquarium.

Doradidae (Spiny Catfishes)

Home: Tropical South America.

Bottom-fishes of compact shape, armed with spiny bony plates, with one pair of upper jaw and two pairs of lower jaw whiskers.

Care: Undemanding, hardy even with temporary cooling. Like soft substrates, many species burying themselves deeply in the sand. Set aquarium plants in pots! Reproduction almost entirely unknown.

Amblydoras hancockii (CUVIER & VALENCIENNES, 1840)

15 cm, 25°C, G - W - N

15 cm	25°C	G-W-N	

Home: Central and northeastern South America.

Bizarrely shaped. The dorsal fin spine is smooth anteriorly and posteriorly, not serrated as in most other catfishes. When removed from the water, it utters growling noises.

Breeding unseccessful as yet. Parents are said to construct a nest of plant parts and to guard the eggs.

Amblydoras hancockii. Photo by B. Kahl.

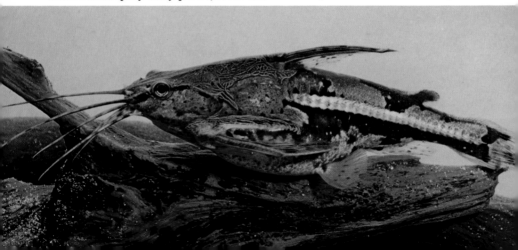

Platydoras costatus (LINNE, 1766)
(Chocolate Spiny Catfish)
24 cm, 25°C, G - W - N

24 cm	25°C	G-W-N

Home: Amazon and Guyana.
Attractive white markings on gray ground, especially in youth. Tail fin deeply forked and marked with gray-white. Undemanding.
Acanthodoras spinosissimus is of very similar appearance, distinguished by its rounded tail fin.

Siluridae
A catfish family distributed throughout Eurasia. Skin completely naked. Head broad, usually with two pairs of long barbels. Long anal fin, short or no dorsal fin.
Kryptopterus bicirrhis (CUVIER & VALENCIENNES, 1839) (Glass Catfish)
10 cm, 26°C, G - S - W

10 cm	26°C	G-S-W

Home: Southeast Asia.
Glass-like transparent body. Like to stay still in a school in open water.
Care: Must have sufficient open swimming space. Day-active. Will not take food from the bottom. Feed preferably live food!
Very similar is the species *K. macrocephalus*, originating on the Sunda Islands, which differs, however, by having numerous dark spots on the upper side.
Siluris glanis LINNE, 1758 (Wels)
3 m, 18°C, A - H

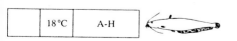

	18°C	A-H

This gigantic European catfish is a ravenous, night-hunting fish that grows to 3 m in length. Young fish can easily be kept in the cold-water aquarium. No demands regarding water and food. Rapid growth. Keep individually. Older animals are more difficult to care for.

Chacidae (Frogmouth Catfishes)
Tadpole-like catfishes with a very broad mouth. Only one genus (*Chaca*) with two barely distinguishable species ranging from India to the Greater Sunda Islands. Animals from Malaysia to Borneo look brown-red; the Indian form (*Chaca chaca*) is rather gray. *C. bankanensis* is the more common species. Eyes very wideset. Two barbels in the corners of the mouth that can be set into worm-like motion. When small fish try to grab this bait, they are eaten.
Care: Not a fish for the community aquarium! After adaptation, will also take tubifex and food pellets.

Pangasiidae
Home: Southeast Asia, widely dispersed.
Anal fin long, deeply-cut tail fin. Also lively during the day. Closely related with the equally day-active African family Schilbeidae.
Pangasius sutchi FOWLER, 1937 (Siamese Shark)
20 cm, 25°C, (G) - S - W - N

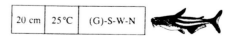

20 cm	25°C	(G)-S-W-N

Home: Central Thailand.
The iridescent silvery color makes this a popular species.
Care: No special water requirements, will take food of all kinds ,

sometimes even vegetarian food. Rapid growth with good diet. Only suitable for larger aquaria, so provide sufficient swimming space!

Clariidae

Home: Africa, tropical Asia.

Elongated, carnivorous fishes with elongated anal fin and four pairs of long barbels. Adipose fin lacking. Voracious fishes that are suitable only for the dedicated aquarium since they usually grow quite large. Undemanding in regard to water quality. Able to breathe air. This family includes among others the *Clarias* species (long dorsal fin, terminal mouth) and the genus *Heteropneustes* (short dorsal fin, mouth undershot).

Mochocidae

A purely African family with several genera. Head armored, body not armored. Species of the genus *Synodontis* are regularly offered for sale.

Synodontis (Upside-Down Catfishes)

Of the about 140 species, only a small number can be described here. Young animals are often marked differently than adult specimens. Many are characterized by their often root-like branched barbels and by an often strikingly large adipose fin. The tail fin is forked.

Peaceful, night-active fish, some of which frequently swim belly-up and rest in the same position. They like to draw together into small groups at night, therefore keep several if possible. Offer hiding places for day rest. Undemanding animals. Exact guidelines for reproduction and raising are missing. At least a few species lay their eggs while mouthbrooding cichlids are spawning, allowing the cichlid to brood the eggs.

Synodontis angelicus SCHILTHIUS, 1891 (Angelicus Catfish)
25 cm, 25°C, (G) - S - W - N

| 25 cm | 25 °C | (G)-S-W-N |

Home: Western and central Africa.

Beautiful species! Young fish colored violet with irregular white spots. The coloration fades in age. One variation shows, in addition to the spots, four or five wavy vertical stripes on its body.

Synodontis flavitaeniatus BOULENGER, 1906
12 cm, 25°C, G - S - W - N

| 12 cm | 25 °C | G-S-W-N |

Home: Tropical West Africa (where it attains about 20 cm in length).

Yellowish with irregularly wavy chocolate-brown lengthwise bands. Anal and dorsal fins with dark dots arranged in stripes.

Synodontis nigrita CUVIER & VALENCIENNES, 1840
22 cm, 25°C, G - S - W - N

| 22 cm | 25 °C | G-S-W-N |

Home: Northeastern and northwestern Africa.

Body irregularly dotted; fins, with the exception of the pectoral fins, striped at right angle to the direction of the rays. In older animals, the dotted pattern fades partly or entirely.

Synodontis nigriventis DAVID, 1936 (Blackbellied Upside-Down Catfish)
10 cm, 25°C, G - S - W - N

| 10 cm | 25 °C | G-S-W-N |

Home: Central Congo region.

Unobtrusively brownish with darker

Kryptopterus bicirrhis. Photo by B. Kahl.

spots. Despite the scientific name *"ni-griventis,"* the abdomen is not always dark. Often rests under leaves and roots with its abdomen turned upward.

Cave spawners caring for their brood. About four days after hatching, the young will eat artemia nauplii; they will assume their preferred upside-down position only after about ten weeks.

Synodontis notatus VAILLANT, 1893 (Black-dotted Upside-Down Catfish)

28 cm, 25°C, (S) - (G) - W - N

28 cm	25°C	(S)-(G)-W-N	

Home: Congo basin.

Basic coloration gray. Characteristic is a dark spot in the center of the body above the beginning of the pectoral fin. There may be several spots present. Frequently imported. Because of its size and digging habits, only suited for larger aquaria.

Pimelodidae

Tropical American species that usually grow large, with three pairs of bar-

265

bels, of which two pairs are on the lower jaw, one pair on the upper jaw. The latter may grow very long. Usually good swimmers.

Pimelodella

Slender, elongated fishes with long adipose fin base and deeply forked tail fin. The common aquarium species are all distinguished by a horizontal black band on the body. Good swimmers and relatively peaceful.

Pimelodella gracilis (CUVIER & VALENCIENNES, 1840) (Slender Pimelodella)
17 cm, 25°C, (G) - W - N

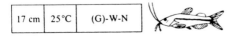

17 cm	25°C	(G)-W-N

Home: Eastern South America.
Lengthwise body band beginning at edge of the gill cover and becoming broader toward the back.
Care: Prefers shaded areas such as root shelters and dark substrates with good edge planting. Not very sensitive

Sorubim lima. Photo by J. Vierke.

about water composition. Omnivorous. Not too small fish for company!
Pimelodella lateristriga (MUELLER & TROSCHEL, 1849)
20 cm, 25°C, (G) - W - N

20 cm	25°C	(G)-W-N

Home: Eastern Brazil.
Differs from *P. gracilus* by its often dark-dotted fin edges. Lengthwise band begins at the snout; adipose fin dark– edged.
Care: Like *P. gracilis.*
Pimelodella vittata (KROEGER, 1874)
10 cm, 25°C, G - W - N

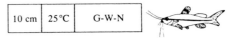

10 cm	25°C	G-W-N

Home: Southeastern Brazil.
Elongated species with a strongly prolonged upper tail fin lobe. Dorsal fin with delicate dark band.
Care: Like *P. gracilis.*

Pimelodus

In body structure and care, this genus closely resembles the genus *Pimelodella.* Most frequently imported is the fish called *P. pictus* by aquarists. It is silvery with large, irregularly distributed black spots. Young are fairly peaceful, but become quarrelsome with increasing age. Some authorities believe that *P. pictus* is the juvenile of *P. clarias,* a fish growing to 30 cm. Additionally, some workers make *P. clarias* a synonym of *P. blochii,* in which case the proper name of the aquarium *P. pictus* would be *P. blochii.*

Sorubim

A monotypic genus with broad, spatulate front part of head.

Sorubim lima (BLOCH & SCHNEI-
DER, 1801) (Shovelnose Catfish)
60 cm, 26°C, A - W - N

60 cm	26°C	A-W-N

Occasionally imported, beautiful animals for the large tank. Heavy eaters:
earthworms, fish. Like to stand head
downward in contact with reed stems.
A dark lengthwise body stripe enhances this camouflage.

Similar is *Pseudoplatystoma fasciatum*, another shovelnosed catfish of
about the same size that can be distinguished by a banded body pattern.

Aspredinidae (Banjo Catfishes)

Bizarrely shaped, flattened. Includes
the subfamilies Bunocephalinae and
Aspredininae.

Bunocephalus (Banjo Catfishes)

The about 20 South American species are so much alike that they are easily confused and are usually offered as
B. knerii or *B. coracoideus*. The animals
are reported to grow to 20 cm in length
but grow only slowly. Night-active;
during the day they lie about in the
tank as though dead.

Care: Temperature not above 24°C.
Use a glass for capturing them. In a net
they get easily tangled up and injure
themselves.

Malapteruridae (Electric Catfishes)

The family includes only two African
species, only *Malapterus electricus*, the
electric catfish, being imported. The
fish will grow to 1 m in length, eats a
lot, and grows rapidly.

Only young, to be kept singly, are
suited for the aquarium. Their electric
organ serves to obtain prey and to defend themselves. Diet consists of dead
fish, worms, heart meat. Temperatures
between 23 - 30°C.

Callichthyidae (Armored Catfishes)

The catfishes best suited for the
aquarium. Most are small animals, active during the day, that are harmless
and relatively insensitive. Characteristic are two rows of bony plates on each
side of the body, arranged in a che-
vron-like pattern. South American.
Two subgroups: the larger armored
catfishes, genera *Callichthys*, *Dianema*,
Hoplosternum, etc., and the smaller armored catfishes, genera *Aspidoras*,
Brochis, *Corydoras*, etc. The larger species are usually more elongated with a
less deep-bodied appearance.

Brochis

Closely related to the genus *Corydoras* and similar in care and breeding.
The most noticeable difference is the
considerably longer dorsal fin, with ten
or more rays.

Brochis splendens CASTELNAU, 1855
(Short-bodied Catfish)
8 cm, 25°C, G - S - W - N

8 cm	25°C	G-S-W-N

Home: Upper Amazon.

Greenish iridescent on the sides.
Very deep, laterally compressed body.
Breeding not very productive. *B. coeru-
leus* is a synonym.

Callichthys

Only one species. Differing from the
vey similar genus *Hoplosternum* by the
dorsal armor, which is not firmly connected to the side armor, and by the
greater distance betwen the dorsal fins.

Callichthys callichthys (LINNE, 1758)
(Slender Armored Catfish)
18 cm, 25°C, G - W - N

Corydoras schwartzi. Photo by J.
Vierke.

18 cm	25 °C	G-W-N	

Home: Eastern South America.
Peaceful nocturnal or crepuscular (dusk-active) fish. Offer hiding possibilities. Interesting propagation behavior: constructs foam nest under broad leaves of floating plants. The nest is guarded by the father, who occasionally utters grunting noises. Young hatch after four or five days. After they become free-swimming may be fed with ground tubifex.

Corydoras
Very popular genus rich in species (over 100). Compact, high-backed animals with short caudal peduncles and forked tail fins. Short downward-directed barbels.

As inhabitants of standing, often oxygen-poor waters, they are equipped for intestinal breathing of atmospheric air.

Care: Insensitive toward water values and temperature. In small groups of the same or similar species they are excellently suited for the community aquarium. However, there should be sandy substrate, at least in some places. In sharp-edged gravel substrate they easily injure their barbels.

Breeding most advantageous in tanks of 100 - 200 liters with a water level around 20 cm. Frequent water changes! Water rich in oxygen, clear, and bacteria-free. Use two females with about four to six males. Males are slimmer and smaller, and often their dorsal fin spine is markedly more elongated than in females. For pairing, the male pinches the barbels of the female with his pectoral fin ray and presses the female to the side of his abdomen. Following this, the eggs are released and go immediately into a pocket formed by the abdominal fins of the female, where they are believed to be fertilized. The female attaches the eggs to rocks, roots, plants, or the glass of the aquarium.

The brood hatches after five to eight days. The young can be fed with brine shrimp nauplii, Grindal worms and microworms.

Corydoras aeneus (GILL, 1858) (Aeneus Catfish)
 6 cm, 25°C, G - S - W - N

Home: Venezuela and Trinidad and farther south to the La Plata region.

Metallic iridescent. Care and breeding unproblematic. Very common in the American aquarium hobby.

Corydoras arcuatus ELWIN, 1939 (Skunk Catfish)
 5 cm, 25°C, G - S - W - N

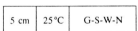

Home: Amazon region.

Strong dark stripe from the snout, following the profile of head and back, to the base of the tail, where it bends sharply and tapers to go to the lower edge of the tail fin.

Corydoras hastatus EIGENMANN & EIGENMANN, 1888
 3 cm, 25°C, G - S - W - N

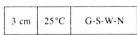

Home: Mato Grosso region.

A species that remains small, with dark lengthwise body stripe that is enlarged into a diamond-shaped spot on the caudal peduncle and has a light

edge. Lively tiny fish that like to swim in open water. Small aquaria are sufficient with not too large fellow tankmates. Very similar is *C. pygmaeus.* Breeding not very productive.

Corydoras julii STEINDACHNER, 1906 (Leopard Catfish)
 6 cm, 25°C, G - S - W - N

Home: Lower Amazon.

Characteristic is a large black spot in the dorsal fin, a black zigzag lengthwise body band, and a spotted pattern that is often blended into stripes. The gill covers are shimmering gold-green. Very similar are *C. trilineatus* and *C. bondi.* The latter lacks the dorsal fin marking. Unproblematic care.

Corydoras melanistius REGAN, 1912
 6 cm, 25°, G - S - W - N

Home: Northeastern South America.

Body covered with many irregular black dots. Wide black eye stripe. A black spot at the beginning of the dorsal fin that runs into the fin.

Corydoras nattereri STEINDACHNER, 1877 (Blue Catfish)
 7 cm, 25°C, G - S - W - N

Home: Eastern Brazil.

Basic body color bluish green. Back as well as a lengthwise body stripe with particularly intense coloration. No other markings. Attractive species.

269

Corydoras paleatus (JENYS, 1842)
(Peppered Corydoras)
7 cm, 25°C, G - S - W - N

Corydoras trilineatus. Photo by B. Kahl.

7 cm	25 °C	G-S-W-N	

Home: Lower Amazon.

The pale body is covered with a reticulation or network of black lines. In the dorsal fin is a striking black spot. An attractive species.

Dianema

Slender catfishes with pointed heads when viewed from the side, with the eye at middle or below middle of head. Large, forked tail fin.

Dianema longibarbis COPE, 1871 (Porthole Catfish)
9 cm, 26°C, G - S - W - N

9 cm	26 °C	G-S-W-N	

Home: Entire Amazon region.

Good, lively swimmer. Harmless. Predominantly nocturnal. Small black dots all over the body, much larger at midside (portholes). Foam nest builder. More rarely seen is *D. urostria*,

which is easily recognized by its tail fin, which is marked on a white ground with five striking black horizontal stripes.

Hoplosternum

Closely related to *Callichthys*, but back armor firmly connected to the side plates. Tail fin straight or slightly emarginate at back edge, not forked.

Hoplosternum littorale (HANCOCK, 1828) (Hoplo)
18 cm, 25°C, G - W - N

18 cm	25 °C	G-W-N	

Home: South America.

Solid gray-brown. Prefers twilight. In spite of its size, completely harmless and undemanding.

Care: For breeding, use large tanks. Constructs foam nest under broad leaves in the breeding aquarium, also under styrofoam sheets. Productive species.

Hoplosternum thoracatum (CUVIER & VALENCIENNES, 1840) (Port Hoplo)
18 cm, 25°C, G - W - N

18 cm	25°C	G-W-N

Home: Panama to Paraguay.
Red-brown with a large number of black spots over the entire body and the fins. Care like *H. littorale.*

Loricariidae (Plated Catfishes)

Fishes of northern and central South America into Central America, in flowing waters. Very strong armor and often bizarrely shaped. Suction mouth.

Care: Soft and medium-hard water. Nocturnal. Do not like to swim about. Need shelters or, even better, caves. Some species popular as algae-eaters. For spawning caves, flower pots on clay pipes are readily accepted. Father cares for and guards the eggs. It is essential that young be offered vegetable food, too!

There are very many species, most known under a wrong name. Exact determination of the species is often impossible for the hobbyist. In addition, there have been name changes in recent times. The species known as *Loricaria filamentosa* now is called *Dasyloricaria filamentosa; Loricaria parva* now is called *Rineloricaria parva.* In both instances these are very elongated species that strongly resemble *Farlowella.* They differ, among other things, in the positions of their dorsal and anal fins. Both species have repeatedly been bred.

Farlowella. Photo by B. Kahl.

Ancistrus (Bristle-nosed Catfishes)
About 30 species. Males are usually characterized by antenna-like, often repeatedly forked bristles on the snout and gill covers. Although most species grow to about 15 cm in length, they are harmless; known as good algae-eaters. Breeding possible. Most frequent sold are the species *A. cirrhosus* and *A. dolichopterus.*

Farlowella (Stick Catfishes)
Stick-like, elongated fishes usually with elongated rostrum (front part of head). Dorsal and anal fins are directly opposed. About 40 species known. Harmless animals that grow to 20 cm in length.

Hypostomus (Plecostomus Catfishes)
This genus, better known under the nonusable name *Plecostomus,* includes about 70 species, most of which cannot

271

be distinguished by the aquarist. Abdomen without plates. Large-headed fishes, usually provided with large fins; can grow to 60 cm in length.

Care: Not suited for small aquaria. Undemanding, good algae-eaters. Twilight-active. Like to eat blanched lettuce.

Otocinclus (Sucker Catfishes)

Grow to only 4 - 6 cm. Have laterally positioned eyes and bodies somewhat reminiscent of Chinese algae-eaters. Often with dark lengthwise body stripe. Eager algae-eaters that absolutely require vegetable foods. Higher aquarium plants remain unmolested. Breeding similar to *Corydoras*. Determination of the species barely possible for the hobbyist.

Pterygoplichthys (Long-finned Plecostomus)

Includes some species strongly reminiscent of *Hypostomus*, but with 10 - 13 dorsal fin rays (*Hypostomus* species about 7). Harmless animals for large aquaria that may grow quite large. They are often bizarrely patterned and are quite attractive because of their large dorsal and tail fins.

ATHERINIFORMES

Belonidae (Needlefishes)

This includes only a few freshwater species in a mostly marine family. They are elongated and have dorsal and anal fins beginning far back on the body. Quick, carnivorous fishes with long, strongly toothed jaws. Freshwater species grow to 30 cm and require correspondingly large aquaria! Must have live foods. *Potamorrhaphis guianensis* from South America and *Xenentodon cancila* from Southeast Asia are imported occasionally.

Hemiramphidae

Closely related to Belonidae. However, upper jaw considerably shorter than the lower jaw and movable in relation to the skull. Three freshwater genera are known to be imported: *Dermogenys*, *Hemirhamphodon*, and *Nomorhamphus*. All are surface fishes of Southeast Asia with internal fertilization and are viviparous.

Dermogenys pusillus VAN HASSELT, 1823 (Malayan Halfbeak)

7.5 cm, 25°C, G - (S) - H

7,5 cm	25°C	G-(S)-H	

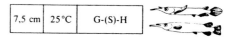

Home: Southeast Asian flowing waters.

Peaceful fish that live on insects falling into the water. In aquarium, cover surface partially with floating plants since the fish are easily frightened. Will also accept dry food, but will need occasional live food. For breeding, add fruitflies. The young are about 1 cm long at birth. With unsatisfactory diet, the females abort.

Nomorhamphus celebensis WEBER & DE BEAUFORT, 1922 (Celebes Halfbeak)

9 cm, 25°C, G - H

9 cm	25°C	G-H	

Home: Celebes.

Fins reddish with black edges (with the exception of the tail fin). Males colored more intensively, with age developing a dark-colored flap on the end of the lower jaw. Will enter middle water levels. In care and breeding less problematic than *Dermogenys*. Viviparous. Parents go after their young! Similarly cared for is their very close relative *N. liemi*.

Cyprinodontidae (Killifishes)

Cyprinodontidae, the killifishes, furnishes some of the most colorful aquarium fishes. At present, these are 54 genera with some 500 species known, the overwhelming majority of which come from tropical America and from Africa. It is obvious that within this framework, only the most important representatives can be dealt with in detail.

Among the killifishes there can be differentiated, depending on their spawning behavior, plant-spawners and bottom spawners. Some of the bottom-spawners are not satisfied with depositing their spawn **on** the substrate. They virtually dive into the swampy substrate of their home waters and deposit their eggs there, **in** the sand or mud. An explanation for this behavior is found in the fact that in the dry season these waters will more or less dry out. The old fish die when a year or less of age (annual fishes), while the eggs in the substrate survive. Even in aquarium surroundings, such fishes will rarely grow older than a year.

With some exceptions, killifishes are loners. For this reason, many species are well suited for being kept in pairs in a miniature tank. In the community aquarium, it is possible to combine them with fishes of about the same size. The aquarium should be sufficiently planted and well covered. Most species are good jumpers! Live food should be given whenever possible.

For more detailed information about the breeding of the plant-spawners, see *Aphyosemion australe;* about the breeding of a bottom-spawner, see *Cynolebias*.

Aphyosemion (Lyretails)

Home: Western and central Africa. Distributed throughout the Congo basin and in the savanna region bordering it in the north.

Small, slender killies with pronounced sex dimorphism. Males often very colorful, females smaller and mostly brownish. Surface-fishes requiring lower temperatures (22 - 24°C) and neutral water. Soft water. Acid pH should be avoided.

The northern species of the savanna regions are predominantly bottom-spawning annual or short-lived fishes, the rain forest species mostly plant-spawners. Many species are easy to breed, especially species with adhesive eggs laid on a spawning mop or on peat fibers. The majority of the species are not annuals. Only the species *A. walkeri, arnoldi, robertsoni, sjoestedti, deltaense,* and *filamentosum* are typical annual fishes. Their eggs need a dry period of several weeks.

At present, 89 species are known; that is almost one-fifth of all the killifish species!

Care: Most advantageously kept in a densely planted tank with floating plants. Surface fishes. Males often quarrelsome, so if possible keep more females than males.

Aphyosemion australe (RACHOW, 1921) (Cape Lopez Lyretail)
5.5 cm, 22°C, G - A - W

5.5 cm	22°C	G, A-W	
			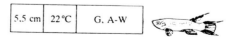

Home: Congo to Gaboon.
Peaceful and undemanding fish. Males more colorful.

Care: Even beginners can be successful in breeding this species. A breeding tank of about 10 liters content with delicate water plants is good. Before stocking, keep the sexes separated for some time and give them a varied live food diet. Stock several breeding fish, since individual males are occasionally sterile. The eggs are hardy. They may be collected daily by hand and transferred into nursery bowls. Hatching occurs after 10-14 days. The young will immediately eat brine shrimp nauplii. Quick-growing young fish must be kept separately, since they would kill or eat their smaller siblings. Occasionally yellow and chocolate brown color varieties of this species appear in the trade.

Aphyosemion bivittatum (LOENNBERG, 1895) (Two-striped Lyretail)

5 cm, 22°C, G - A - W

5 cm	22°C	G, A-W	

Home: West Africa, in small and medium-sized flowing waters from Togo to Guinea.

Two dark, lengthwise stripes, especially strong in the female. Colorful males with especially well-developed dorsal fin. The species can be bred as a plant- spawner, but with unsatisfactory hatching results. The collected eggs may be kept dry for two to three weeks.

Similar in behavior and breeding are the species *A. loennbergii, A. multicolor, A. splendopleure,* and the larger *A. riggenbachi.*

Aphyosemion bualanum (AHL, 1924) (African Swamp Killie)

5 cm, 20°C, G - A - W

5 cm	20°C	G, A-W	

Home: Running waters of the steppe regions of eastern Cameroon and of the Central African Republic.

A peaceful fish, very easy to keep and breed in the aquarium. Not annual. The species is split into many populations that differ in coloration. An attempt should be made to keep the different color variations pure.

Aphyosemion calliurum (BOULENGER, 1911) (Blue Calliurum)

5 cm, 22°C, G - A - W

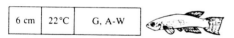

5 cm	22°C	G, A-W

Home: Southern Nigeria.

Undemanding plant spawner that resembles *A. australe* in care and breeding. Splendid coloration.

Aphyosemion christyi (BOULENGER, 1915) (Christy's Lyretail)

6 cm, 22°C, G - A - W

6 cm	22°C	G, A-W

Home: Central Congo basin.

Males ochre with red dots. Closely related are the species *A. elegans, A. cognatum, A. rectogoense, A. lamberti,* and *A. melanopteron.* They are all somewhat sensitive fishes. Breeding not quite easy. The water must be soft and slightly acid. Plant spawners.

Aphyosemion cinnamomeum CLAUSEN, 1963 (Cinnamon Killie)

5 cm, 22°C, G - A - W

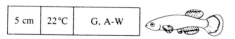

5 cm	22°C	G, A-W

Home: High plains of western Cameroon.

Males attractively cinnamon-brown in the rear half of body; bottom-spawner, not annual.

Aphyosemion exiguum (BOULENGER, 1911)

4 cm, 22°C, G - A - W

4 cm	22°C	G, A-W

Home: Northern Gaboon and eastern Cameroon.

Peaceful, attractive species. Closely related to *A. bualanum* and, like that fish, unproblematic in care and breeding.

Aphyosemion filamentosum (MEINKEN, 1933) (Togo Lyretail)

5.5 cm, 22°C, G - A - W

5,5 cm	22°C	G, A-W

Home: Swamp regions of southwestern Nigeria.

Closely related to *A. arnoldi* and like it a bottom-spawner with seasonal fish characters. The development of the eggs lasts one to five months.

Aphyosemion gardneri (BOULENGER, 1911) (Gardner's Lyretail)

6 cm, 22°C, G - A - W

6 cm	22°C	G, A-W

Home: Nigeria and western Cameroon (occurring in several color varieties).

Easy to keep and breed, but often aggressive. Provide hiding places! Live food! Plant-spawners, but frequently better bred as bottom-spawners. The eggs then need about one month dry rest.

Aphyosemion gulare (BOULENGER, 1901) (Yellow Gularis)

8 cm, 22°C, G - A - W

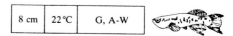

8 cm	22°C	G, A-W

Home: Southern Nigeria.

Large, beautifully colored seasonal fish that should be given large feedings of live food. Relatively aggressive. Bottom- spawner. Development period of the eggs about two months.

Aphyosemion labarrei POLL, 1952 (Labarre's Lyretail)

5 cm, 22°C, G - A - W

5 cm	22°C	G, A-W	

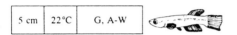

Home: Region of the lower Zaire River near Madimba.

Body of the male bright blue, red-dotted. Plant-spawner.

Aphyosemion sjoestedti (LOENNBERG, 1895) (Blue Gularis)

12 cm, 24°C, G - (A) - W

12 cm	24°C	G(A)-W	

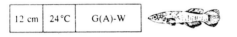

Home: Southern Nigeria and swamp regions of Cameroon.

Beautiful and hardy fish, but requiring live food and often quite aggressive. Not too small tanks! Eggs are deposited in the substrate and require a rest period of about two months for development.

Aphyosemion walkeri (BOULENGER, 1911)

6 cm, 22°C, G - A - W

6 cm	22°C	G, A-W	

Home: Ghana, Ivory Coast.

Species split into many color populations. It should be attempted to keep the variations pure. Bottom-spawner, care and breeding relatively easy. The eggs develop best after a rest period of about two months.

Aplocheilus

Home: Tropical Asia.

Surface fishes of pike-like structure. Hardy, can even be bred in hard and slightly alkaline water. Do not combine with smaller tankmates. Breeding as for *Epiplatys*.

Aplocheilus lineatus (CUVIER & VALENCIENNES, 1846) (Striped Panchax)

10 cm, 23°C, G - A - W - N

10 cm	23°C	G, A-W-N	

Home: Southern India.

Beautiful, hardy fish. Characteristic are several vertical body stripes. Females with more rounded fins than males. Plant-spawners. Collect the eggs! Young hatch after only about 14 days.

Very similar in looks and behavior is *A. dayi* from Sri Lanka. The nominate form is unstriped, but there is also a subspecies, *A. d. werneri*, that strongly resembles *A. lineatus*.

Aplocheilus panchax HAMILTON-BUCHANAN, 1822 (Blue Panchax)

7 cm	23°C	G, A-W-N	

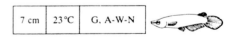

Home: Southeast Asia, Indonesia.

Robust fish occurring in several variations. A black spot at the base of the dorsal fin. Breeding easy.

Cynolebias

Found mostly in the coastal zones of Brazil and the La Plata states, inhabiting small temporary pools and puddles. The eggs are deposited in the bottom before the waters dry and survive the dry period, which lasts for months.

Includes about 25 species of mostly rather deep-bodied annual fishes with considerable sex dimorphism. Males are larger and much more colorful and have more fin rays than the females.

Care and Breeding: Dedicated tank. Before stocking for breeding, separate the sexes for a time. Temperatures around 20°C. For breeding, use boiled and rinsed peat. The thickness of the peat layer should correspond at least to the length of the breeding fish. When the eggs of the females are exhausted after some weeks, remove the peat, squeeze slightly dry and store moderately damp to "tobacco- damp" in a plastic bag or tin can. Provide periodical airings (danger of mold!). After two to four months, add fresh water. Since not all larvae hatch immediately, the rest of the peat should be dried again and the procedure repeated after about one month. The young will eat newly hatched *Artemia* nauplii right away, and with a good diet they grow extremely quickly.

Aplocheilus lineatus. Photo by B. Kahl.

Cynolebias bellottii STEINDACHNER, 1881 (Argentine Pearl Fish)
   7 cm, 17°C, A - N

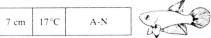

7 cm	17°C	A-N

Home: La Plata region.

Male dark blue with whitish dots arranged in vertical rows; during courtship, almost black. Female brownish with dark spots. Both sexes with blackish band extending from the nape through the eyes. Very similar in appearance is *C. nigripinnis* from the same area. However, it grows to only 5 cm in length and lacks the eye band of *C. bellottii*. Both species are easy to breed.

Cynolebias whitei MYERS, 1942 (White's Pearl Fish)
   8 cm, 20°C, A - N

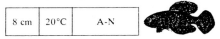

8 cm	20°C	A-N

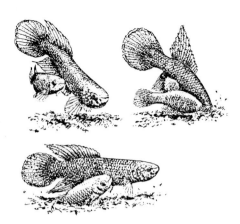

Pearlfish *(Cynolebias whitei)* spawning (from Wickler).

Home: Southeastern Brazil.
Male red-brown with greenish dots and lines. In the anal fin is an orange band. Dorsal and anal fin not rounded as in the vast majority of *Cynolebias* species, but with long points.

Epiplatys
Home: Western and central Africa.
Robust, pike-like killifishes closely related to the Asian genus *Aplocheilus*. Quiet surface fishes.
Care and Breeding: Plant-spawners. Egg-laying lasts for weeks. Transfer spawning plants regularly to separate nursery tanks, since the parents pursue the young fish. Sort young according to size. In the nursery tank, provide a current to bring the food (initially brine shrimp nauplii) to the mouths of the young. The young will not actively search for food! By observing these guidelines, breeding is not difficult.

Epiplatys dageti POLL, 1953 (Red-chinned Panchax)
5 cm, 23°C, G - W

5 cm	23 °C	G-W	

Home: Liberia and Ghana.
Body bronze-colored with five or six dark vertical bands. Males with red throat. Lower tail fin rays usually elongated. Several subspecies are known. Peaceful fish that are easily cared for and bred.
Epiplatys sexfasciatus GILL, 1862 (Six-banded Panchax)
10 cm, 23°C, G - W

10 cm	23 °C	G-W	

Home: Ghana to Gaboon.
Very robust fish of which there are several subspecies. Sides shining, metallic, with red partly black-edged dots on the scales. Non-paired fins greenish, blue, yellow, or orange, depending on origin. Do not combine with too small fish!

Fundulus (Topminnows)
Home: About 30 species and subspecies mostly from eastern North America to the Great Plains (a few to the west coast and northeastern Mexico).
Care: Undemanding as regards water chemistry and temperature. Dry food is readily accepted. Not for the community aquarium. Breeding in the aquarium sometimes difficult. Cool wintering, warm for breeding!

Jordanella (Florida Flagfish)
This genus consists only of the

North American species *J. floridae*, the Florida flagfish. A robust and attractive fish. Peaceful. Grows to 6 cm in length. Suited for small, densely-planted tanks. Good algae-eater. Likes to eat dry food that is based predominantly on vegetable matter. Males larger. Breeding temperature about 24°C. Over the course of several days, the fish deposit 20 - 30 eggs daily on the bottom. Brood hatches after five to ten days.

Lucania (Rainwater Fishes)

Includes *Lucania goodei* from Florida, which grows to about 5 - 6 cm, and *L. parva*, widely distributed throughout coastal eastern North America. Both species are colorful. For their care, hard water is necessary; if needed, table salt may be used to make it harder! Water around 20°C (in winter around 14°C). Breeding not difficult; parents are spawn eaters.

Nothobranchius (Fire Killies)

About 25 species of often very colorful annual fishes most from East Africa, a few in Central Africa. Care not always easy. Adapt only gradually to changed water values. Eat a lot. Bottom-spawners. Eggs require a dry phase.

Nothobranchius korthausae MEINKEN, 1973 (Korthaus's Notho)

5 cm, 23°C, A - W

5 cm	23°C	A-W	

Home: The island of Mafia off Tanzania.

Males with dark-edged body scales, fin edges often light. Breeds in soft, acid water, Dry phase for the eggs one to three months.

Jordanella floridae. Photo by B. Kahl.

Nothobranchius palmqvisti (LOENN-BERG, 1907) (Palmqvist's Fire Killie) 4.5 cm, 23°C, A - W

Nothobranchius korthausae. Photo by B. Kahl.

Home: Regions near the coast of Tanzania and Kenya.

Body shimmering blue, each scale edged in red. Tail fin red. Dorsal and anal fin strongly brown-netted. Female with small dark spots on body.

N. foerschi is of similar appearance but has an only faintly patterned anal fin. Of this species there is a completely yellow color variety.

Oryzias (Ricefishes)

Small schooling fishes of tropical Asia. They are easy to keep in medium-hard water at about 23°C; however, it is better to use soft water for breeding. Frequently the eggs hang from the genital papilla of the female for some time after spawning before they are rubbed off on plants.

Among the tiniest fish is *O. minutillus.* The males grow to 1.2 cm at most, the females attaining lengths of 1.7 cm.

Pachypanchax

Only the species *P. playfairi,* originating in the Seychelles and Madagascar, is known with regularity in the aquarium. The greenish shimmering fish, covered with red dots, grows to 10 cm in length. It has strikingly protruding scales, especially on its back.

Care: Live food. Aggressive, thus hiding places must be provided. Female with rounded anal fin. The fish spawn in plant thickets. Temperature around 24°C.

Procatopus
Home: African rain forests.
Schooling fishes of the African rain forests. Body beautiful iridescent blue.
Care: Since the fishes come from flowing waters, equip the aquarium with filter. Temperatures around 23°C, water medium hard (susceptible to diseases in soft water). The fish lay their eggs in narrow cracks. For breeding, offer pumice stone, cork, or similar materials.

Pseudepiplatys
Pike-like small fish that is very close to the genus *Epiplatys* and was included with it for a very long time. Only one species.
Pseudepiplatys annulatus
BOULENGER, 1915 (Clown Killie)
4 cm, 23°C, G - A - W

4 cm	23 °C	G, A-W	

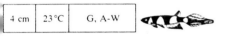

Home: Guinea, Sierra Leone, and Liberia.
Very attractive, with three thick, black vertical body bands. Males with colored fins.
Care: Likes floating plant cover. Raising of the young difficult, since they are very small and initially will not yet eat brine shrimp. Breeding otherwise like *Epiplatys*.

Pterolebias
South American genus consisting of five or six species. Bottom-diving annual fishes that are propagated like *Cynolebias* species.
Pterolebias longipinnis GARMAN, 1895 (Common Longfin)
12 cm, 24°C, A - (G) - W

12 cm	24 °C	A(G)-W	

Home: Brazil, Argentina.
Males with magnificent veiled fins.
Care: Soft, slightly acid peat water. For their development, the eggs need a rest of about three months.

Rivulus
A genus of tropical America that is rich in species. The determination of many species is problematic. Hardy and resistant surface fishes. Enjoy jumping (cover aquarium especially well!). In nature, many species seek new swimming quarters by aimed jumps across land. In the aquarium, the fishes sometimes lie on the leaves of swimming plants, partly or entirely in the air. Breeding not always easy. Sexes same size, but males more colorful; female usually with a dark spot at upper base of tail fin. Requires rich planting. The eggs are deposited near plants.

Roloffia
Home: Western Africa.
Very closely related to *Aphyosemion*, even identical in the opinion of many scientists. The fish need good feedings of live food and temperatures around 22°C. Males usually very aggressive among each other and toward females not ready for spawning.
Roloffia geryi (LAMBERT, 1958)
4.5 cm, 22°C, G - A - W - N

4.5 cm	22 °C	G, A-W-N	

Home: Forest and savanna regions from Gambia to Sierra Leone.
Both sexes with zigzag band extending in a lengthwise direction across the body.
Care: Unproblematic. As with all small species of *Roloffia*, it is best to allow the eggs to hatch without a drying period.

Roloffia occidentalis (CLAUSEN, 1966)
(Golden Pheasant)
8 cm, 22°C, G - A - W - N

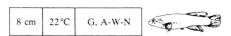

| 8 cm | 22°C | G, A-W-N | |

Home: Sierra Leone.

Especially colorful species. Male with reddish horizontal stripes on the gill covers and colorful caudal fin.

Care: Easy in care and breeding, but lively and relatively aggressive. Not too small tanks! Females need hiding places. The eggs require a dry period of about three months.

The same is true for the species *R. monroviae* and *R. toddi*. Formerly, *R. occidentalis* had been confused with *Aphyosemion sjoestedti*, which has completely different colors.

Terranatos

Monotypic genus. The only species formerly was placed in the genus *Austrofundulus*, and some workers now place it in *Cynolebias*.

Terranatos dolichopterus (WEITZMAN & WOURMS, 1967) (Saberfin Killie)
4 cm, 23°C, A - W

| 4 cm | 23°C | A-W | |

Home: Venezuela, in small, shaded ponds with acid, very soft water.

This striking fish is brown-olive with dark brown spots. A dark vertical line crosses the eye. Fins blue-green; the dorsal and anal fins very long, sickle-shaped.

Care: Acid, very soft water. Live food! Breeding is not easy. For their development, the eggs need a dry interval of four to six months.

Poecilidae (Livebearers)

Center of distribution in Central America. As eager devourers of mosquito larvae, some species have been introduced to other continents in often futile and ecologically dangerous attempts to control insects.

The 20 genera contain about 150 species. Almost all are ovoviviparous, thus not really viviparous in the strict biological sense. True viviparity means that the eggs are not only protected in the body of the mother but are directly nourished by the mother during their development. True viviparity occurs in the related families Goodeidae and Jenynsyiidae.

Sexually dimorphic. The smaller males are recognizable by the anal fin that has been transformed to a movable fertilization organ (gonopodium).

Schooling fishes that live near the surface but which are not as dependent on the schooling unit as are tetras and barbs.

Care and Breeding: Easy for most species, as long as the water is neither soft nor acid. The majority of livebearers need medium-hard to hard water, which possibly should also be alkaline. Tap water usually meets these requirements. Sensitive to nitrogen-containing waste products (ammonia, nitrite, nitrate), so do not forget regular water changes!

Belonesox

This genus consists only of the species described here.

Belonesox belizanus KNER, 1860 (Pike Livebearer)
20 cm, 25°C, N - H - A

| 20 cm | 25°C | N-H-A | |

Home: Swamp regions in Central America.

Care: Use a large, densely planted single-species tank, otherwise the females will eat their "only" 10-cm-long males. Floating plants. Heavy feedings of live food, especially fish, but also worms and larger insects and crustaceans.

For breeding, keep pregnant females separate. Duration of pregnancy 30 - 50 days. Litter size up to 100. Separate the young from the mother as soon as possible. They measure 2.5 - 3 cm at birth and will immediately eat water fleas (daphnia).

Gambusia

A genus consisting of some 30 species. These are mostly unobtrusive animals that are very hardy and have been introduced into many areas. Omnivo-rous, with algae as supplement. For breeding, put females singly in well-planted tanks, since they eat their young. Only a few species have attained aquarium significance.

Gambusia affinis (BAIRD & GIRARD, 1853) (Mosquitofish)

8 cm, 19°C, A - (S) - N - H

8 cm	19°C	A-(S)-N-H	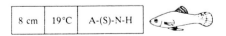

Home: Eastern North America.

Males grow to only 4 cm in length. Very resistant, but less suitable for community aquarium because aggressive. Winter at 10 - 12°C.

283

Girardinus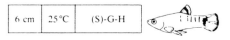

Home: Cuba and Costa Rica.

Small, usually unobtrusive, peaceful fishes. Seldom seen in the aquarium. Most likely to be found is the Cuban *G. metallicus*, sometimes imported through Europe. Care and breeding simple.

Heterandria

Home: North and Central America. Only two species.

Heterandria formosa AGASSIZ, 1853 (Least Killifish)

3.5 cm, 20°C, A - (S) - W - N - H

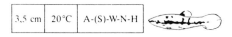

3,5 cm	20°C	A-(S)-W-N-H

Home: Coastal, North Carolina to Louisiana.

The males grow to only 2 cm maximum. Peaceful. Black spot on dorsal fin.

Care: Aquarium (preferably 20 liters plus) stocked densely with delicate plants so some young will always survive without our help. No special requirements concerning water and food.

Poecilia

This genus includes the former genera *Lebistes*, *Limia*, *Mollienesia*, and many others. At present, about 30 species are included in it.

Poecilia melanogaster GUENTHER, 1866 (Black-bellied Limia)

6 cm, 25°C, (S) - G - H

6 cm	25°C	(S)-G-H

Home: Jamaica, Haiti.

Lively shimmering steely-blue fish. Older males with orange throat and abdomen.

Care: Sufficiently planted, medium-

Poecilia melanogaster. Photo by B. Kahl.

sized aquarium. Give live food and green algae. Not to be combined with *P. nigrofasciata*, since this would lead to undesirable hybridizing.

Poecilia nigrofasciata (REGAN, 1913) (Humpbacked Limia)
6 cm, 26°C, (S) - G - H

6 cm	26 °C	(S)-G-H

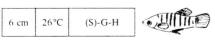

Home: Hispaniola.
Striking because of 8 - 12 pronounced vertical lines. Older males have a somewhat curved back and a fan-like dorsal fin. Lively and peaceful. Somewhat more difficult to keep than the previous species. Can adapt only slowly to new water conditions. One litter produces only about 10 - 30 young, but they measure easily 1 cm at birth.

Poecilia reticulata PETERS, 1859 (Guppy)
6 cm, 24°C, G - (S) - N - H

6 cm	24 °C	G-(S)-N-H

Guppy, breeding males. From top to bottom: lower sword, round tail, spade tail, delta tail.

Home: Northern South America, Trinidad.

The small males are adorned with all the colors of the rainbow, but the larger females are plain. At about monthly intervals they give birth to 20 - 60 young fish, a large part of which will grow up without assistance in a well-planted single-species tank. Undemanding, completely unproblematic fish.

Wild guppies — although much more interesting for behaviorists than the cultivated forms — are rarely ever obtainable in the trade. Instead, many aquarium varieties with fantastically colored, usually veil-shaped fins in the males are offered. In many instances even the females have colorful and elongated fins. For the breeding of new varieties a large number of aquaria are necessary, in addition to knowledge of genetic rules and the standards (which are binding, predetermined breeding goals). But even someone who does not aspire to winning prizes for outstanding guppies at national and international exhibitions may raise his young guppies into big and well-developed fish if the feeds them well from the start (brine shrimp) and changes the water frequently.

Poecilia sphenops CUVIER & VALENCIENNES, 1846 (Sphenops Molly)
6 cm, 27°C, G - (S) - H

6 cm	27 °C	G-(S)-H

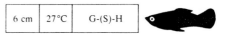

Home: Central America (will often go into brackish water).
Care: Needs harder water in the aquarium (prefers an addition of 10% sea salt) and warmth. In addition to normal food, requires algae or food

flakes manufactured from a vegetable base.

Much more frequent than the normal silvery form is the black molly, a deep black aquarium variety. Some varieties have the upper and lower tail fin rays elongated (lyre-tail molly). Breeding easy. In densely planted tanks the young will grow up unmolested by the parents. Will often turn black only with increasing age.

Poecilia velifera REGAN, 1914 (Yucatan Sailfin Molly)

18 cm, 27°C, (S) - A - G - H

18 cm	27°C	(S)-A, G-H

Home: Mexico (Yucatan peninsula). With large, sail-like dorsal fin with 18 -19 rays.

Care: Give as hard water as possible (brackish water better), much algae for food (vegetable food flakes as substitute), and a large aquarium with sufficient open swimming space. For raising the young, large algae-filled tanks with brackish water are also important.

Is easy to confuse this species with the more common sailfin molly, *P. latipinna*, which has 14 rays in the dorsal fin. This species should be kept in only 22 - 25°C. Also similar is *P. petenensis*, whose tail fin is elongated into a short spike on the lower edge. Crosses between these species as well as xanthic (yellowish) animals are often offered for sale.

Priapella

The attractive blue-eyed livebearer, *P. intermedia*, from southeastern Mexico belongs to this genus. These fish need a large aquarium (over 100 liters) and have to be kept in a school. Water clear, moving, 25°C. Dry food with much vegetable content, occasionally fruit flies if possible.

Xiphophorus

Some of the most popular aquarium fishes belong to this genus: the common swordtails and platies. In addition, there are seldom-seen wild species like *X. montezumae* and *X. pygmaeus* that are very difficult' to keep. (These wild forms come from typically soft water areas.) Aquarium fishes are in many instances hybrids, so accurate scientific determination of names for these species are often not possible for the aquarium forms.

Xiphophorus helleri HECKEL, 1848 (Swordtail)

12 cm, 23°C, G - (S) - N - H

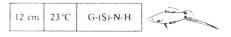

12 cm	23°C	G-(S)-N-H

Home: Mexico and Guatemala.

The adult males are characterized by a sword-like continuation of the lower rays of the tail fin. Greenish, with red lengthwise stripes. Impressive courtship swimming! Wild form much more lively than the aquarium forms, therefore especially recommended.

Care: To be kept only in 22 to at most 25°C. Provide a medium-sized aquarium with sufficient free swimming space. In small aquaria have only one male!

The aquarium varieties have often been hybridized with *X. maculatus*. They are less temperamental than the wild form and require higher temperatures (around 25°C), but are sometimes sensitive. There are pure-red *helleri* aquarium varieties (red swordtails), red with black fins (wagtail helleris), forms with markedly elongated fins (lyretailed helleris), and many others.

Tranfer pregnant females into separate densely planted tanks!

Xiphophorus maculatus (GUENTHER, 1866) (Platy)

   6 cm, 24°C, (S) - G - N - H

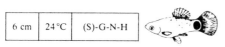

| 6 cm | 24 °C | (S)-G-N-H |

Home: Southern Mexico, Guatemala, Honduras.

The plain original form is of no aquarium significance. Instead bright red aquarium forms (red platy), forms with black tail fin base (moon platy), and other forms are offered for sale, which all are recommended even for the beginner. Lively, peaceful, and un-

Xiphophorus helleri. Photo by B. Kahl.

demanding fish. Excellent for the community aquarium. Males have no swords. Breeding easy.

Xiphophorus variatus MEEK, 1904 (Platy Variatus)

   7 cm, 22°C, (S) - G - N - H

| 7 cm | 22 °C | (S)-G-N-H |

Home: Rapidly flowing waters of Mexico.

Somewhat slimmer than *X. maculatus.* Body often with irregular spots, steel- blue. Dorsal and tail fins frequently colored. Lively, peaceful.

Care: Not demanding, but do not keep too warm! Offer additional plant food. Here also there are many aquarium varieties. Male without sword. For breeding, the temperature may be raised for a short time to 26°C.

Goodeidae

About 40 species, all from the highlands of Mexico. Relatively high-backed animals. Viviparous.

Xenotoca eiseni (RUETTER, 1896) (Red- tailed Goodeid)

7 cm, 22°C, G - A - N - H

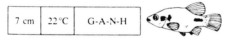

7 cm	22 °C	G-A-N-H

Home: Lakes and rivers of the Mexican highlands.

Adult males with noticeably narrow caudal peduncle and deep, rather elliptical body. Caudal peduncle with bright orange-red band in the rear half. The fertilizing organ (gonopodium) of the male is modified from the anterior anal fin rays and slightly separated from the other rays.

Care and Breeding: Simple. Peaceful fish. 20 - 60 young per litter.

Jenynsiidae

Widely distributed in South America south of the Amazon. It is interesting to note that the animals are built in such a manner that each can fertilize or be fertilized only on either the right or the left side.

Most easily obtained is *J. lineata*. They grow to 12 cm in length. Need medium— hard water of about 25°C with a slight current. Omnivorous. Aggressive, therefore not suitable for the community tank.

Anablepidae (Foureyed Fishes)

Three known species. Live in the coastal brackish waters of the Amazon. Perfectly adapted to life at the surface. Their eyes are divided in such a manner that in normal swimming position they can see with each eye simultaneously under water and in the air. Like the Jenynsiidae, because of the construction of the fertilization organs only partners of opposite build can mate.

Care: Keep in large, special aquaria with surface areas as large as possible. These lively fish grow to about 20 cm in length! Add some salt to the water. Temperature 24 - 28°C. Food: live crickets and grasshoppers, small fishes, mussel meat, dry food. The young — about 3 - 20 per litter — measure 3 - 5 cm at birth.

Atherinidae (Silversides)

Formerly included also the Australian rainbowfishes and blue-eyes, now in families Melanotaeniidae and Pseudomugilidae. Today the family contains only one species of aquarium significance.

Bedotia geayi PELLEGRIN, 1907 (Madagascar Rainbow)

15 cm, 24°C, S - G - N - H

15 cm	24°C	S-G-N-H

Home: Madagascar.

Problem-free fish. There are variations belonging to the same species that lack the red in the tail fin. In the aquarium, the lively schooling fish usually attain a length of only 7 cm.

Care: Peaceful, omnivorous. Medium to hard water, somewhat alkaline. For breeding, use a planted aquarium. Recommended is the addi-

tion of 1 teaspoon table salt for 10 liters of water. Continuous spawner; will daily deposit some eggs among the plants. Will not chase the young. Young will eat brine shrimp nauplii right away.

Telmatherinidae
Home: Celebes.

Slender schooling fish, males with filamentous soft dorsal and anal fins.

Telmatherina ladigesi AHL, 1936 (Celebes Rainbow)

7 cm, 22°C, S - G - H

7 cm	22 °C	S-G-H

Home: Mountain rivers of Sulawesi (Celebes).

Care: Peaceful. Sensitive to nitrates; regular partial water changes essential. Breeding like *Bedotia geayi*.

Melanotaeniidae (Australian Rainbowfishes)

Lively schooling fishes from the Australia-New Guinea region. Two

Glossolepis incisus. Photo by J. Vierke.

dorsal fins. Prefer hard, clean water and frequent water changes. Peaceful and hardy. Breeding like *Bedotia*. Eggs covered with filamentous appendages. *Iriatherina werneri* from New Guinea and northern Australia looks more like *Telmatherina* than other Australian rainbows.

Glossolepis

At least five species from New Guinea only. Only one is commonly found in aquaria.

Glossolepis incisus WEBER, 1908 (New Guinea Red Rainbowfish)

15 cm, 22°C, S - G - N - H

15 cm	22 °C	S-G-N-H	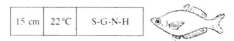

Adult males magnificently orange-red. Females brassy, smaller. Peaceful but lively schooling fish.

Care: Larger aquaria with sufficient open swimming space. Otherwise unproblematic.

Melanotaenia

Includes aquarium fishes popular because of their modest requirements and attractive coloration. All are to be kept and bred as described for the family. Some species are still called by the generic name *Nematocentris*, but that name is a synonym of *Melanotaenia*.

Melanotaenia fluviatilis CASTELNAU, 1878

10 cm, 20°C, S - G - H

10 cm	20°C	S-G-H

Home: Northeastern Australia and southern New Guinea.

Males with dark fin edges and orange- red gill covers. Is often erroneously called *M. nigrans*. However, they are a completely different species.

Care: Needs hard water!

Similarly colored is *M. sexlineata*, but it has six narrow dark, lengthwise body stripes.

Melanotaenia maccullochi. Photo by J. Vierke.

Melanotaenia maccullochi OGILBY, 1915 (Dwarf Australian Rainbow)

7 cm, 22°C, S - G - N - H

7 cm	22°C	S-G-N-H

Home: Northeastern Australia.

Quite frequently available. Highly recommended, hardy fish. Beautiful, lively, and peaceful. Breeding in medium—hard water easy. Well-fed parents are not spawn-robbers. Young hatch after seven to ten days in 25°C.

Pseudomugilidae (Blue-eyes)

Home: New Guinea, Australia.

In appearance the blue-eyes are reminiscent of their close relatives the Australian rainbows and resemble them also in care and breeding. The species *Pseudomugil signifer*, which grows to only about 4.5 cm, is sometimes available.

GASTEROSTEIFORMES

The stickleback group contains mostly small and predominantly marine species. Included in this order are the relatives of sticklebacks, trumpet-fishes, and pipefishes.

Gasterosteidae (Sticklebacks)

Family of small marine and freshwater fishes frequently with interesting spawning and brood-caring behavior, distributed through North America and Europe. Sticklebacks need hard water and large amounts of live food.

Syngnathidae (Pipefishes)

About 300 species are known, but only a few are truly freshwater fishes. Distinguished by a characteristic, elogated body shape and ring-like plates. Males with breeding pouch on the abdomen for the development of the brood.

Enneacampus ansorgii BOULENGER, 1915 (African Freshwater Pipefish)
15 cm, 26°C, A - H

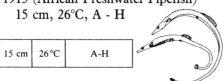

15 cm	26°C	A-H

Home: Brackish and coastal freshwater of western Africa.

Very beautiful animals with red abdomen and bright blue spots on their flanks. Formerly called *Syngnathus pulchellus* in the aquarium literature.

Care: Hard tap water (or add salt). Live food (brine shrimp, cyclops, daphnia).

Breeding sometimes successful. Brackish water! Raise young with brine shrimp nauplii.

CHANNIFORMES (SNAKEHEADS)

Home: Africa, tropical Asia.

Sedentary carnivorous fishes with large mouths and elongated bodies. Fin spines lacking. Provided with additional labyrinth organs (accessory breathing organ). About 30 species known, of which some grow to more than 1 m.

Care: Special aquarium or combination with large fish.

PERCIFORMES

Order of fishes richest in forms and species, divided into 20 suborders. These perch-like fishes usually have two dorsal fins, the anterior one of hard rays (spines), the posterior one consisting of soft rays that are usually branched at least toward the tips.

Percoidei

Sub-order of Perciformes richest in species, with about 70 families, the majority of which are marine.

Lobotidae

Family with few species. Frequently lobe-like broadened soft-rayed parts of the dorsal and anal fins. Robust carnivorous fishes.

Datnioides quadrifasciatus (SEVASTIA-NOV, 1809((Many-barred Tiger fish)
30 cm, 26°C, A - (G) - N - H

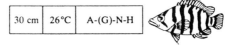

30 cm	26°C	A-(G)-N-H

Carnivorous fish from the river estuaries of southern and southeastern Asia, that occasionally are imported as young specimens. Young with about eight vertical dark bands on a silvery ground. Remarkably large head, small tail. Second spine of the anal fin saber-shaped.

Care: Suitable for combining with fish of about the same size. Easily adapted. Fresh or brackish water. Food: earthworms, larger pond food.

Centropomidae (Snooks and Glass Perches)

Aquarium species with glassily transparent high bodies. Dorsal fin in two parts. Most species are marine.
Chanda ranga (HAMILTON- BUCHANAN, 1822) (Glassfish)
   7 cm, 24°C, A - G - H

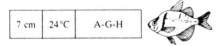

7 cm	24°C	A-G-H

Home: Clear, flowing waters of India, Burma, and Thailand; sometimes also in brackish waters.
Care: Hardy fish. Not too soft water; if needed, add salt. Prefers live food! For breeding, set several pairs in a tank planted with fine-leaved plants. Increase readiness for spawning by raising of the temperature and adding fresh water. Morning sun! Raising difficult! Offer smallest cyclops nauplii. The young do not search actively for food.

Recently, imported fish covered with fluorescent paint have appeared in the trade. What cruelty to animals!

Centrarchidae (Sunfishes)

North American basses and sunfishes with well developed brood care. Cold- water fish! Larger species especially well- suited for garden ponds.
Centrarchus macropterus (LACEPEDE, 1802) (Flier)
   10 cm, 19°C, A - G - H

10 cm	19°C	A-G-H

Home: Eastern USA.
Will grow to 16 cm in the wild.
Care: Live food! Larger, planted aquarium with sandy substrate. Hard water. Winter cool.
Breeds in single-species aquarium. Eggs laid in nest cleaned in sand. Male cares intensively for the brood.
Elassoma evergladei JORDAN, 1884 (Everglades Pygmy sunfish)
   3.5 cm, 18°C, A - N

3.5 cm	18°C	A-N

Home: Southeastern USA.
Very pretty. Recommended for the mini-aquarium. Male black-blue, with sparkling dots.
Care: Undemanding, but needs live food. In a planted single-species tank breeding is easy, especially after cool wintering. Not spawn-eaters.
Lepomis gibbosus (LINNE, 1758) (Pumpkinseed Sunfish)
   20 cm, 17°C, A - G - N - H

20 cm	17°C	A-G-N-H

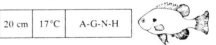

Home: Eastern North America; widely transplanted as a panfish.
Imported into many other areas, including Europe. Remains smaller in the aquarium. Sexually mature at 10 cm. Males very colorful.
Care: For larger cold-water tanks and garden ponds. Care and breeding like *Centrarchus macropterus*.
Mesogonistus chaetodon BAIRD, 1954
   30 cm, 18°C, A - G - N - H

10 cm	18°C	A-G-N-H

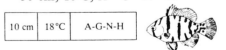

Home: New Jersey to Florida, in standing and slowly flowing waters. Now usually placed in the genus *En-*

neacanthus. A species worthy of recommendation for the cold-water aquarium.

Care and Breeding: Like *Centrarchus macropterus*. Live food!

Percidae (True Perches)

Home: Inland waters of the northern temperate zone.

Carnivorous fishes usually with two separate dorsal fins. For the aquarium, young of the yellow perches *(Perca flavescens* and *P. fluviatilis)* are the ones most likely kept. Darters *(Etheostoma, Percina)* are also popular with North American coldwater aquarists.

Care: Live foods of all kinds; water as cool as possible.

Scatophagidae (Scats)

Home: Coastal waters of Southeast Asia to Australia.

Brackish water animals that temporarily tolerate freshwater and full marine situations. Peaceful, omnivorous; will often attack the aquarium plants! Not suitable for planted aquaria. Frequently available: *Scatophagus argus*.

Badis badis burmanicus. Photo by J. Vierke.

Toxotidae (Archerfishes)

Surface fishes of the coastal regions of southern and southeastern Asia to Australia. *T. jaculator* and *T. chatareus*, which is more suitable for the freshwater aquarium, are regularly available in the stores.

Badidae

Small perch-like fishes originating in southern Asia. Peaceful. Formerly grouped with *Nandus*.

Badis badis (HAMILTON-BUCHANAN, 1822) (Badis, Chameleon Fish)

8 cm, 26°C, A - (G) - N

8 cm	26°C	A (G)-N	

Home: Standing waters in India and Burma.

The sexes can be recognized by their abdominal line. Even with good diet, the markedly larger males tend to have a hollow belly. Females, on the other hand, are rounder.

Care: Ideal for the mini-tank. Provide cave hiding places! Must have live foods! Not infrequently, the red badis, a subspecies or species (*B. b. burmanicus*) from Burma is offered. Care and breeding like the blue badis, *Badis badis badis*.

Nandidae

Carnivorous fishes not suitable for the average community aquarium. Compact and large-headed. Mouth large, with protrusible jaws. Quiet animals that wait for their prey in camouflage coloration; predominantly twilight-active.

Care: Well-planted aquaria with root as hiding places. Prefer live foods (fish), but can usually be accustomed to pieces of meat and pellets. Soft water!

Monocirrhus polyacanthus HECKEL, 1840 (Leaf fish)
  9 cm, 25°C, A - W

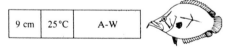

| 9 cm | 25°C | A-W | |

Home: Amazon and Guianas.

Both sexes with tendril on lower jaw. Spawns on plant leaves. Father cares for family, so remove mother. Young hatch after three to four days.

Nandus nebulosus GRAY, 1830)
  12 cm, 25°C, A - (G) - W - N

| 12 cm | 25°C | A (G)-W-N | |

Home: Thailand, Malayan peninsula, and Greater Sunda Islands.

Care: In small aquarium or together with larger fishes. Very similar is the larger *N. nandus* found from India to Thailand. However, it has smaller scales.

Polycentrus schomburgki MUELLER & TROSCHEL, 1848 (Schomburgk's Leaf Fish)
  10 cm, 25°C, A - (G) - W

| 10 cm | 25°C | A (G)-W | |

Home: Northeastern South America.

Remains small in captivity. At spawning time male become velvety black with turquoise dots.

Care and Breeding: Like *Monocirrhus*.

Cichlidae (Cichlids)

Distributed almost exclusively in Central and South America and in Africa. More than 600 species. Often colorful fishes with interesting behavior, especially brood-care behavior. Since they are frequently territorial, there are often problems getting compatible combinations. Based on their brood care, we distinguish between open breeders and hidden breeders. The latter have fewer eggs that, however, are larger and need more time for development. The cave breeders as well as the mouth brooders are included with the hidden breeders. Within the family, mouthbrooding has developed repeatedly and independently in different groups.

Aequidens

South American genus. Usually fairly large cichlids, but also some very peaceful, small species. Some species, like *A. paraguayensis*, are mouthbrooders, but the majority are open breeders.

Aequidens curviceps AHL, 1924 (Flag Cichlid)
  8 cm, 26°C, G - W

8 cm	26°C	G-W

Home: Amazon.

Beautiful, peaceful little fish that does not dig. Males with more elongated fins. With varied diet, breeding not difficult. Open-breeder; spawns on rocks. Biparental care.

Care: Suitable for the planted community aquarium. Requires frequent partial water changes.

Aequidens dorsigerus HECKEL, 1840 (Red-breasted Flag Cichlid)
  12 cm, 26°C, G - W

12 cm	26°C	G-W

Home: Rio Paraguay.

In courting pattern, both sexes are red on the throat and chest. Males with black, golden-edged spot in the center of the dorsal fin.

Aequidens pulcher. Photo by B. Kahl.

Care and Breeding: Like *A. curviceps.* Suited for planted community tanks.

Aequidens pulcher GILL, 1858 (Blue Acara)
  17 cm, 24°C, A - (G) - N - W

17 cm	24°C	A (G)-N-W

Home: Venezuela, Colombia, and Panama.

One of the most beautiful cichlids. Adult males usually with more elongated dorsal and anal fins. Does relatively little digging, yet not a fish for well-planted community aquaria.

Care: Cichlid tank. Food: coarse live food, pellets, large flakes. For breeding, stock in pairs. Provide spawning rocks. An open-breeder with biparental care. This species is in many instances still called *"Aequidens latifrons."*

To be kept and bred in the same way are the somewhat more peaceful but less colorful species *A. maronii* and *A. portalegrensis*.

Apistogramma (South American Dwarf Cichlids)

Small cichlids of South America with marked sex dimorphism. Cave breeders. Put no more than one male and two or three females into a small or medium- sized aquarium. Polygamy is customary, and only the females look after their brood. *Apistogramma* species prefer soft, slightly acid water. Suitable for combination with tetras and other small soft–water fish.

Apistogramma agassizii (STEINDACHNER, 1875) (Agassiz's Dwarf Cichlid)

10 cm, 26°C, G - W

10 cm	26°C	G-W

Home: Amazon.

Males larger and more colorful, with spatulate tail fin. There are several color variations, including predominantly yellow or red males.

Care: Well suited for the community aquarium. Provide caves and roots as hiding places. As far as possible, give live food. For breeding, use two or three females for each male if possible and a large tank with sufficient breeding caves. Soft water.

Apistogramma bitaeniata PELLEGRIN, 1936

9 cm, 27°C, G - A - W

9 cm	27°C	G-A-W

Home: Upper Solimoes and upper course of the Amazon proper.

A very beautiful species. The considerably larger males have elongated dorsal fin flaps. Cave breeders. There also exists a wine-red variation whose relationship to the species has not yet been assured.

Apistogramma agassizi. Photo by J. Vierke.

Apistogramma bitaeniata. Photo by J. Vierke.

Care: Suitable for the community tank. Sensitive to medication. Frequent partial water changes necessary. Water as soft as possible. Live food.

Synonyms: *A. kleei, A. klausewitzi.*

Apistogramma borellii REGAN, 1908 (Umbrella Dwarf Cichlid)

7 cm, 25°C, G - W - N

7 cm	25°C	G-W-N

Home: Rio Paraguay.

Male blue-yellow with very tall, sail-like dorsal fin.

Care: Excellent for the community aquarium. Undemanding fish. Breeding relatively easy; stock in pairs and provide a breeding cave. Female usually cares for brood reliably.

For years the species was known under the name *A. reitzigi.*

Apistogramma cacatuoides HOEDE-MAN, 1951 (Cockatoo Dwarf Cichlid)

8 cm, 25°C, G - W - N

8 cm	25°C	G-W-N

Home: Guianas.

Males with elongated dorsal fin and two-pointed tail fin.

Care: Breeding easy. Use one to three females per male. Breeding caves!

The species formerly was incorrectly known by the name *A. borelli.* We can differentiate a gray variation (often with red spots in the tail fin), a turquoise form (often with yellow tail fin spots), and the unspotted blue form.

Apistogramma iniridae KULLANDER, 1979

7 cm, 26°C, G - A - W

7 cm	26°C	G-A-W

Home: Rio Iniridia in the upper Orinoco region.

Male with high dorsal fin and large, rounded tail fin with sketchy vertical striping.

Care and Breeding: Like *A. agassizii.*

Apistogramma pertensis (HASEMAN, 1911) (Amazon Dwarf Cichlid)
7 cm, 25°C, G - W

7 cm	25°C	G-W	

Home: Central Amazon region.
Rounded tail fin provided with delicate vertical bands.
Care and Breeding: Like *A. agassizii.*

Apistogramma steindachneri REGAN, 1908 (Steindachner's Dwarf Cichlid)
10 cm, 25°C, G - W

10 cm	25°C	G-W	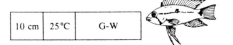

Home: Northeastern South America.
One of the larger dwarf cichlids, yet well suited for the community aquarium. Male larger and more colorful than female, with elongated tail fin tips. Establishes a relatively large territory. Cave breeder.

Care: Plant well and use shelters of roots, rocks, and similar items. Live food; likes dry food less.
This species was often sold under the names *A wickleri* and *A. ornatipinnis,* which are synonyms.

Apistogramma trifasciata (EIGEN-MANN & KENNEDY, 1903) (Three-striped Dwarf Cichlid)
6 cm, 27°C, G - W

6 cm	27°C	G-W	

Home: Amazon, also south of the Amazon watershed in plant-rich bays. Split into several subspecies. Males with very high, feather-like elongated dorsal fin membranes anteriorly.
Care: Give live food as much as possible. Suitable for the well-planted community tank. For breeding, put several females with one male and use

Apistogramma trifasciata. Photo by J. Vierke.

a corresponding number of breeding caves. Establishes relatively large territories!

Astronotus
Astronotus ocellatus (CUVIER, 1829) (Oscar)
33 cm, 24°C, A - W - N

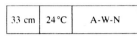

33 cm	24 °C	A-W-N

Home: Amazon basin and Parana system.

Sex differentiation difficult. Substrate spawner. Parents guard young. Several color varieties are known, the most popular being the red form (red oscar).

Care: Magnificent fish for the large aquarium. Combination with other large cichlids possible. Equipment: large rocks, roots, floating plants. Food: earthworms, goldfish, meat, trout food, etc.

Aulonocara
Best known is the species called *A. nyassae*, endemic in Lake Malawi, Africa. Grows to 18 cm in length. A popular fish for the hard-water large cichlid tank because it is very colorful. Temperatures around 24°C. Mouthbrooder.

Chromidotilapia
Mouthbrooder from the coastal waters of western Africa. Need hard to medium- hard water.
Chromidotilapia guentheri (SAUVAGE, 1882) (Guenther's Mouthbrooder)
18 cm, 25°C, A - N - H

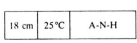

18 cm	25 °C	A-N-H

Home: Western Africa.
Beautiful, but often aggressive fish.
Care: Cichlid tank. Breeding in pairs. Female with reddish abdomen. Spawning on rock or in hole. Mouthbrooders. Parents take turns guarding young.

Cichlasoma
Usually large cichlids of Central and South America. Adult males are larger than females and often have elongated dorsal and anal fins as well as a protuberance on the forehead. Most species are suitable only for specially equipped large cichlid tanks with appropriate companion fishes. Often excellent brood care. Biparental family.
Cichlasoma cyanoguttatum (BAIRD & GIRARD, 1854) (Texas Cichlid)
30 cm, 20°C, A - N

30 cm	20 °C	A-N

Home: Texas and northern Mexico.
Care: Beautiful, large cichlid for the cichlid tank. Needs rocks, roots, floating plants, and a filter, plus frequent additions of fresh water. In old water the fish easily get ulcers. Is often called *Herichthys cyanoguttatus*.
Cichlasoma festivum (HECKEL, 1840) (Flag Cichlid)
20 cm, 24°C, G - W - N

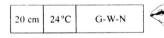

20 cm	24 °C	G-W-N

Home: Amazon and western Guyana.
Very peaceful, does not dig. Sexes almost impossible to differentiate externally. Open-breeder. Parental family.

Care: Planted tank with rocks and roots. Can be combined without second thought with fishes that are not too small.

299

Cichlasoma meeki (BRIND, 1918) (Firemouth)
15 cm, 23°C, A - (G) - N

15 cm	23°C	A (G)-N

Home: Central America — Yucatan. Very beautiful cichlid that sometimes digs. Females usually smaller than males. Open-breeder; parental family. Crossing with *C. nigrofasciatum* possible.

Care: Possible to keep in community aquarium. Secure plant roots with rocks. Not too small fellow inhabitants. Coarse live food, trout food, meat, dry food flakes.

Cichlasoma nigrofasciatum (GUENTHER, 1869) (Convict Cichlid)

15 cm	23°C	A (G)-N

Home: Central America from Guatemala to western Panama.

Females usually smaller than males, with rounded fins and reddish zones on the abdomen. Spawn in open on rocks or in artificial caves. Both parents care eagerly for the brood.

The albino form is misleadingly called "Congo Cichlid."

Care: Digs a lot, therefore has only a limited suitability for the community aquarium.

Cichlasoma octofasciatum (REGAN, 1903) (Jack Dempsey)
20 cm, 23°C, A - N

20 cm	23°C	A-N

Home: Central America — Mexico to Honduras.

Splendid display fish. Sexes very similar. Open-breeders, parental family. The species formerly was most often called *C. biocellatum*.

Care: Only suitable for a large cichlid tank. Digs a great deal. No plants. Filter! Food: goldfish, earthworms, trout food, meat.

Cichlasoma septemfasciatum REGAN, 1908
12 cm, 23°C, A - N

12 cm	23°C	A-N

Home: Eastern slopes of Costa Rica and Panama.

Beautiful peaceful fish that digs at spawning time. It was once thought that this species was identical with *C. spilurum; C. cutteri* is a synonym.

Cichlasoma severum (HECKEL, 1840) (Severum)
20 cm, 25°C, A - W - N

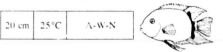

20 cm	25°C	A-W-N

Home: Northern Amazon basin and Guyana.

Very beautiful and normally peaceful; during spawning season, however, quarrelsome. Males with stronger red-brown head markings. Breeding not always easy, since often choosy when selecting a partner.

Care: Cichlid tank. Coarse live food (small earthworms, fish, meat), occasionally fresh lettuce leaves.

Cichlasoma spilurum (GUENTHER, 1862) (Blue-eyed Cichlid)
12 cm, 23°C, A - N

12 cm	23°C	A-N

Home: Eastern coast of Belize, Guatemala, Honduras.

Peaceful, hardy fish for the cichlid tank. Older males larger, often with forehead protuberances. Breeding easy. Eggs are placed preferably in stone caves. Biparental family, persevering care.

This species is not identical with *C. cutteri* (see *C. septemfasciatum*). It hybridizes with *C. nigrofasciatum*.

Crenicara (Checkerboard Cichlids)

Of the four known species of this genus, only the following is frequently offered for sale:

Crenicara filamentosa LADIGES, 1959 (Checkerboard Lyretail)

10 cm, 25°C, G - W

10 cm	25°C	G-W	

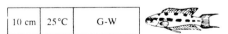

Home: Central Amazon region.

Males with beautiful colors and extended tail fin tips. Breeding successful only in optimal water qualities. Open-spawners. Mother cares for brood.

Cichlasoma spilurum. Photo by J. Vierke.

Care: Suited for the well-planted community tank. Water soft and acid (peat additive). Sensitive to water deterioration. Live foods, occasionally dry food.

Crenicichla (Pike Cichlids)

Elongated carnivorous fishes. About 30 South American species, often beautifully colored. Suited only for the single-species aquarium.

Crenicichla lepidota HECKEL, 1840 (Peacock Pike Cichlid)

20 cm, 24°C, A - W - N

20 cm	24°C	A-W-N	

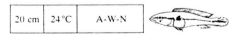

Home: Amazon basin.

Extremely predaceous fish that likes to hide under plants and roots near the bottom. Males with long dorsal and anal fin extensions.

301

Care: Water not too hard. Eats fish, large water insects, earthworms. For breeding, offer large spawning caves; also said to breed in the open. Care of the brood mainly by the male.

Eretmodus

Only one known species. Together with the closely related genera *Tanganicodus* and *Spathodus,* it is one of the cichlids of Lake Tanganyika, Africa.

Eretmodus cyanostictus BOULENGER, 1898 (Striped Goby Cichlid)
8 cm, 25 °C, A - G - N - H

8 cm	25 °C	A-G-N-H

Home: Lake Tanganyika.
Peaceful and friendly to plants. Rather comical bottom-fish.

Care: Community aquarium possible, but single-species tank better. Many stone constructions, caves. Water not too soft. Frequent water changes! Live and dry foods.

Breeding difficult, since pair formations are of long duration. Mouthbrooders with territories. Allow parents to care for the brood together!

Etroplus

The only truly Asiatic genus of cichlids (others in the Middle East); only three species. One of them *(E. canarensis)* is very rare and completely unknown in the aquarium.

Etroplus maculatus (BLOCH, 1795) (Orange Chromide)
8 cm, 26 °C, G - N - H

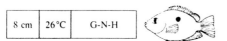

8 cm	26 °C	G-N-H

Home: Southern India and Sri Lanka.
Recommended, peaceful cichlid. Plant-friendly. The larger males are colorful. Breeding not difficult. Open-breeders.

The young feed initially on their parents' body slime.

Care: Accept live and dry foods.

Etroplus suratensis (BLOCH, 1790) (Banded Chromide)
15 cm, 24 °C, A - H

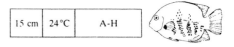

15 cm	24 °C	A-H

Home: Coastal regions of Sri Lanka and India (here to 40 cm length!).

Peaceful fish, despite their size; however, because they are plant-eaters they are unsuited for the community tank. Sex differences unknown.

Care: Food: live food (fishes, earthworms), meat, lettuce, balanced spinach. Require large aquaria, some salt addition advantageous. For breeding, add 2-3 teaspoons of sea salt per 10 liters of water. Open-breeders, parental family.

Geophagus (Eartheaters)

Peaceful South American cichlids that show all transitions from open-breeders *(G. brasiliensis)* to the highly specialized mouthbrooders *(G. steindachneri)*. The name "Geophagus" means "earth eater" and refers to the animals' peculiarity of taking the substrate into their mouths to sift it for something edible. The aquarium should have a sandy substrate, at least in places; plants have to be protected by rocks against being uprooted.

Geophagus jurupari HECKEL, 1840 (Demon Fish)
26 cm, 25 °C, A (G) - W

26 cm	25 °C	A (G)-W

Home: Guianas.
Decorative fish. Completely harmless toward other fishes. Chews substrate searching for food, therefore poorly suited for the average community aquarium. The

spawn is usually deposited on rocks. After about 24 hours, the parents continue to care for the spawn in their mouths. Release of the young occurs after about ten days. Parental family.

Care: Special cichlid tank setup with sandy substrate. Eats smaller live foods (tubifex, mosquito larvae) and dry food.

Geophagus steindachneri EIGENMANN & HILDEBRAND, 1910 (Redhump Geophagus)

25 cm, 26 °C, (G) - N

25 cm	26 °C	(G)-N	

Home: Colombia, in the Cauca and Magdalena systems.

A peaceful fish that digs relatively little. Males larger, with forehead bump. No territory formation. Mouthbrooder. The female releases the young after about 20 days. Set her apart during carrying time and do not feed. Young will immediately eat *Artemia*. Mother-protected family.

Geophagus steindachneri. Photo by J. Vierke.

Care: Can be kept in planted community tanks with fishes that are not too small, but cichlid tanks better. Eats coarse live food, small fishes, earthworms, pellets, and food flakes.

This species has been called *G. hondae* and *G. magdalenae* at different times. Interesting courtship. Dummy egg (?) in the corner of the mouth.

Geophagus surinamensis (BLOCH, 1791) (Surinam Geophagus)

28 cm, 25 °C, A (G) - N

28 cm	25 °C	A (G)-N	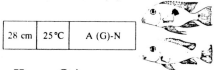

Home: Guianas.

Males with extended posterior fin rays. Spawn on rocks. Shortly before hatching, pick up the eggs and care continues in the mouth. Parental family.

Care: Single-species or cichlid tank with sandy substrate. Live and dry foods.

Haplochromis

An African cichlid genus that contains more than 200 species (but lately broken by some workers into many genera). Most of the species originate in Lakes Malawi and Victoria. Most with striking sexual dimorphism (males and females differ in size and coloration). The females care for the eggs and larvae in their mouths. The males have so-called egg-spots at the rear end of the anal fin that serve as decoys to entice the female to spawn in the nest cavity and also in the fertilization of the eggs. The female collects the eggs in her mouth before they can be fertilized; during the female's attempt to grab the decoy eggs on the male's anal fin, she sucks up the sperm, which now can fertilize the spawn in the female's mouth.

Haplochromis burtoni GUENTHER, 1893 (Burton's Mouthbrooder)
15 cm, 26 °C, A (G) - N

15 cm	26 °C	A (G)-N

Home: Africa.
Very beautiful fish.

Care: Combination with robust fishes in larger community aquarium possible but a single-species or cichlid tank is preferable. Will dig out spawning cavities! Undemanding as regards water composition and food.

For breeding, combine a male with several females. Females smaller, less colorful, with less striking anal fin spots. Females mouthbrooders. Keep spawn-carrying females separate. Raising of the young, which swim free after 15-20 days, easy. (Placed with the genus *Astatotilapa* by some authors.)

Haplochromis compressiceps (BOULENGER, 1908) (Malawian Eye-biter)
25 cm, 24 °C, A - H

25 cm	24 °C	A-H

Home: Lake Malawi, Africa.
Impressive because of its enormous wedge-shaped and elongated head.

Care: Quiet fish for the cichlid tank, better yet for the planted single-species aquarium. Is said to sometimes bite the eyes out on other fishes! Will take living and dry foods; eats small fishes.

Haplochromis moorii BOULENGER, 1902 (Blue Lumphead)
25 cm, 24 °C, A - H

25 cm	24 °C	A-H

Home: Lake Malawi, Africa.
Decorative, large blue cichlid.

Care: Cichlid tank with partial sandy substrate. Water hard, slightly alkaline; needs regular partial water changes. Accepts live and dry foods.

Breeding: Mouthbrooder. Isolate spawn-carrying female.

Hemichromis

African open-breeders. Very beautiful but very aggressive toward each other and toward other species. Take good care of their brood.

Hemichromis bimaculatus GILL, 1862 (Jewel Cichlid)
15 cm, 24 °C, A - N

15 cm	24 °C	A-N

Hemichromis bimaculatus. Photo by B. Kahl.

Home: Northern and tropical Africa.

Very beautiful fish but extremely aggressive. Females usually redder than males. Open-breeders. Parental family. There are two different forms of the jewel cichlid that perhaps belong to different species.

Care: Best is a single-species tank with rock constructions and hardy plants. No demands concerning food and water quality.

Hemichromis fasciatus PETERS, 1857 (Five-spotted Hemichromis)
    25 cm, 24°C, A - N - H

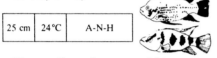

Home: Central western Africa.

Extremely quarrelsome but beautiful cichlid. In the wild, a fish-eater.

Care: Large single-species tank with many possible hiding places. Coarse live foods (including earthworms) and meat.

Herotilapia

Genus of Central American cichlid close to the genus *Cichlasoma*. Only one species.

Herotilapia multispinosa (GUENTHER, 1869) (Rainbow Cichlid)
    14 cm, 23°C, A - N

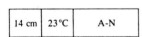

Home: Costa Rica and Nicaragua.

A relatively peaceful species that, however, should be kept in a cichlid tank if possible. Undemanding, beautiful fish. Males with longer, pointed dorsal and anal fin extensions. Breeding very easy. Open-breeder. Parents take good care of the brood.

Julidochromis

Slender cichlids from the rocky bank zone of Lake Tanganyika. In the aquarium need medium-hard alkaline water and as many cave hiding places as possible. Five species.

Julidochromis marlieri POLL, 1956 (Marlier's Julie)
    15 cm, 25°C, A - N

Home: Rocky regions of Lake Tanganyika.

Care: Single-species or cichlid tank with many rocks and stone caves. Plant friendly. Combining with others of the same species may initially be very difficult, but become friendly after an adaptation period. Eat live or dry foods. Sensitive to transfer into different water! Cave-breeders. Keep young with parents. The same applies to *J. regani*.

Julidochromis ornatus BOULENGER, 1898 (Julie)
    9 cm, 25°C, A - G - N

Home: Lake Tanganyika.

Beautiful black and yellow cichlid. Female larger, plumper. Cave-breeder. Leave young in the tank with the parents. They are not persecuted by the parents and may establish new colonies.

Care: Most effective in single-species tanks. However, housing in beautifully planted community tanks is possible. After adaptation, peaceful toward each other. Need many rock constructions with caves. Be careful when transferring into other water. No special demands concerning food. These guidelines also apply for *J. dickfeldi* and *J. transcriptus*.

Labeotropheus

From Lake Malawi. Have strikingly undershot mouths with obvious "nose." Only two species are known.

Labeotropheus fuelleborni AHL, 1927 (Fuelleborn's Mbuna)

15 cm, 25°C, A - N - H

15 cm	25°C	A-N-H

Home: Lake Malawi, Africa.

Care: Cichlid tank with rock constructions and roots. Only hardy plants. Water slightly alkaline. Live food, beef heart, dry food, balanced spinach, and lettuce. Breeding not particularly difficult. The females are mouthbrooders. If possible, mouthbrooding fish should be isolated without chasing them too much when catching them.

Labeotropheus   trewavasae   FRYER, 1956 (Red-top Trewavasae)

15 cm, 25°C, A - N - H

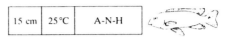

15 cm	25°C	A-N-H

Home: Lake Malawi, Africa.

Similar to *L. fuelleborni* but slimmer. Large number of regional color variations.

Care and Breeding: Like *L. fuelleborni.*

Labidochromis

Mouthbrooders from Lake Malawi. Like all mbuna cichlids, to be kept in medium-hard, slightly alkaline water. Relatively undemanding. Sexes not always easy to differentiate.

Julidochromis dickfeldi. Photo by J. Vierke.

Lamprologus

Home: Lake Tanganyika and Congo region.

Species of very diverse appearance. Eat predominantly live food. Not mouthbrooders. Deposit their eggs on rocks or similar structures, often hidden in caves or cracks.

Lamprologus brichardi POLL, 1974 (Brichardi, Lyretailed Lamprologus)
10 cm, 24°C, G - N - H

| 10 cm | 24°C | G-N-H |

Home: Lake Tanganyika, Africa.

Beautiful, lively fish, occasionally aggressive. Undemanding.

Care: Possible to keep in community tanks with hardy companion fishes. Needs many stone caves and will not destroy plants. Water medium-hard to hard, alkaline. No particular food requirements. Breeding best in single- species aquarium. Cave-spawners. Parents will not persecute young. In the single-species aquarium it has been observed that the older siblings sometimes help the parents in caring for the brood. Former name: *Lamprologus savoryi elongatus.*

Lamprologus congoensis SCHILTHUIS, 1891 (Congo Lamprologus)
15 cm, 24°C, A - W

| 15 cm | 24°C | A-W |

Home: Regions of the rapids in the Congo River (Zaire).

An elongated cichlid inhabiting the bottom. Sometimes aggressive. Females frequently smaller than males. Breed in hiding places under rocks and roots.

Care: Single-species or cichlid tanks with rock constructions, many caves,

and roots and driftwood.

Very similar in care and breeding is *L. werneri.*

Lamprologus leleupi POLL, 1956 (Lemon Cichlid)
10 cm, 24°C, A (G) - N - H

| 10 cm | 24°C | A (G) N-H |

Home: Lake Tanganyika, on rocks in 5-20 m depth.

Sex differentiation difficult. Breeding in single-species tanks uncomplicated. Cave-breeders. The young may remain with their parents for a long time. In addition to the popular golden-yellow form, there is also a blackish race as well as a slenderer yellow form.

Care: Planted single-species tank with many rock constructions and caves.

Melanochromis

Fishes occurring only in Lake Malawi; closely related to the genus *Pseudotropheus.*

Melanochromis auratus (BOULENGER, 1897) (Auratus, Malawi Golden Cichlid)
11 cm, 25°C, A - N - H

| 11 cm | 25°C | A-N-H |

Home: Lake Malawi, Africa, on rocky substrate.

Magnificent fish, sometimes aggressive. Submissive males usually have the same coloration as females. Careful when purchasing! Mouthbrooders in the female sex.

Care: Two or three females per male. Cichlid tank with rocks and caves. Take live and dry foods, and in addition algae.

Similar guidelines apply for the care of the similar, somewhat smaller *Melanochromis johanii* (formerly called *"Pseudotropheus daviesi"*).

Nannacara

South American genus poor in species (close to the genus *Aequidens*).

Nannacara anomala REGAN, 1905 (Golden Dwarf Cichlid)
9 cm, 25°C, G - W - N

9 cm	25 °C	G-W-N

Home: Venezuela and Guyana.

Recommended, beautiful dwarf cichlid. Females smaller than males, with shorter dorsal and anal fin tips.

Care: Well planted community aquarium. Cave hiding places. Undemanding fish.

Breeding not difficult. Equip with breeding caves such as flowerpots. In small aquaria, remove father after spawning. Mother cares for young.

Nanochromis

Dwarf cichlids from central and western Africa. In care and breeding they are very similar to the *Apistogramma* species of South America, preferring a well-planted aquarium with root shelters and caves. Provide soft, somewhat acid water, but water of medium hardness is also tolerated.

Nanochromis nudiceps (BOULENGER, 1899)
8 cm, 25°C, A - W

8 cm	25 °C	A-W

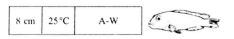

Home: Lower Congo in quickly flowing waters.

Secretive fish that can be aggressive, especially toward others of the same species. Females with swollen abdo-

mens. Stock in pairs for breeding. Cave-breeder. Biparental family.

Care: Best in a single-species tank provided with rocks and roots. Prefers to eat live foods, but will also take artificial food.

Possibly identical with *N. parilus*.

Neetroplus

Central American fish close to the genus *Cichlasoma*.

Neetroplus nematopus GUENTHER, 1869 (Little Lake Cichlid)
14 cm, 24°C, A - N

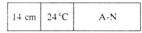

14 cm	24 °C	A-N

Home: Nicaragua and Costa Rica, in rocky zones close to the bottom of lakes.

Lively, not always peaceful fish. Male larger than female, with steeper forehead. Cave-breeders. Biparental family.

Care: Should have rocks and caves in the aquarium also. Fine sand substrate.

Papiliochromis

South American species with at present only one species kept in the aquarium. *Microgeophagus* has been accepted as the correct name by American ichthyologists.

Papiliochromis ramirezi (MYERS & HARRY, 1948) (Ram, Butterfly Dwarf Cichlid)
6 cm, 27°C, G - W

6 cm	27 °C	G-W

Home: Colombia and Venezuela, in plant-rich, quiet, warm water zones of the rivers.

Beautiful and very peaceful. Unfortunately, short-lived.

The female is most easily recognized by its rose-colored abdomen. Spawning in the open, in cavities or on rocks. Biparental family; do not always take good care of the brood.

Sometimes a gold-colored variety is offered; in care and breeding like the original form.

Care: Plant-rich community tank. Sensitive to old water.

The Ram found in eastern Bolivia is said to belong to another species *(P. altispinosa)*.

Pelmatochromis

Small to medium-sized cichlids from tropical western and central Africa. Some species originally included in this genus are today placed with the genera *Pelvicachromis, Thysia,* and *Chromidotilapia.*

Pelmatochromis thomasi

(BOULENGER, 1915) (African Butterfly Cichlid)

10 cm, 25°C, G - W - N

10 cm	25°C	G-W-N	

Pelvicachromis pulcher. Photo by J. Vierke.

Home: Sierra Leone, southeastern Guinea, and western Liberia.

Peaceful, plant-friendly fish.

Care: Community aquarium. Water soft to medium-hard and neutral to acid. No special food requirements.

Breeding is easy. Stock in pairs (females are smaller and more rounded than males). Open-breeders. Biparental family. The parents often do not take good care of the brood. Some authors place this species with the genus *Hemichromis.*

Pelvicachromis

Western and central African dwarf cichlids. Frequently beautifully colored. Cave-breeders with sexual dimorphism. Females more colorful!! Mother families; in many instances, the father may participate in brood care of the older young.

Pelvicachromis pulcher (BOULENGER, 1901) (Kribensis)
10 cm, 24°C, G - N

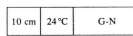

10 cm	24°C	G-N

Home: Coastal regions of western Africa. Will enter brackish water.
Very beautiful, peaceful fish.
Care: Excellent addition to a beautifully planted community aquarium. Living and breeding caves of rocks and coconut shells. Live or dry food. Undemanding regarding water values.
Breeding is easy. Stock in pairs with flowerpot cave. Males have to be removed after spawning, since otherwise they may be killed by the females. Formerly *Pelmatochromis kribensis.*

Pelvicachromis taeniatus (BOULENGER, 1901) (Striped Kribensis)
10 cm, 24°C, G - W - N

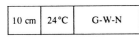

10 cm	24°C	G-W-N

Home: Distributed through different regions of western Africa in several color forms.
For typical males the dark-edged body scales form a netted pattern. The smaller females are more colorful.
Care and Breeding: Like *P. pulcher.*

Pseudocrenilabrus
Very interesting small mouthbrooders from Africa that make no special demands on either food or water quality. Relatively peaceful, thus suitable for community aquaria. During the reproductive period, however, they dig spawning cavities in the substrate. The species now included in this genus formerly were placed with the genus *Haplochromis* and then were designated as *Hemihaplochromis* for awhile.

Pseudocrenilabrus multicolor (HILGENDORF, 1903) (Dwarf Egyptian Mouthbrooder)
8 cm, 24°C, G - N

8 cm	24°C	G-N

Home: Eastern Africa.
Relatively peaceful, small mouthbrooders.
Care: Undemanding with regard to water quality and food. For breeding, use two to four females per male. Isolate mouthbrooding females. Propagation possible even in the community aquarium.

Pseudocrenilabrus philander (WEBER, 1897) (South African Mouthbrooder)
12 cm, 24°C, G - N

12 cm	24°C	G-N

Home: Southern Africa.
The males are shimmering golden-green and have an orange anal fin tip.
Care: Undemanding in every respect. One male should be kept with several females, and the mouthbrooding females should be isolated. Raising of the young easy.
A frequently imported subspecies (*P. p. dispersus*) remains markedly smaller.

Pseudotropheus (Mbunas)
Includes a large number of popular mouthbrooding rock-dwelling cichlids from Lake Malawi. Usually decorative fishes. Together with a few other closely related genera (*Melanochromis*, etc.) from this region, they are called "mbuna."
Care: Best kept in large tanks divided by rock constructions into many territory- like zones, together with a

number of related species. Serious fights then usually are avoided. However, plant growth does not often last in such tanks, especially since the fish require alkaline water. In smaller aquaria the necessity of keeping only a few fish often poses problems. Breeding in the typical mbuna tank is not difficult. The most advantageous breeding temperature lies around 26°C. Water not too hard (around 10° DH is favorable), pH value in the alkaline range. Trap egg-carrying females in a glass and transfer with the water into a separate aquarium with water of the same quality. Capture is easiest at night in a dark tank, using a flashlight.

Pseudotropheus livingstonii (BOULENGER, 1899) (Livingstone's Mbuna)
15 cm, 24°C, A - N

Home: Lake Malawi.

The males are more colorful than the females and have an egg-spot in the anal fin.

Care: Undemanding mouthbrooder for the cichlid tank. Will accept hiding places in caves, but in its home the fish lives in the empty snail shells of the genus *Lanistes* — at least in its young stages.

Externally very similar and with a corresponding mode of living is the dwarf snail cichlid *(P. lanisticola)*. It is said to grow to a maximum of 6 cm.

Pseudotropheus tropheops REGAN, 1921 (Tropheops)
15 cm, 25°C, A - N

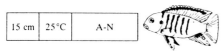

Home: Rocky coasts of Lake Malawi.

Sexes of different color. Male usually with dark blue base coloration and black vertical bands, with golden-yellow egg- spot in the anal fin. Females very variable in coloration.

Pseudotropheus zebra BOULENGER, 1899 (Zebra)
15 cm, 25°C, A - N

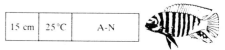

Home: Lake Malawi.

The males normally are larger and more colorful than the females and have well-marked egg-spots on the anal fin. In addition to the normally blue-black males, there are also other natural forms (bright blue, red zebra, etc.). Among the females also there are several different colors and patterns.

Care: Fish for the cichlid tank equipped with rock constructions and caves. Aggressive. Keep one male with several females. Occasionally add some lettuce to the food.

Pterophyllum (Angelfish)

The representatives of this genus rightfully belong to the most popular of aquarium fishes. They are very decorative, peaceful, and plant-friendly. In addition to the two species described here, there is also the long-nosed angelfish, *P. dumerilii,* which is very rarely seen.

Pterophyllum altum PELLEGRIN, 1903 (High-finned Angelfish)
16 cm, 27°C, G - W - S

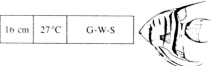

Home: Upper Orinoco.

This species (its status is controver-

sial!) is said to differ from *P. scalare* mainly by the course of the vertical bands: the gray vertical band that follows the black eye band runs through the beginning of the pectoral fins completely around the neck; Then follows another black band. Sexual differences very difficult to detect.

Care: Keep several in a well-planted community tank. Easily startled. Large Angels occasionally eat small tetras (neons)!

Pterophyllum scalare (LICHTENSTEIN, 1823) (Angel fish)

15 cm, 26°C, W - N - S

15 cm	26°C	W-N-S

Home: Amazon.

Quiet schooling fish; territorial. Outside of the breeding period, sexual differences are difficult to recognize. In breeding angels the sexes can be recognized by the shape of the genital papilae. The female has a blunt, broad-ended papilla, the male a pointed pa-

Sarotherodon mossambicus. Photo by J. Vierke.

pilla. There are many color varieties: gray, black, yellow, marbled, veil-finned, etc.

Care: Well planted community aquarium. Peaceful, but will sometimes eat small fish (neons). Accepts live and dry foods.

Sarotherodon

These mouthbrooders, originally included in the genus *Tilapia*, are without exception very large cichlids from Africa and the adjacent Middle East. Fully–grown fishes are barely suitable for amateur aquaria. Listed here is only the best-known and perhaps most beautiful species.

Sarotherodon mossambicus (PETERS, 1825) (Mozambique Mouthbrooder)

40 cm, 25°C, A - N

40 cm	25°C	A-N	

Home: Originally eastern Africa, today worldwide in the tropics.

Males larger, darker than females. Sexually mature at 10 cm length. Females mouthbrooders.

Care: Recommended only for large display tanks. Give them rocks and roots, but not plants. No special requirements concerning water quality. Food: coarse live food (fishes, earthworms), meat, also rolled oats.

Spathodus

The two *Spathodus* species, like the closely related species of the genera *Eretmodus* and *Tanganicodus*, inhabit the rocky coastal zones of Lake Tanganyika. They need medium-hard, clear, alkaline (pH 8-9 water).

Spathodus erythrodon BOULENGER, 1900 (Blue-spotted Goby Cichlids)
   8 cm, 25°C, A - N

8 cm	25°C	A-N	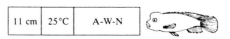

Home: Rocky banks of Lake Tanganyika.

Comical bottom-fish, peaceful and plant-friendly.

Care: Special tank with rocky caves (may also be combined with *Julidochromis ornatus, J. transcriptus,* or *Tropheus*). Accepts live and dry foods. Frequent water changes necessary.

Breeding difficult: territorial mouthbrooders. Do not separate parents caring for the brood.

The same also applies to *Tanganicodus irsacae* and the larger *Spathodus marlieri*.

Steatocranus

A few species from the region of the rapids of the Congo River (Zaire).

Steatocranus casuaris POLL, 1939 (Lionhead Cichlid)
   11 cm, 25°C, A - W - N

11 cm	25°C	A-W-N	

Impressive but aggressive. Form territories on the bottom. Males markedly larger than females, with age developing high forehead protuberance. Cave-breeders. Mother family.

Care: Need large tank with many rocks, roots, and caves. Put two to four females with one male . Combination with surface fishes possible. Accepts live and artificial foods.

Symphysodon (Discus Fish)

Widely distributed in the Amazon region and the area of the Orinoco. Very popular fish because of its round, flat shape and the often striking coloration. It comes from acid, very miner-

Young *Symphysodon* grazing on the adult.

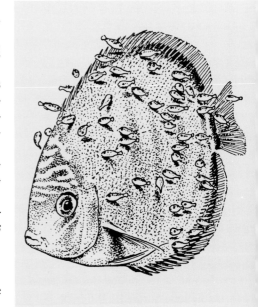

al-poor waters. For correct care and best breeding potential it should be given corresponding water. For keeping, a medium degree of hardness is often sufficient. Discus should not be kept under 26°C and should be provided as often as possible with a wide variety of live foods.

Symphysodon aequifasciata PELLEGRIN, 1903 (Discus)
18 cm, 28°C, A - G - W

18 cm	28°C	A-G-W

Home: Amazon, Orinoco region.

No definite sexual distinctions. Stock in pairs. Substrate-spawner (on upside-down flowerpots). Biparental family. Young animals at first feed on skin secretions of the parents. For this reason, artificial raising — especially by amateur aquarists — cannot be considered practical.

Care: Needs well-planted community tank with roots. Sedate fellow inhabitants. Special tank better. Several specimens can be kept in a tank. Water soft and acid (pH around 6). Frequent partial water changes. Food: varied, live food as much as possible. Not a fish for the beginner. Easiest to keep and breed is the brown discus; other subspecies are the green and blue discus.

Symphysodon discus HECKEL, 1840 (Discus Heckel)
20 cm, 28°C, A (G) - W

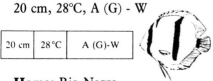

20 cm	28°C	A (G)-W

Home: Rio Negro.

Differs from *S. aequifasciata* by having the central vertical band especially clearly marked. Decorative, peaceful.

Care: Well-planted community aquarium or — better — special aquarium. Not a fish for beginners! Otherwise, care and breeding like *S. aequifasciata.*

Teleogramma
Elongated bottom-fishes from the Congo basin.

Teleogramma brichardi POLL, 1959 (Brichard's Slender Cichlid)
12 cm, 23°C, A - W

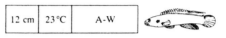

12 cm	23°C	A-W

Home: River rapids region in the vicinity of Stanley Pool (Pool Malebo) in the Congo.

Males darker than females. Females soft red on the abdomen. Cave-breeders.

Care: Aggressive bottom-fish for the special aquarium well equipped with rock caves and roots. It is best to keep several females with one male. Provide clean water by means of motorized filter! Takes live and artificial foods.

Telmatochromis
Slender cichlids from Lake Tanganyika, reminiscent of *Julidochromis.*

Telmatochromis bifrenatus MYERS, 1936 (Striped Telmat)
8 cm, 25°C, A - G - N

8 cm	25°C	A-G-N

Very peaceful fish. Female plumper than male.

Care: Requires many rocky constructions with caves for hiding. Suited for planted community aquaria.

Breeding like *Julidochromis;* cave-breeder. Water alkaline and of medium hardness.

Very similar in appearance is *T. vittatus,* which is identical in care and breeding. Both species have a lengthwise body band extending from the mouth to the beginning of the tail fin. In *T. bifrenatus*, in contrast to *T. vittatus*, the band is overlaid with a zigzag stripe typical of the species.

Thysia

This includes only one species that formerly was placed with the genus *Pelmatochromis*.

Thysia ansorgii (BOULENGER, 1901) (Five-spot African Cichlid)

13 cm, 25 °C, A - G - N

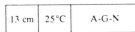

Home: Coastal regions of West Africa.

Care: Relatively peaceful, undemanding fish that is suited for the well-planted community aquarium. Offer roots and other shelters. Not more than one male in the aquarium, since otherwise they will fight.

Females can be recognized by the shining silvery anal spot. Spawns under rocks or in caves with wide opening. Mother cares for the brood. In smaller tanks, the male should be removed.

Tilapia

Genus of rather large cichlids widely distributed throughout Africa and the Near East. After removal of the mouthbrooding forms, which were placed in the genus *Sarotherodon*, only open-breeders remain in the genus. They are only suitable for large unplanted aquaria. The majority are plant-eaters!

Tilapia mariae BOULENGER, 1899 (Tiger Tilapia)

20 cm, 25 °C, A - N

Home: Lower courses of the rivers and streams in the coastal regions of West Africa.

Persevering, peaceful fish, but aggressive when caring for the brood. Open-breeder with biparental family.

Care: Large cichlid tank with rocks and roots. Plant-eaters! Take live food, dry food, rolled oats, lettuce.

Tropheus

Thus far, three described species occurring only in Lake Tanganyika. *Tropheus* species should be kept in small schools. If possible, bring them into the aquarium together as young fish. Fish purchased later are relentlessly battled and not accepted into the group!

Tropheus duboisi MARLIER, 1959 (Duboisi)

12 cm, 25 °C, A - N - S

Home: Rocky regions of Lake Tanganyika, in a depth of 5-15 m.

Females mouthbrooders. Young leave the mouth only after about one month.

Care: Aquarium with rocky zones offering hiding possibilities. Live and dry food.

Tropheus moorii BOULENGER, 1898 (Moorii)

12 cm, 25 °C, A - N - S

Home: Lake Tanganyika, upper regions of rocky bank zones.

No certain external sex characteristics. Of this species, almost 20 geographical races are available. Especially beautiful are the yellow-red, tail striped, emperor, and double spot forms.

Care: In schools. Rocks with many hiding places. Live and dry foods. Water medium hard, alkaline.

For breeding, the water should lie between 10 and 15° DH and have a pH value of 7.5-8. Breeding temperature about 26 °C. Maximum of ten eggs per spawning! Females mouthbrooders.

Uaru

Attractive large South American cichlid. Thus far, only one species known whose requirements and behavior are strongly reminiscent of the discus.

Uaru amphiacanthoides HECKEL, 1840 (Uaru, Triangle Cichlid)

30 cm, 28 °C, A - W - (S)

30 cm	28 °C	A-W-(S)

Home: Mineral-poor waters of Amazonia and Guianas.

Peaceful fish. Open-breeder. Biparental family. During their first days the young fish graze off a skin secretion produced by the parents.

Care: Several fish together. Large, not too bright single-species tank decorated with rocks and roots. Needs soft, acid water and frequent partial water changes. Accepts live foods (mosquito larvae, water fleas), small fish, little pieces of meat, lettuce, small pieces of apple, and other vegetable foods. Eats a lot; filter!

Anabantoidei (Labyrinth Fishes)

A suborder composed of about 75 species, with many popular and interesting aquarium fishes. These fishes are distinguished by the possession of a labyrinth organ that allows them in addition to the regular gill breathing of dissolved oxygen, to breathe atmospheric air. For this they regularly need to go to the surface in order to exchange the air in their labyrinth cavity. This is a hollow space provided with tissue folds that is found above the actual gill cavity. To this suborder belong the following four families.

Anabantidae

Includes the Asiatic genus *Anabas* and the two African genera *Ctenopoma* and *Sandelia*. These fishes have thorn-like processes (spines) on the gill covers.

Anabas (Climbing Perch)

Only one species, but frequent in all parts of southern and southeastern Asia. Food fish!

Anabas testudineus (BLOCH, 1795) (Climbing Perch)

23 cm, 26 °C, A - W - N

23 cm	26 °C	A-W-N

Relatively peaceful toward others of its species. The fish survives the dry periods in its home by burrowing into the drying muck. Occasionaly leaves its home waters and searches for new waters, walking across the land.

Care: For larger tanks without plants. Combine with robust fishes, cichlids. Cover aquarium well! Omnivorous.

Females heavier bodied than males. For breeding, stock in pairs. No care for the brood.

Ctenopoma

An African genus with about 25 species. We recognize two types: those that care for their brood and those that do not care for their brood. Those that care for their broods are usually beautifully colored bubblenest builders with sexual dimorphism that defend their territories (including *C. ansorgii*, *C. nanum*, *C. damasi*). The often larger species that don't care for their brood, on the other hand, are not territorial and have no sexual dimorphism. They are less aggressive toward others of the same species and therefore much easier to keep (including

C. kingsleyi, C. acutirostre, C. oxyrhynchus).

Ctenopoma ansorgi (BOULENGER, 1912) (ornate Ctenopoma)

8 cm, 25°C, A - G - W

8 cm	25°C	A-G-W

Home: Cameroons; hidden in the bank region of rivers.

Males sometimes splendidly colored. Stock in pairs. Bubblenest builders. Male cares for family.

Care: Single-species or well-planted community tank. Water soft and slightly acid. Live food, occasionally prepared food taken. These guidelines also apply to the rare *C. damasi* from Uganda.

Ctenopoma fasciolatus BOULENGER, 1899

8 cm, 24°C, A - G - W - N

8 cm	24°C	A-G-W-N

Home: The Congo region, in clear, vegetation-rich waters.

Males colored more strikingly than females. Peaceful and hardy.

Care: Accepts mixed small live foods and dry food. For breeding use soft, slightly acid water. Stock in pairs. Bubblenest builders. Male care for family.

Ctenopoma kingsleyi GUENTHER, 1896 (Kingsley's Ctenopoma)

19 cm, 26°C, A - (G) - N

19 cm	26°C	A (G)-N

Home: West African, in running waters.

Peaceful and long-lived.

Care: Suitable for well-planted community aquaria, if the other fishes fit as far as their size is concerned. Occasionally easily startled. Accepts coarse pond

Ctenopoma oxyrhynchus. Photo by B. Kahl.

food, earthworms, trout food, etc. For breeding, in pairs. Breeds in a quiet place, not too bright. No care for the brood; spawn-eaters.

Note: This species is probably identical with *C. petherici*. The similar, somewhat smaller *C. maculatum* is less peaceful.

Ctenopoma oxyrhynchus BOULENGER, 1902 (Mottled Ctenopoma)

10 cm, 24°C, A - (G) - W - N

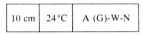

Home: Congo basin.

High-backed species with pointed snout.

Care: Well-planted community aquarium. Companion fishes must not be too small! No special requirements for food. For breeding, stock in pairs in soft water in a tank that is not too bright. Do not care for the brood.

The similar *C. acutirostre* is much more timid and choosier with its food. However, both species can be kept together quite well.

Belontiidae

To this fish family from tropical Asia belong many popular, very highly recommended aquarium fishes. All care for their brood, and many of them can be propagated relatively easily.

Belontia

The species of this genus are the largest in the family. Peaceful, but when they fall into the mood for caring for their brood, they may kill smaller fishes. Plant friendly. Well-suited for combining with medium to large and very large catfishes and other bottom-fishes. Can also be combined with medium-sized *Cichlasoma* species.

Belontia hasselti (CUVIER, 1831) (Java Combtail)

19 cm, 26°C, A - G - W - N

Home: Malayan peninsula to Borneo and Sumatra, in slowly flowing virgin forest waters.

Long-lived. Sexes difficult to differentiate. Breeding as for *B. signata*. Care for brood.

Special traits: Sometimes the animals will show sleeping behavior during the day also. Lie flat on the bottom (imitation of a dried leaf).

Care: Plant aquarium well. No special food demands.

Belon tia signata (GUENTHER, 1861) (Combtail)

16 cm, 26°C, A - (G) - W - N

Home: Sri Lanka, in zones along the banks of standing and slowly flowing waters that are rich in hiding places.

Long-lived. Sexes difficult to tell apart.

Care: Coarse pond food, small fishes, small earthworms, dry food, trout food. It is most advantageous to obtain four or five young fish, allowing pair formation to take place by itself. Later, keep in pairs. Well-planted single-species or community tank with hardy fishes.

Stock in pairs. Take good care of the brood. Female participates in care of the brood. Family may remain together until the young are almost grown.

Betta (Fighting Fishes)

Home: Southeastern Asia and the East Indies.

About 20 species, among them many

mouthbrooders, but the bubblenest builders are more colorful and for this reason more popular. Breeding usually easy. All species are suited for combination with other fishes, despite the name "fighting" fish. However, in smaller aquaria only one male of the bubblenest- building species should be kept, since otherwise the males might fight each other.

Betta coccina VIERKE, 1979
   4.5 cm, 27°C, A - (G) - W

4.5 cm	27°C	A (G)-W

Home: Surroundings of Jambi, central Sumatra.

Extremely elongated, dark wine-red fish. Peaceful, but often shy. Males often with a dark greenish iridescent spot in the center of the body.

Care: Densely planted tank with quiet tankmates. Bubblenest builders.

Betta imbellis LADIGES, 1975 (Peaceful Betta)
   5 cm, 27°C, A - G - W - N

5 cm	27°C	A-G-W-N

Betta pugnax. Photo by J. Vierke.

Home: Along the edges of rice paddies in Malaysia and southwestern Thailand.

Males with magnificent fins and colors, larger than females. Relatively peaceful. Bubblenest builders. Father cares for family.

Care: Ideal for the well-planted mini- tank. In larger tanks (over 70 cm side length) three or four males may be kept at once. Floating plants! Undemanding concerning water quality and food.

The same is also true of *Betta smaragdina.*

Betta pugnax (CANTOR, 1850)
   10 cm, 24°C, A - G - W - N

10 cm	24°C	A-G-W-N

Home: Slowly and rapidly flowing waters of southern Asia.

Longer-finned than *B. taeniata.* Adult males with elongated central tail fin rays. Very quiet and peaceful.

320

Care: Densely planted tanks. Coarse live food (including small earthworms), dry food. Breeding not easy. Soft, clean water. Provide a current! Mouthbrooder in the male sex.

The species is identical with *B. brederi* and closely related to *B.anabatoides.*

Betta splendens REGAN, 1910 (Siamese Fighting Fish)

7 cm, 27°C, G - W - N

7 cm	27°C	G-W-N

Home: Thailand and Cambodia; probably naturalized on the Malayan peninsula.

The wild form rarely grows longer than 6 cm. Today, veil-finned aquarium varieties in many different colors are offered almost exclusively.

Care: No special demands on water and food. Combine as indicated in the description of the genus.

For breeding, stock in pairs. The larger males have much more splendid fins and colors. Provide hiding places for the female! Bubblenest is preferably built in floating plants. Father cares for family.

Betta taeniata REGAN, 1909

7 cm, 25°C, A - G - W - N

7 cm	25°C	A-G-W-N

Home: Southeast Asia, in slowly flowing waters.

Relatively short-finned, without elongated tail fin.

Care and Breeding: Like *B. pugnax.*

Closely related to the smaller *B. picta* from Sumatra, which is kept quite similarly. *B. picta* is easier to breed than the other mouthbrooding species of *Betta*.

Colisa

Four species from India and Burma. Differ from the larger *Trichogaster* species by their long-based dorsal fin. Males very colorful. Magnificent aquarium fishes. Bubblenest builders. Breeding easy. Occasionally these gouramis will spit at dry food that remained stuck to the aquarium glass above the water surface. When defending their territories, the males sometimes feign an attack on intruders while uttering a menacing growling sound.

Colisa chuna HAMILTON-BUCHANAN, 1822 (Honey Gourami)

4.5 cm, 26°C, A - G - N

4.5 cm	26°C	A-G-N

Home: Lowlands of northeastern India.

Peaceful, lively fish. Males in display coloration brown-red with blue-black throat.

Care: Mini-tanks and quiet community aquaria. No special demands on water and food. For breeding, stock in pairs.

Colisa fasciata (BLOCH & SCHNEIDER, 1801) (Giant Gourami)

12 cm, 25°C, G - N

12 cm	25°C	G-N

Home: Lowlands of northern India.

Relatively peaceful fish. Males colored more strongly, with pointed dorsal fins.

Care: Community aquarium. Undemanding. For breeding, stock in pairs.

Colisa labiosa (DAY, 1878) (Thick-lipped Gourami)

Colisa labiosa. Photo by J. Vierke.

9 cm	25°C	G-N

Home: India and Burma.

Even more peaceful than the somewhat larger *C. fasciata*. At spawning time the color of the male turns almost to black. Otherwise like *C. fasciata;* this fish is sometimes considered a geographical race of the latter.

Colisa lalia HAMILTON- BUCHANAN, 1822 (Dwarf Gourami)
5.5 cm, 26°C, G - N

5.5 cm	26°C	G-N

Home: Plant-rich waters of the north Indian lowlands.

One of the most beautiful and interesting aquarium fish. Peaceful and lively. Unfortunately short-lived.

Care: Community aquarium. No demands regarding food and water, but do not keep too cold!

Breeding easy. Stock in pairs; the smaller females are less colorful than the larger males. Male will build compact bubblenest incorporating plant material.

All details also apply to the aquarium color varieties called the red dwarf gourami, blue dwarf gourami, and the rainbow lalia.

Macropodus (Paradise Fishes)

Three southeastern Asiatic species.

Macropodus concolor AHL, 1937
12 cm, 25°C, G - N

12 cm	25°C	G-N

Home: Southeast Asia.

Adult male has a large tail fin that is often spread like a fan during courtship.

Care: Not too small, well-planted community tank. No special water and food requirements. Breed in not too hard water. Bubblenest builder.

Macropodus opercularis LINNE, 1758
(Paradise Fish)
  9 cm, 23°C, G - N

9 cm	23°C	G-N

Home: Eastern Asia from Korea to South Vietnam, in rice paddies and standing waters.

Beautiful, very undemanding fish. Adult males with greatly elongated tail and anal fin tips and long tail fin lobes.

Care: For larger, well-planted community aquaria with not too sensitive inhabitants. Breeding easy. Bubblenest builders.

Pet shops also offer blue varieties as well as yellow and white color forms.
Malpulutta

Only one species from Sri Lanka. Exhibits characteristics relating it to the genus *Parosphromenus*, which it resembles greatly in care and breeding.
Malpulutta kretseri DERANIYAGALA, 1937 (Malpulutta)
  9 cm, 26°C, A - W

9 cm	26°C	A-W

Macropodus opercularis. Photo by J. Vierke.

Home: Sri Lanka, hidden in standing and slowly flowing waters.

Decorative but sensitive fish. The males reach an overall length of 9 cm. Of this, more than 3.5 cm is the elongated tail fin. The smaller females have much shorter tail fins.

Care: For the single-species or miniature tank. Not too hard, slightly acid water. Hiding places. Live food.

Parosphromenus

A genus presently including four species of very delicate and secretive labyrinth fishes of the Malayan peninsula and India that are suited for the mini–tank.

Parosphromenus filamentosus VIERKE, 1981

4 cm, 27°C, A - W

4 cm	27°C	A–W

Home: Lives hidden in plant-rich, slowly flowing waters of southeastern Borneo.

Males in display coloration are very beautiful. Both sexes have thread-like tips to the tail fin rays. Females smaller, less intensely colored than males.

Parosphomenus filamentosus. Photo by J. Vierke.

Breeding easy. Stock in pairs. Cave-spawners. Father cares for family.

Care: Well planted mini-tank with soft, slightly acid water. Live food. Closely related is *P. deissneri*, the licorice gourami, which is much more difficult to care for and breed. Other species: *P. parvulus* (with maximum 3 cm overall length, the smallest labyrinth fish) and *P. paludicola*.

Pseudosphromenus

At one time the species of this genus were placed with the genus *Macropodus*. However, the fish differ in anatomical characteristics and reproductive behavior.

Pseudosphromenus cupanus CUVIER & VALENCIENNES, 1831 (Spike-tailed Paradise Fish)

8 cm, 25°C, G - N

8 cm	25 °C	G-N

Home: Southern India and Sri Lanka. Hidden, but frequent in grassy ditches.

Peaceful, undemanding fish. The females (!) assume a black coloration at the time of reproduction. Otherwise, sex differences as in *Trichopsis;* hold in front of light in a glass!

Care: Well-planted community aquarium. Breeding easy if stocked in pairs. Likes to construct its bubblenest under the ceiling of a cave. Father cares for family.

Old name: *Macropodus cupanus cupanus*.

Pseudosphromenus dayi KOEHLER, 1909 (Day's Paradise Fish)

7 cm, 26°C, G - W -N

7 cm	26 °C	G-W-N

Home: Southeast Asia.

Lives well-hidden. Undemanding and peaceful. The sexes can be differentiated by the more splendid formation of the fins and the coloration of the males. Breeding easy. Stock in pairs. Like to establish bubblenest under the horizontally standing leaves of *Cryptocoryne*. Father cares for family.

Care: Well-planted community aquarium; also suited for smaller tanks.

Sphaerichthys

Mouthbrooders originating in Malaysia and Indonesia. Closely related is the monotypic genus *Parasphaerichthys* from northern Burma, which, however, is of no aquarium significance.

Sphaerichthys acrostoma VIERKE, 1979

9 cm, 28°C, A - W

9 cm	28 °C	A-W

Home: Swampy forests of southern Borneo.

Slimmer and larger than the well-known chocolate gourami with different markings. Mouthbrooder, but not bred thus far. Peaceful.

Care: Single-species tank. Needs soft, acid water and small live food.

Sphaerichthys osphromenoides CANESTRINI, 1860 (Chocolate Gourami)

5 cm, 28°C, G - A - W

5 cm	28 °C	G-A-W

Home: Malayan peninsula, Sumatra, Borneo. Not rare in slowly flowing waters.

Frequently imported, attractive fish that is sensitive, however. Sexes difficult to differentiate. The dorsal fin of larger males is longer and somewhat pointed. Mother is mouthbrooder; will often eat the spawn. Young leave the mouth after about two weeks.

Care: Single-species tank or quiet community aquarium. Good planting. Water soft, slightly acid.

Trichogaster

A genus from southeast Asia that includes four species. It furnishes some larger but at the same time very peaceful and beautiful animals for the community aquarium.

Trichogaster leeri (BLEEKER, 1852)
(Pearl Gourami)

12 cm, 27°C, G - (S) - W - N

12 cm	27°C	G-(S)-W-N

Home: Overgrown standing or slowly flowing waters of the Malayan peninsula to Sumatra and Borneo.

Male with longer dorsal fin and more colorful than female.

Care: Warmth-loving! Ideal for well- planted community aquaira. Very peaceful. Do not combine with tiger barbs. No special food requirements.

For breeding, 30°C. Stocking in pairs. Sensitive to disturbances. Bubblenest builders. Father cares for family. Some males will occasionally construct mounds of sand under their nests for no apparent reason.

Trichogaster leerii. Photo by B. Kahl.

Trichogaster microlepis (GUENTHER, 1861) (Moonbeam Gourami)
18 cm, 27°C, G - (S) - W - N

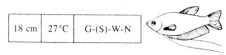

18 cm	27°C	G-(S)-W-N

Home: Plant-rich waters in Thailand and Cambodia.

Very peaceful, decorative fish. Dorsal fins of older males are longer and less rounded than those of the females.

Care: For the large, well-planted community aquarium. Breeding like *T. leerii.*

Trichogaster trichopterus PALLAS, 1777 (Blue Gourami, Three-spot Gourami)
15 cm, 26°C, G - N

15 cm	26°C	G-N

Home: All of southeastern Asia; frequent in plant-rich waters.

Hardier than the other species of *Trichogaster.* Dorsal fin of the female shorter and more rounded than the male.

Care: Undemanding. For well-planted community tanks. Breeding fairly easy. Stock in pairs in not too small aquarium.

In the trade there frequently are available color varieties of *T. trichopterus* whose care is the same: golden gourami, silver gourami, marbled ("Cosby") gourami and the blue gourami ("sumatranus"). Very peaceful also is the related species *T. pectoralis*, which, however, grows to more than 20 cm.

Trichopsis (Croaking Gouramis)

The genus *Trichopsis* consists of three species that are all distinguished by a remarkable characteristic: during courtship and the generally harmless

fights, the animals will sometimes utter quite audible growling sounds. These sounds are produced by violent vibrations of the pectoral fin, whose ligaments glide across special bones.

Trichopsis pumilus (ARNOLD, 1936) (Pygmy Gourami)
3.5 cm, 27°C, A - G - W - N

3.5 cm	27°C	A-G-W-N

Home: Surroundings of Bangkok, Thailand.

Small, very secretive fish. In transmitted light the ovary of the female may be clearly seen as a triangle which is pointedly elongated toward the tail. When stocked in pairs, breeding is not difficult. The bubblenest is constructed preferable in caves or under plant leaves.

Care: Well suited for smaller, beautifully planted tanks. Undemanding.

Trichopsis schalleri LADIGES, 1962 (Three-striped Croaking Gourami)
6 cm, 26°C, G - W - N

6 cm	26°C	G-W-N

Home: Thailand.

Very closely related to *T. vittatus.* Markings are paler.

Care and Breeding: Like *T. vittatus.*

Trichopsis vittatus CUVIER & VALENCIENNES, 1831 (Croaking Gourami)
7 cm, 26°C, G - W - N

7 cm	26°C	G-W-N

Home: Frequent throughout southeastern Asia; prefers plant-rich bank zones.

Peaceful, undemanding fish. Sex differences as in *T. pumilus*.

Care: For densely planted community aquaria. When stocked in pairs, breeding not difficult. Likes to construct its bubblenests in flowerpot caves. Breeding aquarium not too small. Provide hiding places. Father cares for family.

Helostomatidae

This family includes only one genus with one highly specialized species. Its gill apparatus is transformed into a filter that enables it to gather planktonic food.

Helostoma temmincki CUVIER & VALENCIENNES, 1831 (Kissing Gourami)

30 cm, 26°C, A - G - W - N

30 cm	26°C	A-G-W-N

Home: Southeastern Asia, mainly in standing waters.

Peaceful fish. Impressive is the harmless mouth-pressing (kissing) during courtship and fights. In addition to the wild green form there is a pink color variety.

Care: Good fish for the community aquarium. Takes very small live food. They also like fine dry food and rolled oats. Many fish starve in the aquarium! Plankton-eaters.

For breeding, stock in pairs. Females ready for pairing are markedly plumper. Do not care for their brood. Spawn–eaters.

Osphronemidae

The Osphronemidae are represented by only one species.

Osphronemus goramy LACEPEDE, 1802 (Giant Gourami)

70 cm, 26°C, A - N

70 cm	26°C	A-N

The largest labyrinth fish. Distributed throughout southern and southeastern Asia as a food fish. Occasionally the young, pointy-headed fish appear in pet shops. They are attractive but eat a lot, grow rapidly, and are often quarrelsome. Plant-eaters!

Care: Only for large aquaria without plants. Keeping with large cichlids possible. No demands regarding water and food. Breeding in the aquarium hardly possible. Build spherical plant nests about 20 cm below the surface.

LUCIOCEPHALOIDEI

Pike-like surface fish provided with a labyrinth organ. Closely related to the Anabantoidei and probably merely highly specialized fish derived from that suborder. Only one species.

Luciocephalus pulcher (GRAY, 1830) (Pike Head)

18 cm, 24°C, A - W

18 cm	24°C	A-W

Home: Malaysia and Indonesian islands.

Elongated carnivorous fish with an enormous mouth.

Care: Suited only for single-species tanks. Requires soft, slightly acid water. Eats small fishes (especially likes half– grown black mollies!), insects. Mouthbrooder. Breeding is difficult.

Helostoma temminckii. Photo by B. Kahl.

BLENNIOIDEI (BLENNIES)

Almost exclusively marine bottom fishes of elongated shape with abdominal fins positioned under the throat or chin.

Blennius

Of the 25 European species, one lives in the lakes and fresh waters around the Mediterranean: the freshwater blenny *(Blennius fluviatilis)*. Hardy and very droll, but sometimes aggressive. Grows to 15 cm.

Care: It is best to prepare a larger tank with many cracks between the rocks for this species. Harder water, if necessary, add salt.

GOBIOIDEI (GOBIES)

About 600 predominantly marine forms, of which some have migrated to fresh waters. Abdominal fins frequently grown together into a sucking disc; two dorsal fins. Swim bladder usually lacking.

Eleotridae (Sleepers)

Family very rich in genera and species. It includes the genera *Mogurnda* and *Oxyeleotris* among others. Bottom fishes, usually carnivorous in adults that need live food and medium-hard to hard water that must not be acid. Water that is too soft may be hardened with one to five teaspoons of salt per 10 liters of water.

Eleotris

Distributed worldwide.

Mostly sea and brackish water animals. Need an addition of salt. Therefore not to be kept in the planted aquarium for any length of time. Frequently quarrelsome.

Hypseleotris

Southeast Asian to Australian genus with some purely freshwater forms.

Some beautiful species, like *H. compressus* from the coastal regions of southern New Guinea and *H. cyprinoides* from Sulawesi (Celebes).

Mogurnda

Occasionally, *Mogurnda mogurnda*, may be sold. These fish, which grow to 18 cm in length and are attractively colored during courtship, can be bred relatively easily in temperatures around 27°C. One should put several females with one male. The eggs are stuck onto a rock. The male cares for the brood. These predaceous fish should be kept only with larger fish. Become very tame.

Gobiidae (Gobies)

Home: Distributed worldwide.

Fishes living predominantly in the sea. Abdominal fins generally grown together into a sucking disc.

Brachygobius nunus (HAMILTON-BUCHANAN, 1822) (Bumblebee Goby)

4 cm, 26°C, A - G - N - H

4 cm	26°C	A-G-N-H

Home: Common bottom fish throughout all of Southeast Asia and the East Indies in waters near the coast, in pure freshwater as well as in brackish water.

Droll, harmless fish.

Care: As eaters of small live foods they are suited especially for the mini-tank. Obtain several specimens. Hiding places in caves and snail shells should be provided. One teaspoon of salt per 10 liters of water is recommended.

Breed after addition of freshwater. Cave spawners. Father cares for the brood. Remove adults after hatching!

Very similar with its pattern of golden- yellow rings is *B. xanthozona* from Sumatra, Java, and Borneo. *B. nunus* has the anal and dorsal fins edged with black, yellow, or colorless. The outside edges of the fins of *B. xanthozona* are dark. The rarely imported species *B. aggregatus* has an entirely light-colored anal fin.

Stigmatogobius sadanundio (HAMIL-TON-BUCHANAN, 1822) (Knight Goby)

8 cm, 25°C, A - (G) - S - H

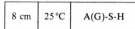

8 cm	25°C	A(G)-S-H

Home: Southeast Asia.

Pretty, lively fish.

Care: Best in very slightly brackish water. Tank not too small; cave or root shelters. Keep several fish.

Periophthalmidae (Mudskippers)

Home: Widely distributed in Indo-Pacific and eastern Atlantic tropical swamp regions.

The fish can move quickly on land by crawling or jumping. In addition to the well-known genus *Periophthalmus*, the genera *Boleophthalmus* and *Scartelaos*, among others, are also included here.

COTTOIDEI

Almost all purely marine fishes, of which a few species have come to inhabit fresh waters. The following species is excellently suited for the coldwater aquarium:

Cottus gobio LINNE, 1758 (Miller's Thumb)

17 cm, 14°C, A - N - H

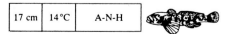

17 cm	14°C	A-N-H

Home: Europe and northern Asia, in clear streams in meadows and mountains.

Bizarrely shaped fish with enormous pectoral fins. Will become tame.

Care: Eats live foods of all kinds. Needs cool, clear, possibly moving water. The temperature in spring may vary between 5 and 16°C; do not keep over 20°C for extended periods! Equip aquarium wth rocky hiding places and caves.

Breeding possible in early spring. Spawns hidden under rocks or in caves. Male cares for brood.

MASTACEMBELOIDEI (SPINY EELS)

Home: In freshwater and brackish regions of southern and southeastern Asia and tropical Africa.

Elongated eel-like fishes with a movable continuation of the snout. Dorsal fin with a posterior, soft-rayed part connected to an anterior fin of numerous low spines. More than 40 species.

Many spiny eels are attractively and colorfully marked. Twilight animals living in hiding. Sometimes become quite tame.

Care: Eat live food, especially worms and other bottom animals. Do not combine with small fish! Ideal tank for spiny eels would be an aquarium with a muddy, soft substrate, slightly brackish water, and dense plantings! However, this cannot be easily realized in the aquarium!

TETRAODONTIFORMES

This order includes, in addition to the puffers, the marine triggerfishes and filefishes, among others.

Tetraodontidae (Puffers)

Predominantly marine fishes, some species of which are pure freshwater forms. Puffers have a set of four sharp teeth that resemble the beak of a parrot. With this they like to crack the shells of snails. When in danger, the fish are able to pump air or water into an extension of their stomach and bloat themselves into a spherical shape. In the aquarium, we find mainly species of the genera *Tetraodon* and *Carinotetraodon*. Some species have been spawned in captivity. The males (sometimes several at the same time) attach themselves with their teeth to the female during spawning.

Tetraodon

A genus fairly rich in species. Much given to nibbling of fins. In the aquarium need caves or root shelters in order to hide from each other.

Tetraodon fluviatilis (HAMILTON-BUCHANAN, 1822)
    20 cm, 25°C, A - (G) - H

20 cm	25°C	A(G)-H

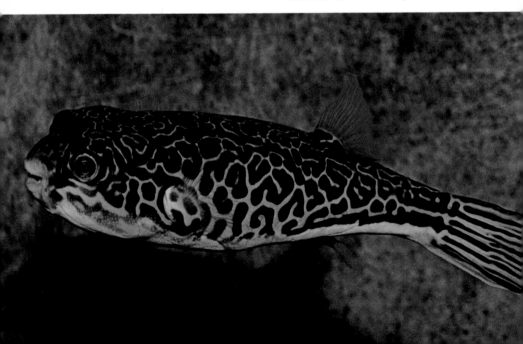

Home: All of southern and southeastern Asia to the Philippines.

Numerous dark spots on greenish-yellow ground. Frequently imported as small specimens that often develop into brawlers in the aquarium. Rapid growth!

Care: The fish is omnivorous but should occasionally be given snails as food. The addition of salt enhances its well-being.

Tetraodon mbu BOULENGER, 1899
    75 cm, 25C, A - W

75 cm	25°C	A-W

Home: Central and lower Congo.

Beautiful freshwater fish with characteristic very long fin.

Care: Since the species grows very large, suited principally for display aquaria. Snail-eaters. Given to biting.

Tetraodon mbu. Photo by J. Vierke.

Tetraodon palembangensis BLEEKER, 1852 (Figure-eight Puffer)
   20 cm, 24C, A - (G) - N

Tetraodon palembangensis. Photo by A. Roth.

20 cm	24°C	A(G)-N

Home: Fresh waters of Thailand, Sumatra, and Borneo.

Distinctive yellow net pattern and eye spots at the bases of the dorsal and tail fins. Most popular puffer species, mostly peaceful, but will sometimes turn out to be a fin-eater given to biting and pulling off plant leaves. Snail exterminator.

Tetraodon schoutedeni PELLEGRIN, 1926
   10 cm, 25C, A - (G) - N

10 cm	25°C	A(G)-N

Home: Lower course of the Congo.

More peaceful than the other species, but will sometimes molest plants. Has been bred in single-species aquaria. Males considerably smaller than females. Open- spawners that release the eggs near the surface.

THE BREEDING
OF FISHES

Very many species of fishes can be induced to reproduce in the aquarium only at relatively great cost and with a sizable portion of prudence, experience, and patience. With many species, breeding has not been successful so far. On the other hand, many species of fishes propagate almost or entirely without our help in the aquarium. Of course, the tank then must be equipped and stocked in a suitable manner!

Safeguarding the Brood in a Community Aquarium

In its broadest interpretation, the simplest breeding of fishes begins with the removal of guppy and swordtail fry from the community aquarium and their transfer to a special container in order to save them from pursuit by the larger inhabitants of the tank.

With species who care for their brood, we have the option of removing the spawn or the larvae that are not yet capable of swimming from the community aquarium (thus safeguarding them) and raising them separately. If our aquarium is suitably equipped and not too densely inhabited, those fish that care for the brood often have the opportunity of fighting for and establishing a breeding territory, which they then use for spawning and for the care of fry not yet able to swim. But once the young swim free, this state is usually over: in the closeness of a community aquarium, only few fish parents have a chance to really raise their young. This is where the aquarist should interfere.

We are most likely to save the complete spawn or brood from cichlids and labyrinth fish. With mouthbrooding cichlids (*Pseudocrenilabrus, Geophagus*) we don't even have to separate the brooding parent from its brood. We herd it carefully into a glass held in the aquarium and remove it together with the water, being very careful with the transfer! If the fish is startled too much, it will spit out its spawn and will not accept them again! Once a mouthbrooder has been transferred into a tank of its own, there is not much that can go wrong. However, water temperature and quality must be identical to the values of the community tank. The aquarium for our mouthbrooder should be left alone — we do not feed. After one or two weeks, when the young have been released, we may raise them separately from their parent, feeding freshly hatched brine shrimp. It is more beautiful yet to observe the family idyll for some time longer. In suspected danger and at night, the mother will continue to take the little ones into her mouth for a while longer.

Most cichlids stick their spawn to a rock, a root, or a plant leaf. In the community aquarium this is seen quite frequently with *Pterophyllum scalare*, *Aequidens*, and *Cichlasoma* species, and with the ram, *Papiliochromis ramirezi*. If we observe such a cichlid preparing to mate, we may remove the fish after spawning (do not leave the spawn as food for the other inhabitants!) and transfer them into their own not too small breeding tank. With a varied diet of live food, the fish are almost sure to

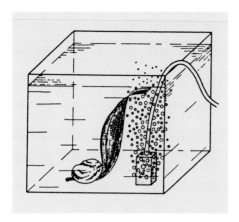

When aeration is used with a rock or leaf to which eggs are attached, the air bubbles should not touch the eggs directly.

spawn again after one to three weeks, and we will be able to observe the fascinating drama of cichlids caring for their brood in all its details. After hatching, the parents move the fry into a specially prepared cavity and continue to care for them there. Many cichlids fasten their newly hatched larvae to plant leaves.

Only when the young rise in a school a few days later and begin their search for food may we feed them. Providing we have hatched *Artemia* eggs in time, we can now put the nauplii into the aquarium in small amounts. We can tell by the orange-colored stomachs of the young fish when they have eaten the little brine shrimp.

Many aquarists find it almost heartbreaking to leave the spawn deposited in the community aquarium as a feast for the other fishes. It is often possible to artificially raise the young of species caring for their brood. However, artificial raising should not be employed regularly, since there is a danger of raising lineages whose behavior degenerates and which in the following generations are not capable of raising their broods normally even under ideal conditions. Among the rams and angels, which are regularly commercially raised by artificial means in large numbers, there are already such lineages. On the other hand, there are situations in which we are forced to use artificial means to preserve rare species.

The eggs of substrate-spawners are transferred to the breeding tank under water in a glass. The nursery tank must be meticulously clean. Disinfect it first with a dark red solution of potassium permanganate and rinse well with clear water until the red coloration has disappeared. We now fill with water from the spawning tank, which we take directly from the filter outflow if possible. To prevent a fungus infestation of the spawn, add Trypaflavin to the water (1g to 600 liters of water) or methylene blue (until the water is a strong blue — overdosing with methylene blue is virtually impossible).

The spawning rock is simply put on the bottom of the nursery tank and a spawning leaf can be weighted with a stone in such a manner that the spawn stands relatively free in the water. Now we place an airstone in the vicinity of the eggs in such a manner that the air bubbles do not directly touch the eggs but furnish them constantly with fresh water. We have to check the spawn daily for fungus-infested eggs or larvae. If necessary, they must be removed — under water, of course! Once the young swim free and eat brine shrimp nauplii, everything will be alright.

Less complicated is the raising of most bubblenest-building labyrinth fishes. Here we distinguish between species whose eggs are lighter than water (they are usually glass-clear) and species whose eggs are heavier than water (they are opaque white). The labyrinth fishes with floating eggs *(Ctenopoma, Trichogaster, Macropodus)* are particularly easy to raise. Since the brood is usually insensitive to infestation with fungus or bacteria, we do not need to take any special measures against fungus infestation. We will also not use a bare nursery aquarium but an old, established aquarium with plants (no snails!). Especially important is a partial covering of the water's surface with floating plants *(Ceratopteris, Riccia)*. The nest with the eggs or the larvae is transferred into the nursery aquarium with a soup plate or a ladle. If possible, the aquarium should be not too small — the larger it is, the larger will be the yield of young fish, of course. When the young swim free, they will always find a certain amount of infusoria as initial food in a nursery tank thus equipped. Infusoria are minute living organisms that are always present in a well-established tank. The little fish will be able to eat brine shrimp nauplii within a week or so of becoming free-

Microorganisms can be very useful as the first foods for the fry of some of the egglaying species. Left to right are a paramecium, or slipper animal, trumpet animal, one of the rotifers.

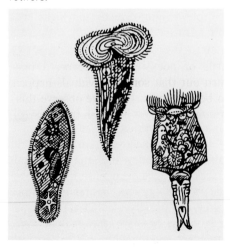

swimming. Once they have reached this stage, they can be raised without further difficulties. Of course, these labyrinth fishes can be bred more intensively with a purposeful feeding of infusoria. In this manner we will obtain larger numbers of offspring.

Labyrinth fishes with sinking eggs *(Trichopsis, Betta, Malpulutta, Pseudosphromenus, Parosphromenus)* also are relatively easy to raise. If possible, do not remove the nest until shortly before the fry become free-swimming. About three days before, the larvae hang below the bubblenest like little commas. Raising can now take place as with the floating egg forms, because the brood-caring father has already bridged the most critical phases. However, sometimes the spawn has to be brought to safety immediately. It may be transferred with or without the bubblenest; usually the eggs will fall to the bottom of the nursery tank sooner or later, anyway. We now need aeration and usually also additions of Trypaflavin or methylene blue. With these species, the water should not be too hard — the *Parosphromenus* and *Malpulutta* species require soft water.

In quite a similar manner, the brood of other fish species may be safe-guarded. Armored catfishes sometimes fasten their spawn directly to the glass of the aquarium. We may carefully scrape it off with a razor blade and transfer it into a shallow nursery bowl (add Trypaflavin and aerate!). After about five to seven days the young will hatch, and they swim after another day. They will immediately eat freshly hatched *Artemia*.

In community aquaria, the *Apistogramma* species spawning in caves will breed occasionally. Sometimes the mothers will appear with a whole swarm of young, which, however, they cannot defend against the fellow inhabitants of the tank for any length of time. We carefully siphon off the young with a hose and put them into a separate nursery aquarium.

Permanent Stocking

A well-planted aquarium that houses fish of only one species may be extremely decorative. In addition, by using such a single-species aquarium many species can be propagated relatively easily. The fish spawn for days or weeks and, under suitable conditions, will prey on their brood little or not at all. In these cases, we talk about permanent stocking. However, most often we will not obtain any mass production in this manner.

Particularly well-suited for permanent stocking are White Clouds (*Tanichthys albonubes*). A 30 liter aquarium will be suitable as a breeding tank. In order to keep from dragging in snails and parasites, scald the sand and disinfect the plants in an alum bath. White Clouds spawn preferably in finely branched plants such as *Myriophyllum* and the tank must be densely planted, at least in part.

For permanent stocking, floating plants are especially important, since they serve as shelter for the young. Here again, *Ceratopteris* and *Riccia* are especially well suited. In the breeding tank thus equipped we put a swarm of 8 to 12 White Clouds. The water must not be too soft, and the temperature should lie between 18 and 21°C. We feed food flakes but also offer freshly hatched *Artemia* on occasion, which the older fish also like to eat. The fish will soon begin to spawn, and shortly we will discover the first young fish, shining almost like neons, among the floating plants.

In a very similar manner most Atherinidae and rainbowfish Melanotaeniidae may be bred. Permanent stocking functions especially well with *Bedotia geayi* and *Melanotaenia maccullochi*. However, we must provide both species with really clean water, which should not be too soft.

More demanding fish, like *Rasbora hengeli*, may also be bred with permanent stocking. As adhesive spawners, they will need some broad-leaved plants (such as *Cryptocoryne*) to which they may fasten their eggs. If we put a school into an adequately equipped aquarium and the water hardness lies between 3 - 6°DH, success should soon follow. They are fed flake food with occasional additions of *Artemia*. Quite suitable for permanent stocking are also *Rasbora maculata* and *Rasbora urophthalma*. These two species also require soft water, if possible not above 3°DH.

If we put no special value on particularly high numbers of offspring, we may also breed by permanently stocking several fish that are infamous as spawn-robbers. We just have to see to it that the parents will always have live food (water fleas, mosquito larvae) — then they will usually molest the brood little or not at all! However, it may turn out that some individuals happen to be cannibals. Once we observe this, we must remove these fish from permanent stock immediately. The planting in these tanks should also be very dense in places, especially on the surface. If in addition we use suitably soft water, we may breed *Nannostomus*, *Epiplatys*, and *Aplocheilichthys* species.

The permanent stocking even of so-called "problem-fishes" such as *Nema-*

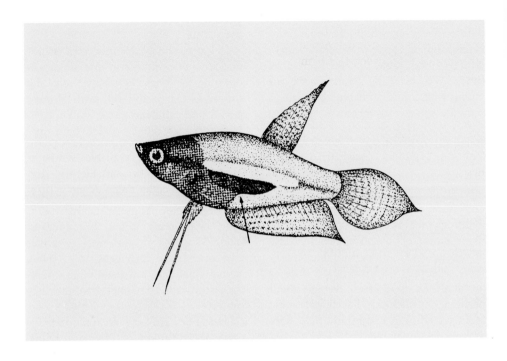

tobrycon palmeri and African tetras of
the genera *Brycinus* and *Phenacogrammus* may even result in offspring. However, for these species we must not
only prepare soft water and sufficient
live food; the tank must be planted
very densely in places and must be provided with floating plants. Since the
young live predominantly on the bottom for the first weeks, we must cover
the actual sand layer with a 3-5 cm
layer of large pebbles. In the cracks between the pebbles, the young may
grow unmolested by their parents.
Once we see the first young swimming
around, we should add *Artemia* to the
food.

The tank for stocking with about
three pairs of emperor tetras should
have a capacity of at least 100 liters.
The most advantageous breeding temperature lies around 24-26°C. Congo
tetras need lower temperatures (22-
24°C) and a larger tank (200-300 liters).

Sexing a labyrinth fish (*Pseudosphromenus
cupanus* is shown) by means of shining a
light behind the fish to reveal the outline of
the internal organs (arrow).

The Actual Breeding Aquarium

For purposeful breeding, the fish are
put in pairs — sometimes also in a
small school — into a specially
equipped aquarium for spawning during short periods of time.

It goes without saying that the
breeding pair must be healthy and
without deformities (which are hereditary in many cases, as is generally
known). Someone who wishes to obtain or breed color and fin varieties of
such fishes as fighting fish, guppies,
and other livebearers must first collect
information about genetic rules and the
principles of selective breeding in specialized literature! (Yes, there is a book
on genetics of aquarium fishes!)

The acquisition of a suitable breeding pair is not always easy. Even animals ready for spawning are not always compatible. In such cases one of the partners must be exchanged and we must wait and see whether the new combination will lead to the hoped-for success. Depending on the species, the sexes may be differentiated according to a wide variety of characteristics. Wherever possible, I have tried to list these characteristics with the description of the species.

Lack of success can often be explained by the fact that two animals of the same sex have been stocked for breeding! When breeding species in which there is no external difference between the sexes, we should try to let the animals find each other in the school. However, females that are ready to spawn can often be recognized by their markedly increased girth. But a very thick body may indicate some illness or disease! They may be animals that, for instance, had no opportunity for spawning for an extended period. Such females will often die of "egg-binding."

Readiness for spawning, especially in the females, may be stimulated by plentiful and varied feeding with live food. Often this even is a prerequisite for successful stocking for breeding purposes. Mosquito larvae in particular enhance the readiness for spawning.

Sometimes a partial water change with a somewhat lowered water temperature is effective, and occasionally the raising of the temperature by a few degrees is helpful. It is especially effective if the fish are separated by sex before breeding, if possible in bare tanks. If after several days they are put together in a relatively "homey" breeding aquarium, they will often spawn on request.

Since eggs and larvae — particularly those of soft-water fishes — are very susceptible to fungal and bacterial infestation, the breeding tank, spawning grid, and spawning plants to be brought in must first be thoroughly cleaned and disinfected (potassium permanganate!).

For most tetras, a tuft of Java moss or a commercially available synthetic spawning mop is satisfactory for spawning. (Weight them down with a glass rod to counteract the buoyancy of the plants.)

In most instances, a spawning grid is very useful. The spawning grid (plastic tubes glued next to each other) is put directly on the bottom of the breeding tank. The eggs drift to the bottom, lodge between the tubes, and are then out of reach for the spawn-eating parents. Instead of the spawning grid, we may use a layer of glass marbles. After spawning — in many instances, we have to wait for this for several days — the breeders must be immediately removed. As long as they are in the breeding tank they must not be fed — food and droppings might cause a too large growth of infusoria. For this reason, the fish are also not fed for 24 hours before stocking. Decisive for the fertilization and development of the eggs are water hardness, pH value, and water temperature. The requirements regarding these values differ from species to species (see specific descriptions).

The spawn and the larvae are checked daily — a magnifying glass is essential for this!

When the fry swim freely, purposeful feeding can begin. In order to encourage the steady growth of the brood, partial water changes should be made every few days. It goes without

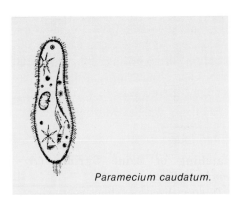

Paramecium caudatum.

tozoans (paramecia), *Artemia* nauplii, finely chopped tubifex, and strained pond plankton. It is essential, above all, that we feed enough! The breeder says: "The young must always be surrounded by food!" On the other hand, we must not feed so much that those food animals that are not eaten die and spoil the water. To establish the correct balance requires sensitivity — and, of course, experience.

Many fishes will accept small brine shrimp nauplii right from the beginning. Raising them presents no problem. In many instances, however, the fry are so small that they cannot handle *Artemia* as first food. Here we must first feed infusoria that we catch in ponds with the finest nets or purchase as breeding stock. It is best to establish a rotifer breeding nursery.

saying that the water removed is replaced only with crystal–clear water of the same temperature, hardness, and pH.

Feeding of the Brood

Many a hopeful breeder has seen his young brood starve. There still are species for which provision of the right food for raising is problematic. However, usually we can make do with pro-

Using one airpump to provide aeration for both hatching brine shrimp cultures and a tankful of baby fish.

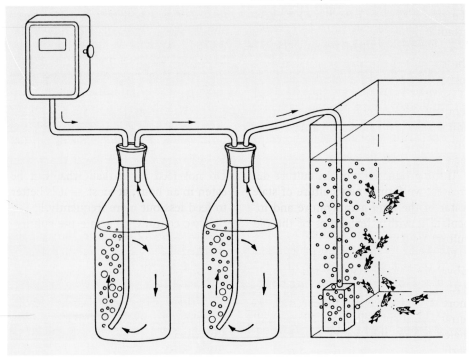

Breeding of Paramecia

Paramecia (slipper animalcules) are an ideal breeding food for most fish broods. In addition, they are very simple to cultivate. However, a *Paramecium* culture does not exactly smell like roses!

It is ideal if we can obtain breeding culture or purchase one through ads in an aquarium magazine. If necessary, we can remove some water from an old aquarium setup or a pond, also removing some of the bottom mud or debris for insurance, and put it into a mason jar or similar glass container (1 or 2 liters). As "food" we add little pieces of potato or carrot to the water. The one-celled animals do not eat directly of the potato or carrot pieces but feed on the decay bacteria that feed on the rotting vegetables. The ideal breeding temperature lies around 20-25°C. After a few days the paramecia can be recognized as small white dots or as a cloud when the glass is held in front of a dark background.

The water and debris removed from the older aquarium or pond is at first mixed with other one-celled organisms, of course. Keeping the culture at high temperatures allows only the slipper animalcules to survive after some time — they are the least sensitive to a lack of oxygen.

If the productivity of the culture decreases, we form a new culture of stale water of the same temperature and inoculate it with a few drops of the old culture medium.

Undemanding fish broods (such as labyrinth fishes) may be fed directly with a dropperful of culture water. For more sensitive young fishes (such as tetras) we should clean the slipper animalcules. For this, we remove a dropperful of the culture liquid and transfer it into a test tube or small bottle. Now close this container with a stopper of cotton and pour clean water on top of the cotton. After some time, the slipper animalcules will swim through the cotton into the clean water. Here we can easily remove them with an eye dropper for feeding.

Hatching of Brine Shrimp (*Artemia salina*)

In specialized pet shops everywhere, you may purchase dry brine shrimp eggs (cysts). Put a pinch into a wine bottle, add a level teaspoon of cooking salt, fill with water, and aerate at a temperature of 25°C. The larvae (nauplii) hatch after one to two days, depending on the temperature. If we put the bottle — no longer aerated! — in a window for a few minutes, the orange-red nauplii will collect on the bottom of the bottle on the side that is turned toward the light. With a hose you now may siphon off some of them and put them through a commercially available *Artemia* sieve. Rinse briefly with fresh water! The little shrimp are thus cleansed of adhering salt water and may be put directly into the breeding tank. However, we should exercise restraint in feeding! In fresh water the little shrimp larvae die relatively quickly and will then spoil the water. Do not feed more than what can be eaten in an hour, at most — it is better to feed less but more frequently.!

If we continue to aerate the culture, we can continue to use it for a few days longer. The shrimp grow very quickly and will soon die in bottles without food. It is best to use two bottles at the same time, using each in turn. We can link them up acording to the washing-bottle principle and thus run both on one pump.

FISH DISEASES

An ounce of prevention is better than a pound of cure — this wisdom also applies to our fishes.

Many diseases in the aquarium appear as stress diseases. Transport, the tight space at the pet shop, the unfamiliar diet, and the repeated adaptation to new water conditions and surroundings weaken many fishes and make them susceptible to diseases that under normal conditions they could easily resist. From this, let us draw a conclusion and let us not constantly experiment with our aquarium, let us not cram it too full, let us remember the regular partial water changes, let us not over-feed, and let us not be stingy with live foods! Aquarists sometimes fear that fish diseases might be brought into the aquarium with live foods and are advised to collect only in waters in which we are sure there are no fishes. However, there are barely any ponds in which there are, with 100% assurance, no carp, minnows, catfish or other small fishes. Had I followed this rule, I would barely have been able to breed any fish other than guppies. The contrary is true, and I want to emphasize my advice again: a variety of live foods enhances the fishes' natural resistance and is their best life insurance!

In the following, I will discuss briefly the different fish diseases and some of their symptoms. Fortunately, most diseases are easy to recognize and simple to treat. On the other hand, fish medicine is a very complicated thing and much can be determined only under the microscope by a specialist — but such conditions are incurable in many instances.

Let us not forget that every fish must die sooner or later! It is certain that in well-kept aquariums, more fish die of old age or of illness caused by old age than in the wild.

Ichthyophthirius multifiliis (White-spot Disease, Ich)

The most frequent and for many the most feared fish disease is *Ichthyophthirius* or, as many aquarists call it, "ich." On the other hand, there is no need for concern if the disease is noticed in time — it is more easily cured than any other common fish disease.

Ichthyophthirius is caused by protozoans that live parasitically under the mucous membranes of the fish. These one-celled organisms can clearly be seen on the skin or the fins of the fish a white dots with a diameter of 0.5-1 mm. If we do nothing, the fish will soon appear to be covered with salt and will die — besides, the other inhabitants of the tank will also be infected. The mature parasites release themselves from their host after some time, and drop to the bottom. Here they encapsulate and divide themselves into a multitude of mobile "swarmer" cells, every one of which may infest a new fish cell.

There are different medications against "ich" available in the trade; they all work very well. However, it is important to meticulously follow the rules for use! Even if sometimes the plants may be slightly damaged, the medication should be put in the concentration indicated directly into the infested aquarium — most of the other fishes are probably already infested. Since the parasites, which dig under the skin, cannot be directly attacked,

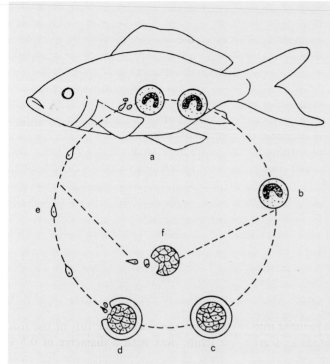

Life cycle of *Ichthyo-
phthirius multifiliis:* **a)**
Fish with parasites. **b)**
Parasite drops to bot-
tom of tank. **c)** At bottom encapsulated
parasite divides to pro-
duce swarmers. **d)** Capsule opens releasing
infective swarmer. **e)**
Swarmer attacks host
fish. **f)** If parasite
leaves host premature-
ly, swarmers formed
directly, without
developing capsule.

but only the swarmers that live in the open water, we must exercise patience until the last white dot has disappeared.

Oodinium (Velvet)

This is a typical stress disease. It attacks mostly fishes that had been kept in excessively cold temperatures. Soft water encourages this disease. Carp, killifishes, and labyrinth fishes are especially susceptible to this disease.

The cause of this disease is again a one-celled organism, this time a dino-flagellate (a type of odd algae). Its developmental cycle corresponds to that of *Ichthyophthirius* and can be successfully fought with the same medications.

Oodinium can also be recognized by white dots, but they are much smaller than with ich. The infested fish appears to be covered with confectioner's sugar, at least in the advanced stage. We really must watch carefully if we want to notice the initial stages. Usually, we take note of this disease when the fish stands listlessly in a corner with folded fins.

Left: *Saprolegnia;* right: *Oodinium.*

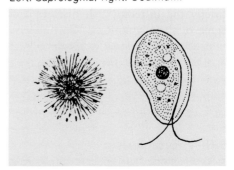

Saprolegnia (Fungus)

If fish are injured (as because of bites or bacterial fin rot) the animals will often be attacked by a fungus that looks like white hair. *Saprolegnia* is best combatted by short baths in salt water. For this, dissolve 20 g cooking salt in 1 liter of aquarium water. Depending on the sensitivity of the fish, give it a short bath lasting from 15 to 40 minutes. Equally proven is a bath for 30 minutes in a potassium permanganate solution (1 g in 100 liters of water). Of course, it is essential to discover and cure the actual cause of the injury.

Bacterial Skin and Fin Rot

Milky, often inflamed areas on the skin and/or torn or rotting fins are the symptoms of skin and fin rot. It too is a pure stress disease, often caused by too low water temperature. Healthy and well cared-for fishes do not contract fin rot! The diseased fish is best treated with a medication against fin rot (Furanace) available in pet shops.

Ichthyosporidium

Another relatively often seen illness is *Ichthyosporidium*, a treacherous fungus. This disease appears more frequently in fish kept under less than optimal conditions, but it may also attack animals that are kept extremely well. Its symptoms are widely variable: sunken or sometimes bloated abdomens, wounds, abscesses, protruding eyes.

The disease is not curable! Fishes that are suspected of *Ichthyosporidium* must be isolated immediately in order to prevent infection of the other inhabitants of the tank!

Fish Tuberculosis

Very similar and almost impossible to differentiate by external symptoms from *Ichthyosporidium* is fish (piscine) tuberculosis. Protruding eyes or bloated bodies and protruding scales (dropsy) may have other causes. However, fishes with these symptoms must be isolated as a preventive measure.

Treatment with the medications available in pet shops may help; however, their chances of success should not be estimated too highly.

Sunken bellies are often merely an indication that the life clocks of our sometimes very short-lived fishes are running down.

INDEX